Against Capital

Experiences of Class Struggle and Rethinking Revolutionary Agency

Against Capital

Experiences of Class Struggle and Rethinking Revolutionary Agency

Edited by Cliff Slaughter

zero books

Winchester, UK
Washington, USA

First published by Zero Books, 2016
Zero Books is an imprint of John Hunt Publishing Ltd., Laurel House, Station Approach,
Alresford, Hants, SO24 9JH, UK
office1@jhpbooks.net
www.johnhuntpublishing.com
www.zero-books.net

For distributor details and how to order please visit the 'Ordering' section on our website.

ISBN: 978 1 78535 094 8
Library of Congress Control Number: 2015949721

A CIP catalogue record for this book is available from the British Library.

Design: Stuart Davies

Printed and bound by CPI Group (UK) Ltd, Croydon, CR0 4YY, UK

CONTENTS

Bring me my Bow of burning gold;
Bring me my Arrows of desire:
Bring me my Spear: O clouds unfold!
Bring me my Chariot of fire!
—William Blake[1]

[T]heory ... becomes a material force as soon as it has gripped the masses ...
—Karl Marx[2]

The philosophers have only interpreted the world in various ways; the point, however, is to change it.
—Karl Marx[3]

The mountain we *must* climb ... is many Himalayas on top of one another ... We must do it ourselves, and we can do it only if we are willing to confront the real stakes and the real obstacles.
—István Mészáros[4]

Acknowledgements

I am particularly grateful to Yassamine Mather, who not only wrote a major part of this book, but must also be credited with the idea behind it.

Thanks are due too to all the other principal contributors: Robert Myers, Tom Owen, Terry Brotherstone, Jonas Nilsson, Raul Zelik, Gabriel Levy, Richard Roman, Edur Velasco Arregui and Janos Borovi. I have also made use of important insights from the writing of the historian and militant Alexei Gusev. Others who have allowed themselves to be quoted at length include Hilary Horrocks, Cathy Milligan, Neil Rothnie and Dave Temple. It goes without saying that they do not all necessarily agree with all the conclusions I draw from their contributions.

For me, István Mészáros, and in particular his books published since the late 1980s – from *The Power of Ideology* (Hemel Hempstead, 1989) and *Beyond Capital* (London, 1995) down to his recent *The Necessity of Social Control* (New York, 2015) – have been a major inspiration and I have benefitted greatly from discussions with him.

The book has, I hope, become more readable as a result of working on late drafts with Terry Brotherstone. It has also had the benefit of Hilary Horrocks' editing skills. Where errors remain, *mea culpa*.

Cliff Slaughter, July 2015

Contributing Authors

Edur Velasco Arregui is a professor of law and labour economics at the Universidad Autónoma Metropolitana in Mexico City, former Secretary-General of Sindicato Independiente de Trabajadores de la Universidad Autónoma Metropolitana, and co-author with Richard Roman of *Continental Crucible: Big Business, Workers and Unions in the Transformation of North America* (2013).

Janos Borovi is a Hungarian-born militant, long based in Paris where he was for many years a teachers' trade-union activist. Although 'not any more a Trotskyist', he remains a communist in the spirit of the Paris Commune, 'fighting for the self-organisation and liberation of the oppressed'.

Terry Brotherstone is an honorary research fellow in history at the University of Aberdeen, a former president of the University and College Union Scotland, co-editor of *The Trotsky Reappraisal* (1994), and author of many articles on labour, socialist, and Scottish history. In the late 1980s and early 1990s he was an arts reviewer for *Workers Press* (London).

Gabriel Levy is author and editor of a wide-ranging blog called 'People and Nature', available at *https://peopleandnature.wordpress.com/*.

Yassamine Mather was born and educated in Teheran. In the 1980s she was a member of the Fedayen (Minority) based in Kurdistan, where she helped set up the organisation's radio station. Later, in Europe, she was a member of the organisation's international committee. She is chair of the Hands of the People of Iran (HOPI) campaign and deputy editor of *Critique: a journal* *of socialist theory* (Glasgow). She writes regularly for *Weekly Worker* (London).

Robert Myers has been a sheet-metal worker and union activist in the aircraft and car industries. A participant in the dissolution of the Workers' Revolutionary Party after 1985, he then worked with political activists in South Africa and played a leading role in Workers' Aid for Bosnia, participating, between 1993 and 2002, in convoys to working-class communities there and in Kosova.

Jonas Nilsson is a Swedish typesetter, who, since 1983, has worked in Barcelona. A survivor of the flawed revolutionary political practices of the last quarter of the twentieth century, he is grateful for what Marxism has taught him: it is this that has allowed him to take part in, and perhaps learn from, the new forms of resistance.

Tom Owen, a practising socialist since joining the Young Socialists at the age of fourteen, has been active in a number of trade unions, principally as an education worker. He is a poet and writer on political and cultural issues who has recently published a translation of the work of the Catalan poet Vicent Andrés Estellés.

Richard Roman is Associate Professor Emeritus of Sociology at the University of Toronto, Associate Fellow of the Centre for Research on Latin America and the Caribbean, York University, co-author of *Continental Crucible* (see above) and a member of Socialist Project (publishing, online, *The Bullet*) and of the Greater Toronto Workers' Assembly.

Cliff Slaughter left the Communist Party of Great Britain after the Soviet Party's twentieth congress and the suppression of the Hungarian Revolution in 1956, since when he has been active in working-class struggles, principally in Britain but also in Namibia, South Africa, Australia and Latin America. His previous books include *Coal is Our Life* (1956), co-authored with Norman Dennis and Fernando Henriques; *Marxism, Ideology and Literature* (1980); and, most recently, *Not Without a Storm: towards a communist manifesto for the age of globalisation* (2006) and *Bonfire of the Certainties: the second human revolution* (2012).

Raul Zelik is a political scientist and an award-winning novelist. A Research Fellow at the Rosa Luxemburg Foundation, Berlin, he writes in both German and Spanish.

First ... A Last Word

by Cliff Slaughter

Against Capital was substantially completed by mid-June 2015 – and many of its parts several months earlier – but I write these final words in Greece in the aftermath of the 5 July 2015 referendum shortly before delivering the book to the publisher. In the referendum, the people of Greece voted to give a defiant and decisive (by 61.31 per cent against 38.69) '*OXI*' ('No!') to the imposition of brutal 'austerity' measures by the country's 'creditors', the major banks in the countries of the European Union and the International Monetary Fund – with 89 per cent of 18- to 34-year-olds in the 'No' camp. Were they organised? Yes – but via smart phones and social media. The referendum result was greeted by mass celebratory demonstrations and dancing in the streets. The joy was communicated internationally – through the internet and television – with, in the background, a city fountain flowing red.

This decision was – and remains – a signal to the masses of people throughout Europe that it is both necessary and possible to reject and oppose the demands of big capital. It highlights brilliantly the aim and content of this book, *Against Capital*. The immediate problems facing the working people of the continent – how to resist the vicious attacks on their basic living standards, how to begin to engage with and overcome the class-war strategy of capital – have now been given a highly visible answer. It is that they must do what the ordinary people of Greece are doing; they must join with them, and all others like them, in an internationalist solidarity counter-offensive against capital and its impositions. In resorting to the plebiscite in Greece, Alexis Tsipras's Syriza government made no call for such international solidarity and joint action, but the Greek people's vote is a resounding correction of that omission.

A central argument of this book is that we should forget those who still say that the problem is how to 'build the alternative leadership'; or who cling to the outworn formula that 'revolutionary consciousness' must be brought to the masses 'from the outside'. No one whatsoever did this – or had to do this – for the Greek masses. Their action is thus a vindication of *Against Capital*'s questioning of what is called 'vanguardism', and also of its recognition of the importance of the growing movements to take over, to occupy, public space.

What next? In Greece the Syriza leadership insisted that the resounding 'No' vote had the limited function and aim of strengthening its hand in negotiations with the powers that be in Europe and the IMF. This was to restrict and mistake completely its significance. Quite apart from the fact that this 'strengthened hand' brought forth nothing but even more stringent impositions, the point is that *No means No*! The real question is how to take forward and spread the struggle, to give its impetus continuity in time and in space, to take steps beyond 'negotiations' and towards the socialist offensive.

Here in Greece I was told by working women days before the referendum: 'This is war. They are making war on us.' Yes, it is class war, and the Greek people have accepted the challenge, they have engaged. It would be a grave mistake to think that they have embarked on an impossible task against an all-powerful adversary. On the contrary. First, they are finding allies in the working classes of other European countries – note that the European Union leaders expressed fear of the danger of 'contagion'. Second, they face a ruling class internationally that is every day losing the ability to deal with the manifestations of its system's structural crisis.

After 50 years of its last resort – the 'neo-liberal' economics and politics initiated by the regimes of Reagan and Thatcher – the limits of the capital system are being reached, and the Greek people have signalled the possibility of a new beginning. Not only are the economic and social consequences of neo-liberalism and its famous 'market' showing gaping wounds, especially since the financial collapse of 2008–09, but everywhere the political (and geo-political) strategy of capital is visibly bankrupt, becoming as actively destructive as its economic imperatives. In the Middle East the only policy is a reliance – changing erratically as convenient (note the shifting US attitudes to Assad in Syria or the Iranian Ayatollahs) – on repressive regimes, together with murderous military interventions resulting in the dispersal and destruction of thousands of communities and the creation of a population of millions of displaced and desperate people. At the same time, the United States, in blind panic about the 'Greater Russia' ambitions of Putin, is supplying thousands of tanks and weapons of war to the countries of Eastern Europe.

In the Greek referendum, young people were to the fore. Understandably so. Youth unemployment stands at a massive 50 per cent. That is socially unsustainable, yet easily comprehensible. As István Mészáros has shown in his *Beyond Capital: towards a theory of transition* (1996), the continued rule of capital has reached the point where its self-reproduction – the essential aim of capital – becomes more and more *destructive*. It is destructive not only of nature and of means of production, but also of the livelihood and the very lives of human beings. For example, at one pole hundreds of millions of young people cannot be employed and cannot look forward to a future with any confidence, while at the opposite pole, as longevity increases, millions of men and women are taken to be a burden on the economy – surplus to requirements, so to speak. Is it any wonder that youth unemployment and pensions were at the centre of the needs that impelled the people of Greece to give their answer to the banks and politicians?

The great question facing the Greek people in the immediate

future is this: what happens now that the Greek parliament has voted – as it did in mid-July – to accept the report-back of Tsipras and his 'negotiators' and the revised (but unyielding) programme of slashing cuts in welfare and living standards demanded by the country's 'creditors'? That question is inseparably connected with the yet-to-be-seen response of the working people of Spain, Portugal, Italy and the rest of Europe to the bold and admirable lead given by the Greek people's '*OXI*'! For their story must surely become a version of the same: as Marx, in the 1860s, warned those who thought that the experience that underpinned his analysis in *Capital* was unique to Britain: '*De te fabula narratur!*' – this will also be your story.

The European civilisation and the idea of 'democracy' that was born in Ancient Greece –which idealist social-democrats like the much-admired philosopher Jűrgen Habermas believed to be the underpinning values of the European Union – now face their greatest challenge since the 1930s and early 1940s. Habermas (see a 16 July 2015 interview at <www.theguardian/commentisfree>) has defined the deal imposed on Greece as 'a manifest claim for German hegemony' that has 'gambled away in one night all the political capital that a better Germany had accumulated in half a century'. But the problem is not German recidivism, a retreat back from 'political sensitivity and post-national mentality': it is rather that – as Habermas recognises – 'the *de facto* relegation of a member state to the status of a protectorate openly contradicts the democratic principles of the European Union'. But, unlike the developments of the 1930s, what is happening today takes place not in the name of nationalist ideology but in that of neo-liberalism, which, as I have said, is capital's 'last resort' – historically, as it were, its last throw of the dice. There can be only one progressive response to the lead that has once again come from Greece – many centuries on from the birth of 'democracy' – and that is for the European working class to respond to the Greek '*OXI*' by hearing it as a call for an international network of solidarity against austerity and the system that lies behind it.

If *Against Capital* can contribute to the development of this response over the next period, it will have served its purpose. It aims to speak to – or rather, engage with – those involving themselves in this struggle. The experiences it highlights show that we need to be done with the old party politics (reformist, 'hard left' or whatever) and with placing reliance on elected (or supposedly 'charismatic') leaders to take responsibility for resisting the attacks of big capital. Rather we need to engage with every form of resistance from below, every new form of fighting organisation. Some of us used to talk a great deal about 'intervening politically'. No! Let us rather participate in the new formations, help to make them work, learn from them. Forget about becoming involved in the 'turmoil' in the British Labour Party, or bemoaning Syriza's inevitable clash with an angry electorate that feels betrayed. These things have to happen. They are evidence both that the old methods are dead and that the new is in gestation.

Preface

by Cliff Slaughter

Inequality in today's world is greater than ever before: inequality of wealth, of opportunity, of access to and participation in the culture created by generations of men and women. Billions of human beings are deprived of freedom by state oppression and by the ravages of war fought in the interests of 'great powers' and the personifications of capital they represent. So destructive are the imperatives of capital accumulation that the very existence of humanity and of the natural environment is more and more under threat.

These are manifestations of the truth advanced more than a century and a half ago by Karl Marx: that a system based on the division of society into classes and the exploitation of the labour of the mass of propertyless workers must come into explosive contradiction with the power and potential of ever-advancing productive forces, which are capable of – but prevented by existing social relations from – delivering material prosperity for all and creative universal intercourse. From this contradiction, which has forced millions of people in every part of the world to fight against exploitation and oppression, flows the necessity of social revolution.

In our century the contradiction between, on the one hand, the rule of capital, and on the other, the necessity and the possibility of creating a truly human society where freedom and equality are the rule, has now reached a new and critical level. Every day it becomes clearer that the elementary natural and cultural conditions of our future are being systematically undermined. The necessity of the fight to put to an end to the exploitative rule of capital has acquired a new urgency. It has become a life-and-death matter.

This book aims to contribute to the clarification of what this means by asking what can be learned from the experiences of past and present movements and struggles. For lessons to be learned, and for the exploited peoples of the world to be rearmed in theory and in practice, we believe that there must be a definitive break from the idea that revolutionary theory must be brought 'from the outside' by a 'vanguard' leadership standing above the struggle issuing commands and prescriptions deriving from its particular dogma. We have tried to define some starting-points for theoretical rearmament, which we see as work that must be part of a committed engagement with every movement of resistance and protest – listening and learning.

These are our concerns. *Against Capital* was inspired in particular by an understanding that the doubts and debates on the left about US and British intervention (supposedly 'humanitarian', of course) in Libya and the Middle East in the wake of the 'Arab Spring' called for new work insisting that the solution to such situations cannot possibly be entrusted to imperialist intervention of any kind. The solution can come only from the self-organisation and independently directed struggle of the ordinary people, developing alongside the fight for international solidarity. This, after all, is only to reassert – in a way urgently relevant today – Marx's great truth: 'the emancipation of the working class is the task of the working class itself!'

To present and analyse the experiences and lessons of the many movements in South America (and their international connections) would require a separate and lengthy treatment (reserved for a later volume). Meanwhile, valuable information can be obtained from numerous internet links, among them the following: La Via Campesina (International Peasant Organisation); the MST – Movimento dos Trabalhadores Sem Terra (Landless Workers Movement); the MTST – Movimento dos Trabalhadores Sem-Teto (Homeless Workers Movement; Urban Occupations, Brazil); the Resistance in the Aguan Valley,

Honduras; The Honduras Solidarity Network; Honduras Resists, blog.

The presentation of the different parts of this book may seem uneven; but that is a reflection of the different experiences of its authors in struggles that themselves have taken many different forms. The unity comes from the underlying causation and aspirations of these struggles and from the fact that all contributors are participants as well as commentators and analysts.

PART I

Introduction: What We Confront

by Cliff Slaughter

In every continent, countless thousands of men and women look for ways to organise and demonstrate for an escape from the oppression and exploitation inflicted upon them. Many of them find themselves victims of murderous wars between conflicting powers, with thousands dying or reduced to homelessness and hopeless poverty. Even in what used to be called the 'advanced capitalist countries' of Western Europe and North America, mass unemployment and attacks on basic standards of living in the name of 'austerity' to solve problems of 'sovereign debt' are more and more the order of the day. Everywhere in the struggles against these conditions youth have been to the fore, more and more of them insisting that the future of humanity is threatened and that a new social order must be founded. We shall argue in this short book that what is at stake everywhere is the necessity to end the rule of capital, and that it is possible to learn from past movements and mistakes in order to move towards that end.

For many years, it was only on very rare occasions that the word 'capitalism' and the name of Karl Marx could be found in our newspapers. Today, in 2015, hardly a day goes by without our seeing them in the European and North American press. We are told that there is too much polarisation of wealth, too much debt, that bankers are paid too much, that there is too much or too little credit or 'quantitative easing', and so on ad nauseam. Some of the commentators report all this as simply matter-of-fact news. Others appear radical, telling us that capitalism 'isn't working' and something should be done about it. But what? With very few exceptions, they offer only suggestions about how to manage the system better and more fairly. On 27 May 2014, TV news programmes informed us that an international conference on 'Inclusive Capitalism' was about to begin proceedings, its intention to deal with 'bad capitalism'! No doubt the initiators of this conference had in mind a 'good capitalism', to be rescued and properly organised. (Has anything been heard of this conference since? Let alone any news of its successes?) In this book we see the problem very differently. The problem is not how to manage the capital system, but how to get rid of it.

Along with the jeremiads about the faults and virtues of capitalism we find reports and commentaries on the state of the working class: has it disappeared? Do people still feel working-class? What happened to the 'old' working class and its culture and consciousness? And so on. Again, our approach here is very different. We do not mean by working-class consciousness the feeling of individual working people about whether or not they are working-class. The workers are a class of wage-earners, the indispensable opposite of capital, its structural antagonist. And so, as for class-consciousness, we focus on the possibilities of a working-class movement aimed at overcoming wage-slavery, with the recognition in theory and in practice that capital has inescapably created, in that movement, what Marx and Engels, in the *Communist Manifesto* of 1848, referred to as 'its own gravediggers'.

The rule of capital now has global reach. In the nineteenth century, when modern socialist ideas and the socialist movement were born, the working class existed in England, soon in Western Europe and the United States, and then, in the last decades of the century, in Russia. Today the working class exists everywhere. In and alongside the working class in many countries there are millions of oppressed and exploited people struggling to find subsistence on the very minimum of resources, and falling victim in massive numbers to famine and disease, as well as the dispersal and destruction of thousands of communities in wars, which have become a savage method of social control. In the older, 'advanced' capitalist countries of Europe and North America, living standards, basic rights and any promise of a future are daily under attack, giving rise to movements of protest, especially of young people. In the countries where ex-Stalinist bureaucrats have become a new capitalist class (particularly China and Russia) a large and growing working class confronts employers who are inextricably integrated with the state machine, together with the transnational corporations who invest there because of the inhumanly low wages and the denial of political and organisational rights imposed by the state. In ex-colonial countries such as those in Africa and the Middle East, millions are awakening (as in the 'Arab Spring') to the necessity of getting rid of the nationalist leaders who abandoned their left-wing, even 'communist' rhetoric as soon as they were in power, turning on the working people, and keeping order on behalf of imperialist powers like the US and Britain.

Egypt provides a compelling recent example. When the workers and youth in Cairo massed in Tahrir Square demanding the ousting of President Mubarak, for decades the head of a government repressing all opposition and protecting US business and strategic interests, newspapers in Britain and the US carried the headline 'Obama: Mubarak Must Stay!' Only days later, as Mubarak's fate was sealed, Obama and the State Department presented the US as the guarantor of a new democracy and the rule of law. In fact the US and its allies have since then, as always, supported and armed the Egyptian military in the imprisonment of tens of thousands of protestors and the murder of some 2,000. US arms sales to Egypt had increased by over 80 per cent by 2014. In Cairo dozens of trade commissioners from the US, Canada and Britain are safely ensconced. Typically, the heroic youth and workers of Egypt are going through bitter experiences in order to absorb the lesson that it is the real source of their plight, the rule of capital, that they must find ways to confront and remove.

The Egyptian experience conforms to a pattern. The US has supported and armed the repressive regime of Saudi Arabia, ignoring its brutal suppression of any demand for human rights and its notorious oppression of women. After encouraging and arming the regime of Saddam Hussein in his invasion of Kuwait, the US claimed to discover 'weapons of mass destruction' in Iraq and, with the support of New Labour's Blair government in Britain, launched the invasion of that country in the name of the 'war on terror'. Since then two million Iraqis have lost their lives. Then came the war in Afghanistan and the barbaric 'drone' bombings. Gaddafi was for some 30 years acceptable as protector of US interests in Libya until the uprising against him, at which point the State Department concentrated only on finding satisfactory successors among his opponents, settling for the highly reactionary assortment of armed militias. Earlier, as the US greatly increased its business relations with Russia, Putin's invasion of Chechnya and South Ossetia was virtually ignored. In China, US business interests grow apace, facilitated by the US administration, while the Chinese state's incarceration of fighters for human rights and freedom of expression is criticised in words but accepted in reality.

In 2014, the Ukraine government led by Yanukovich, seen to be acting in the interests of Putin's Moscow regime, was ousted by popular protests. It was soon replaced by a junta of nationalist and right-wing parties, to which the US and its allies rendered immediate support, knowing that the junta is unable to maintain control without making use of ultra-right and even fascist armed organisations. Meanwhile Russian President Putin took advantage of the crisis and proceeded to the annexation of Crimea and Eastern Ukraine in pursuit of his 'Greater Russia' project, confident in the support of many of the Russian-speaking majority in that region, who mobilised against the junta in Kiev.

In every case of this kind of political and military rule on behalf of capital, we have seen protests and demonstrations, and important signs of consciousness of the need not only for defensive struggles but also for an alternative socialist way of life. Socialists have understood that as well as convictions and aspirations there must be an objective, material basis for the possibility of a socialist future. That basis is the great advance in the forces of production which came with the capitalist system. At a certain point these forces come into contradiction with the social relations based on the capitalist system of exploitation, and the capitalist order must be challenged by its own creation, its structural antagonist, the working class. This was the basis of Marx's anticipation of a social revolution and a socialist future. Is it still justified?

The fantastic growth in productivity, the application of science and technique, the development of what Marx called 'the social brain', has gone far beyond the machine production that Marx analyses in his *Capital*. The contradiction between these means of production and the existing social metabolism, based as it is on capital accumulation derived from 'the theft of alien labour time', is more and more glaring (there are many manifestations, especially in the dominance of finance capital). The 'objective conditions', 'necessary conditions' for a truly human social order are there, increasingly so. *But* we have reached a stage where the uncontrollable imperative of capital accumulation is using the means of production in such a way as to destroy, and threaten the very existence of, the elementary natural and human conditions of such a future social order. *And* is it not a fact that in the nineteenth and most of the twentieth centuries the development of the means of production (large-scale factory production) inevitably brought together many millions of wage-workers in workplaces and towns where they could organise, becoming indeed capital's potential 'gravediggers', the organised movement that could become the agency of social revolution?

Such is the nature of the scientific and technical changes in production in the older, so-called 'advanced' capitalist countries that it is no longer a matter of creating mass-production plants in which thousands, millions of workers can organise themselves. On the contrary, we more and more see that the working environment and the nature of work have radically changed: now we have casualisation, the predominance of 'service industries', de-skilling and 'precarisation'. The self-organisation of large numbers of workers becomes more and more difficult. And to this must be added the persistence of long-term, 'structural' unemployment, particularly for young people, the decline and bureaucratisation of trade unions, the imposition of anti-union laws, and the virtual disenfranchisement of the working class as the so-called socialist and labour parties have become openly pro-capitalist and the betrayals of the old 'communist' parties have given place to their collapse. These agencies have in fact become settled components of capital's system of social control.

At the same time, the 'workshop of the world' (as Britain once was known), where masses of workers are employed in great industrial plants and have the potential to organise, has shifted to China, the Indian sub-continent and parts of Africa and Latin America. Perhaps we should turn on its head Lenin's insistence that after the October 1917 Revolution, socialism in backward Russia could come about only if the Russian workers could 'hold on until the workers of the advanced countries come to our aid'! In Europe and North America must we learn to fight to 'hold on' until the workers of Asia, Africa and Latin America come to *our* aid? We are saying this not out of pessimism or disillusionment (or, God forbid, 'revisionism', as incurable sectarians are certain to say), but because we need urgently to look afresh at the ways in which the exploited and oppressed are beginning to organise and assert themselves.

The twentieth century, however, saw the onset of a new and ever-increasing danger, immeasurably intensifying the urgency of a social revolution; namely, the predominance of the *destructive* side of capital's self-reproduction. The imperatives of capital's system of production have become destructive of the elementary foundations of any future truly human society – on the one hand, through devastating the natural environment and its resources, and on the other, through ruining the potential of human beings, and in millions of cases their very existence. Countless numbers die of starvation in areas of the world now incorporated into capital's 'globalisation', while a few thousand are kept alive by 'charity'. In the old 'advanced capitalist countries', 'austerity' and unemployment, in the name of resolving problems of 'debt' arising from the rule of finance-capital, bring an insoluble crisis in 'welfare' provision. Already in the *Communist Manifesto,* Marx and Engels had seen the writing on the wall when they wrote that:

The bourgeoisie is unfit to rule because it is incompetent to ensure an existence to its slave within his slavery, because it cannot help letting him sink into such a state, that it has to feed him, instead of being fed by him.

In Britain, for example, the ruling class was compelled to concede the benefits of the welfare state at the end of World War Two, but now the depth of the structural crisis is such that this can no longer be 'afforded'. There is no solution for the consequent problems, so that millions will be plunged into a situation of desperate need – the condition for renewed working-class and popular struggle. As Stendhal, writing his long-unpublished autobiographical book, *Vie de Henri Brulard,* in the mid-1830s, put it: 'I have always, as it were by some instinct, despised the bourgeois ... So then according to me, energy was only to be found ... in that class which has to struggle with real needs.'

Marx saw this force of people with 'real needs' in the proletariat of his time: in the ringing closing words of the *Communist Manifesto,* 'Workers of the world, unite! You have nothing to lose but your chains!' Today's proletariat is thousands of times more numerous than in Marx's day; the world ruled by capital in which the proletariat exists is far larger. In terms of living standards, 'nothing to lose' is by no means as true for many of the workers of North America and Western Europe as for those of Asia, Africa and Latin America, but it is highly significant that, as we have noted, in Britain and other countries the 'welfare state' is being systematically destroyed, and in countries like Greece, Portugal, Spain and Italy national indebtedness has brought unemployment and poverty to millions. As we shall try to show, this means that the problems faced by the working class in achieving the consciousness and organisation needed in challenging the rule of capital will differ in important respects in different countries. It also means that the making of a working-class internationalism, a vital component of that consciousness and organisation, involves problems and tasks more complex and demanding than ever before.

We have referred to the 'internal differentiation' of the working class. The class is not only differentiated, it is divided. This is more than a matter of differences between skilled and unskilled, white-collar and blue-collar, low-paid and better-paid workers, etc. Long ago, Lenin identified as one of the sources of opportunism and social-chauvinism in the working-class movement in Britain the existence of a 'labour aristocracy' of relatively well-paid workers, made possible by the fruits of empire and the City of London's international financial dominance. Reformism proved to be of great benefit to the British working class particularly after World War Two. (It was Trotsky who defined the Labour Party – which was to enact the 'welfare state' – as 'a bourgeois workers' party'.) The reforms of the 1945 Labour Government of Clement Attlee were a response to the strong feeling among workers that there must be 'no return to the hungry thirties'. Whatever possibility there was of any sort of revolutionary socialist development in the working class was dispelled by the effect of the concessions won based on the

Beveridge Report, and William Beveridge's 1944 book, *Full Employment in a Free Society*, which included the National Health Service, nationalisation of some industries, and more.

As noted, however, the onset of capital's structural crisis in the late 1960s and early 1970s saw the beginning of a ruling-class offensive against the welfare state, a series of anti-trade-union laws and large-scale privatisations. Margaret Thatcher's governments in the 1980s carried through a campaign to destroy militant trade unionism, culminating in the brutal suppression of the 1984–85 miners' strike and virtual closing-down of the coalmining industry.

The first two decades of the twenty-first century have seen the continuation of this offensive, combined with huge structural unemployment, inability to finance and decline of the National Health Service, abandonment of social housing and rampant privatisation. But it has not been possible, up to the point of writing in 2015, to put an end completely to the 'benefits' system (housing benefit, unemployment pay, family tax credits, etc.) available to several million unemployed and poorly paid workers and their families, many of whom know they are slightly better off on benefits than they would be if working for the miserably low wages available to them. This situation is now creating a division between employed workers and the millions who are daily stigmatised by the media and by politicians as 'benefits cheats', 'scroungers' and so on. The division is exacerbated by the continuous concentration by the mass media – and by party politicians who have made immigration control their key election issue – on the fact that these benefits can also be claimed by immigrants.

All this, it can well be argued, produces a highly contradictory prospect for the relation between the ruling class and the working class, in that the divisions created and zealously fostered by the media and politicians are a very important means of social control, i.e. by dividing the working class, by producing a sub-class of men and women outside the workforce, not engaged directly in the mutually antagonistic but structurally fundamental capital-labour relation that is the source of the class struggle. This division is of course of great advantage to the ruling class, to capital.

On the other hand – and here is the contradiction – governments have taken the road of attacking what remains of the welfare (benefits) system. Insofar as they succeed in this – and it is an offensive that will not abate, being driven by fiscal/financial necessity – they are in practice undermining, even destroying, the very mechanism that we have suggested is for them a vital means of social control. It is a means of social control supported, strengthened, by the reduction of many thousands of employed workers to zero-hours contracts and insecure and individually isolated jobs.

Will the attack on benefits bring only greater impoverishment and desperation? Will it bring a reactionary radicalisation of those who suffer? Will it be the breeding ground for parties of the extreme right? These are certainly dangers, given the decline of trade unions and the bureaucratic conservatism of their leaderships and the 'business-friendly' politics of the Labour Party. In his contribution on Britain in this volume, Tom Owen suggests persuasively that new forms of self-organisation and mutual cooperation will have to develop.

Wherever movements of protest and revolt have developed in recent years, youth have been to the fore. They are able to make use of the new information technology as a basis for organisation, giving them a great advantage, but how are they to arm themselves theoretically, politically, so as to develop the necessary strategy and tactics, together with strong, continuous and renewable organisation? This is a profound question, especially because the source of their problems is, essentially, the same everywhere. That source is the 'globalised' capital system, in the throes of its structural, historical crisis, which has to impose its imperatives in all countries. At the same time, state repression is ever-intensifying. The euphemistically named 'surveillance' is used by the state to monitor and attempt to control every aspect of life, and in particular the intercommunication of young people, from their intimate relationships to their actual and potential participation in protest and occupation movements.

All talk about class struggle being a thing of the past is spectacularly wide of the mark. Under attack from the state's surveillance, young people, students and workers, devise their own defences. In occupations and street actions in the United States, in Britain and in Egypt they immediately found methods of communication that at least temporarily escaped the attention of the authorities. In China, they sought and found the assistance of computer experts who knew how to obstruct the state's 'firewalls'. Some of these experts are now languishing in jail, with long sentences for their 'anti-state activity'. All this is class war, conducted by the state always on behalf of what Marx called 'the personifications of capital'; and this is true whether the capitalists are European and American or Chinese ex-Stalinist bureaucrats. Similarly, the so-called riots in Britain and France in 2011, where young people responded to unemployment and police killings by helping themselves to the consumer goods available in high-street stores, were most certainly a form of response to the ruling class and its state attacks.

The response to these struggles from those who wish to be seen as speaking for the working class has been negative. This verdict is surely true for the leaders of trade unions and parties like Britain's 'New Labour' and the French Socialist Party, who had nothing to say. Hardly surprising, since they had already meekly accepted the anti-union laws of the 'neo-liberal' age, and, in the case of New Labour, declared themselves 'business-friendly'. But the verdict is just as true for the groups and parties to their left. In France, those parties (Force Ouvrière, Ligue

Communiste Revolutionnaire) satisfied themselves with tired comments like 'such actions are fruitless unless the working class comes on to the scene'; and Britain's Socialist Workers Party proved just as pathetic.

While it is tempting to envision a parallel between today's problems of financial crisis, debt, inflation, unemployment and the growth of extreme right-wing and neo-fascist parties in Europe East and West and the days of Weimar Germany and the 1920s and 1930s, there is in fact a decisive difference. Today, unlike the 1920s, there are no mass parties of the working class declaring themselves socialist or communist; the trade unions are much more conservative and bureaucratised, and in Europe the great manufacturing plants and factories have largely disappeared. Antonio Gramsci's insistence on the factory as the basic unit of working-class politics and organisation, for example, would now be misplaced. Furthermore, there is no parallel today with a recent successful proletarian revolution such as had occurred in Russia in 1917. Far from the problem facing the working class being that 'the crisis of humanity is reduced to the crisis of working-class revolutionary leadership' to be met by the 'construction (later the reconstruction) of the Fourth International', as advanced by Trotsky and the Trotskyists, what is at stake is *the reconstitution of the working-class movement itself,* with the internal composition of the working class, and its relation to the so-called middle classes, greatly changed.

Beyond Western Europe, in Iran and the Middle East there have been mass movements of workers and youth, only for the fruits of their sacrifices to be seized, as Yassamine Mather documents in this book, by reactionary religious fundamentalist and military forces, and for severe repression to be meted out. National liberation struggles in Africa, which Robert Myers writes about, have brought the same results. These contributions to parts two and three of this book are complemented by other detailed considerations of such experiences – compelling examples of the problems of organisation and political strategy and tactics facing the working class everywhere in the struggles to come.

The necessary organisational and political rearming cannot be successful without also a *theoretical* rearming. Such a rearming will have to contain from the start a thoroughgoing critique not only of bourgeois ideology but also of revolutionary concepts and theories that belong to an earlier and very different period, and many of which have been dogmatically distorted or misunderstood, with dangerous, even disastrous consequences. In parts four and five, I concentrate on this aspect of the problem before drawing some conclusions in part six.

In brief, what is attempted in what follows is this. Marx's affirmation 150 years ago that the proletarian (socialist) revolution was for all humanity (a 'human revolution') rings so true as to be blindingly obvious. We have globalisation and climate change threatening natural and cultural disaster, and the brutal, dehumanising and barbaric human consequences of rival imperialisms ruthlessly using military conflict to safeguard their continuing exploitation of natural and strategic resources. And the recognition of the need for system-change is now there in all sections of human society, a much more wide-ranging recognition than the understanding of basic needs which first impelled the working class into struggle.

From this point of view, what can be learned from the experiences and struggles here outlined? What basic questions arise in them and flow from them?

First, capital's structural crisis is throwing up all manner of protests, struggles, movements, and at the same time it intensifies the agonising need for a structural change in the social order, beyond the need for reforms or changes of political regime;

Second, the working class as agent of the necessary social revolution has gone through a century of repression, betrayals, mistaken or inadequate theory and practice of leadership, new and radical internal differentiation (national and international): it is left with its basic organisations decimated or bureaucratised, and is politically completely disenfranchised;

Third, the many and varied struggles – 'social movements', national liberation – find themselves reaching a dead end, usurped by enemy forces, or fizzling out, having failed to achieve continuity in space or time. The changes that they may bring about (e.g. change of political regime, as in Southern Africa or the Middle East) leave the people still failing to escape from, and still not adequately arming themselves against, the real cause of their exploitation and oppression, namely the rule of capital;

And last ... the key question: what will be necessary – reconstitution of the working-class movement? international co-ordination? – to overcome this situation, and are there signs of that overcoming?

PART II

Rebuilding: Some Experiences and Lessons

by Cliff Slaughter

What can we make, today, of the well-worn slogan and tactic of a 'united front' of working-class parties? In what country today are there working-class parties, except in the sense that some workers vote for them from time to time? They most certainly do not represent the interests of the working class (or even claim to do so, in most cases). To repeat: the task today is not to change things at the top, in or between parties, but to reconstitute the working-class movement. I would claim that, albeit in the face of great difficulties, in some countries (in particular South Africa) this is beginning, and it will have to be *against* the parties that have deserted and betrayed the working class. In another example, Greece, the working-class movement faces great problems in overcoming the consequences of de-industrialisation and casualisation, membership of the European Union, and the past domination of left politics by the Stalinist Communist Party of Greece, as well as the savage repression inflicted on the working class in the immediate aftermath of World War Two. How can the conflicts in Ukraine begin to be understood without evaluating the consequences of the butchering of over six million Ukrainians by the Stalin regime's forced collectivisation? Stalin's atrocities in Poland, equally, have had a massive effect in shaping the past and present of working-class politics there.

All these examples have this in common: there are protests and demands, even the successful overthrow of existing governmental regimes, but it is only through a series of new struggles and often bitter experiences and disillusionment, that the means will be found to address and confront the real source of oppression, i.e. the capital system as such, against whose conditions it was necessary to rebel in the first place. This is of course no simple matter: the rule of capital is not national or regional but global, and the previous domination and then collapse of Stalinism is also a global phenomenon, which can be understood and – eventually – overcome only on a global scale.

The necessary process of reconstitution must go beyond national boundaries, in our globalised system where there is no longer congruence between economic reality on the one hand, and political power and the arena of political struggle on the other. That is to say: the nation state – even a combination of such states – does not correspond to the economy and has extremely limited means to adapt to or regulate the actual functioning and problems of the economy (so-called 'sovereign debt' being an obvious example). Certainly some of the old 'metropolitan countries' have gained temporary advantages from, say, the European Union or the North American economic 'alliance', in particular the availability of a large new transnational 'reserve army of labour' in Eastern Europe. But they are finding that the social and political problems resulting from this new 'mobility of (cheap) labour' are increasingly difficult to deal with. This is just one example of the nation state's inability to palliate, let alone control, the profound social problems and class struggles which will inevitably flow from the impact of global capital's structural crisis. The intensification of these problems is more and more evident: already in Greece, Spain, Italy, the Middle East, Ukraine, Thailand and elsewhere. It is no accident that we see, in response, the rise of extreme right-wing reactionary forces – neo-Nazi parties, religious fundamentalism, military juntas – and increasingly authoritarian measures, making even more urgent the reconstitution and political rearming of the working class.

Everything said by Trotsky about the betrayals of the working class in the 1920s and 1930s was right, but he greatly underestimated the damage done to the working-class movement. According to Isaac Deutscher, he told Kingsley Martin, editor of the *New Statesman*, in 1937: 'I tell you that in three to five years from now the Fourth International will be a great force in the world', which today seems absurd.[1] Equally underestimated was the benefit (then and later) of those betrayals and defeats to capitalism and its powers of recovery (displacement of its contradictions). Capitalism was in fact able in the advanced countries, after World War Two, to go through two phases of development, namely post-war boom/welfare state, then the monetarist stage from the 1970s.

In the post-war years, the Trotskyist movement's perspective was 'reconstructing the Fourth International'. Again, I suggest that in the virtual absence now of any working-class parties, and given the changed composition and internal relations of the working class, and especially its changed international character, what is at stake is the *reconstitution of the working-class movement*.

The agency of socialist revolution is the working class in movement. This movement will mean the working class arming itself politically for the overthrow of the capitalist state, but *within* that preparation there will be forms of co-operation, organisation and mutual aid which anticipate and actually begin the construction of a socialist society and culture. We should never forget that, as Marx wrote for the rules of the International Workingmen's Association in 1867, 'the emancipation of the working classes must be conquered by the working classes themselves' – from which it surely follows – I quote from my *A New Party for Socialism* (London, New Park, 1996) – that

> the reconstruction of the working-class movement ... is the task of the working class itself. The new party is part of that self-reconstruction; it is not a party 'supplied' to the working class, but one built by the working class.

For 'reconstruction' I would now write *'reconstitution'*.

Only a few years after this was written came, in 2004–06, new advances in electronic communication in the form of social media. These new and technically revolutionary means of communication are now universally available and are already being used, in, for example, the 'Arab Spring', the 'Occupy' and '99%' movements, and the resistance in Greece and Spain in unprecedented ways. The potential for transforming the range and speed of communication between the people engaged in social and political struggles can hardly be overestimated.

Where then do Marxists come in? Surely it is clear that no 'vanguard party', 'centralising', or, as we used to say, 'politicising', these many and varied and original movements against the rule of capital, fits the bill. Instead of 'politicising intervention' in the many and varied forms of resistance provoked by capital's attempt to divert the consequences of it structural crisis – through 'austerity' programmes, destruction of the welfare state and so on – the task is to engage in them, aiding them in developing their independence, contacts, consciousness and continuity. We will need to engage with, fight alongside, and study every form of movement and struggle before an adequate theory can be developed, a theory that can enrich and arm the consciousness of the ever-growing numbers who find themselves driven into conflict with the power of capital. They have the possibility of developing in quite new ways their own contacts, interchanges, networks and forms of solidarity. But there are real limits that must be overcome.

How will it be possible to overcome the separateness in space and time of the many movements and struggles, the absence of a meaningful continuity? Up to the present time, no way has been found to build forms of organisation, networks and threads reaching to the roots of each manifestation of the new movements in order to accumulate experiences and carry the lessons forward in an interlinked continuity of all the struggles of workers and youth. We do not yet know what form of organisation, party or otherwise, can bring together those who learn how to establish those networks, and the responsibility of Marxists is to engage with them, immerse themselves in their struggles, carry out the theoretical work that can digest the experiences and help point the way forward. István Mészáros formulated the basis of an approach to this problem very clearly when, in 1981, he wrote that proletarian unity:

> ... is a problem, a task, a challenge, even an imperative in determinate situations of emergency, but not a spontaneously given actual state of affairs. It may be brought into being for a more or less limited period and for a determinate purpose, but it may never be assumed as an unproblematically persistent condition even after its successful accomplishment in a specific socio-historical situation. On the contrary, *it has to be constantly recreated* under the changing circumstances for as long as the objective grounds of inequality (due to the inherited hierarchical social division of labour and differential rates of exploitation mentioned earlier) remain with us in any form whatsoever, as they are bound to remain for a much longer historical period of transition that one would wish.[2] [Emphasis added.]

If we are right that the new means of communication are highly valuable additional, even transformative, resources for the development of revolutionary organisation, this should not at all be taken to mean that there is no longer a need for the fight on the 'theoretical front'. The contrary is true. We need 'theory', as it is properly understood by Marx, that is as 'a guide to action'. As for the responsibility of Marxists, it is necessary to put an end to the doctrinaire propagandism (and its inevitable consequence in sectarian splits), the *modus operandi* of most if not all of the self-professed 'Marxist' parties and groups.

My argument is that reconstitution of the working-class movement involves overcoming the enormous damage, indeed destruction, inflicted by the betrayals of Stalinism and social democracy, and not at all concentrating on reforming or replacing the existing parties. The massive proletarianisation that has taken place in countries like China, the Indian sub-continent, Latin America and Africa is the unspoken but explosive, inescapably necessary and fatal opposite called into existence by capital's globalised power. There is a new potential basis for socialist internationalism. In the older capitalist countries, the disappearing possibilities of improving or even maintaining the standards of living and the rights of working people through class-collaboration will inevitably bring people into political struggle. They understand more and more that the old working-class parties are totally discredited, but there is the obvious danger that those parties' past betrayals and the weakness and mistakes of the self-styled revolutionary left produce political apathy or a turn to extreme right-wing politics and ideologies.

This essential new socialist internationalism will be built not by doctrinaire pronouncements and outworn formulas. It will only emerge from struggles – and often bitter disillusionments – as workers and young fighters learn that the solutions offered by nationalist, religious-fundamentalist and demagogic 'radical' leaders do not address their deeply felt needs and demands, and that such forces will turn against them once they have power, as has happened, for example, in Egypt and South Africa. Only in the course of these experiences will it become clear that it is the rule of capital itself that must be confronted and overcome, and that the self-organisation of the working class and those who join it must be built within that process. With all manner of differences in historical background and forms of struggle, we can see the same basic problems and prospects in widely separate regional and national contexts. As an introduction, it is useful to have in mind as context the overall historical background, the general characteristics of the stage through which society has passed over the last century. Some years ago, in my book *Not Without a Storm* (London, Index Books, 2005), I advanced the following hypothesis, which I now repeat in a slightly modified form.

Was the twentieth century, as we believed and as we took as the basis of our work and lives, the century of working-class socialist revolution? There was no such revolution in a major, advanced capitalist country except the failed one in Germany – though of course there were many struggles of a revolutionary nature. The Russian October took place in a country where capitalism had only recently begun to develop – and had begun to develop under conditions where capitalism had already become 'imperialism'. Tsarist autocracy stood in the way of Russia's development. Trotsky tried to comprehend this 'uneven and combined development' in countries like Russia with his theory of permanent revolution. In October 1917 he came to agree with Lenin to the – to be sure, very important – extent that they saw the proletariat as the only class able to make the 'democratic' revolution, leading to a workers' state that would then be joined to the proletarian revolution in the advanced countries.

Looking back over the twentieth century, however, we have to acknowledge that there has been no 'bourgeois-democratic' revolution. This suggests that a democratic regime for transition of late-developing nations to capitalism is, in the conditions of the twentieth and twenty-first centuries, impossible. In all ex-colonial countries, the emerging regimes, taking their place (such as it is) in globalised capitalism, have not been in any sense 'democratic'. They have not successfully tackled the 'democratic tasks' of establishing a democratic state, solving the agrarian problem, and so on. 'National liberation' has resulted in bourgeois, non-democratic dictatorships. Where revolutions have overthrown the old regimes – as in China, Russia, South-East Asia – led by communist (Stalinist) parties, with the workers and peasants as the revolutionary force, the resultant regimes have after some decades become capitalist. And the form of capitalism adopted has, inevitably, corresponded to the requirements of the stage that *now* exists in the 'globalised' world arena.

Recognising this, is it too sweeping to say something like the following? Lenin and Trotsky were correct in seeing the need for the proletariat to take the leading role in overthrowing feudalism, serfdom, or whatever *ancien régime* existed. But we have now to go further in analysing the history of the period since their time. It was only via this path – and not via the bourgeoisie – that national capitalist states could be achieved, and this is the *historical role* that the various Stalinist regimes – so-called 'workers' states' – played. They prepared, and then effected, the transition of the nation to capitalism. They did it in an unprecedented way, but they did it. (This estimation of their role in history makes largely irrelevant the interminable debates about the nature of the Soviet Union – 'state capitalism', 'bureaucratic collectivism', 'degenerated and deformed workers' states', 'bureaucratic socialism', not to mention 'really existing socialism'.)

Not only did these states build up the economic infrastructure at least to the point where the new national bourgeoisie (in the first place, ex-Stalinist bureaucrats who plundered state property) could exist and compete in the global capital system. They also created a larger and *disciplined* working class – the creation of which is the main condition necessary for capitalism to begin – with a movement from country to town massive enough for the next step of transition. That next step began with the collapse of Stalinism in 1989–90. In the years 2005 and 2006, large-scale pitched battles were being waged in villages in many parts of China as peasants resisted the seizure of their land for capital investment by members and friends of the 'Communist' state bureaucracy. The tragic consequences for peasant families continue, evidenced by the recent story of four neglected siblings aged between five and thirteen who, having swallowed pesticide, were found dead by a great uncle in the home they occupied alone in a village in the southwest of the country. This far from untypical incident, the London *Times* reported on 12 June 2015, highlighted 'the plight of 60 million children left behind as their parents seek work in fast-growing urban areas', where 'China's apartheid-like system of household registration, called *houkou*, is still used to deny urban social services, including school access, to the rural migrants whose labour has transformed China in recent decades'. The ruthless Chinese predators operating and making themselves wealthy from these expropriations are the heirs of the perpetrators of the land enclosures in England and lowland Scotland, and of the Highland Clearances (to which Marx devoted a large section of *Capital*), which destroyed the peasantry in Britain, creating the mass proletariat necessary for the first transition to industrial capitalism.

Furthermore, the proletariat so prepared and disciplined by the Stalinist regimes is now employed to produce for the 'globalised' market at rates of pay and under conditions that were long ago transcended by workers of the advanced capitalist countries. This gives China, Russia and other ex-Stalinist countries an enormous competitive advantage, a new version of the 'privilege of backwardness', which has immeasurable consequences for every aspect of the global economy.

The historical role and nature of the 'independent', 'national-liberated' regimes in Africa are in essence a derivative of the above characterisation of the Soviet Union. The politicians who came to power on independence came from movements trained and inspired by Moscow. Their 'two-stage revolution' (first the national democratic, then the socialist) is nothing more than a fig-leaf, behind which brutal regimes are imposed on the working people. China, North Korea and South-East Asia (Cambodia, Vietnam, Laos) are in their own ways the same in character.

The foreign policy of Stalinist Russia, including the role of the Soviet bureaucracy as leader of Stalinist ('communist') parties all over the world, as the bureaucracy twisted and turned in its adaptation to the capitalist encirclement, had disastrous effects on the working class and the working-class movement. For example, the post-World War Two history and the present situation of the working class in Greece cannot be understood at all without knowing of the brutal crushing of the Greek Resistance to Nazi occupation by the Churchill government in 1944, a bloody episode made possible only because of the 1944 'percentage agreement' between Churchill and Stalin on the division of spheres of influence in Europe – Eastern Europe for Russia, Western Europe and Greece for the Western powers. On this basis, Soviet troops were ordered not to advance to Greece, delivering the Resistance fighters (led by the Greek Communist Party, who became complicit in what followed because of its subservience to Moscow) to the tender mercies of Churchill.[3] This laid the basis for the decades of military dictatorship and the poisonous residue of right-wing politics behind the neo-fascist 'Golden Dawn' party of today.

In South Africa, the Communist Party (SACP), political core of the African National Congress (ANC), crippled the mass movement against the apartheid regime politically and physically. Politically the doctrine of a 'democratic revolution' was supposed to create the conditions for a struggle for socialism but in practice it produced the corrupt and anti-working-class ANC regime of today; and we shall see below that recognition of how this dogma is so pernicious is central to the revival of socialist politics that is now being derived from bitter experiences by the trade union NUMSA). Physically, the internal ANC regime, modelled on and trained by Soviet Stalinism, tortured and butchered hundreds of young men and women in their own ranks who wanted to take the struggle forward. Some of the most notorious of these atrocities were carried out on the orders of Winnie Mandela, whose activities – and those of the thugs in her so-called Mandela United football club – have, since the end of apartheid, been subject to court cases widely reported in the press and online.

There are strong signs in South Africa – documented in what follows – of a theoretical and practical recognition that 'national liberation' movements in African countries, heavily influenced by the Stalinist bureaucracy through armaments, 'security training' and political indoctrination via 'communist parties', have not resulted in the promised stage of 'democratic revolution' supposedly preceding and preparing the next 'socialist' stage. What is becoming recognised as necessary is the building of a working-class movement for socialism, against the regimes established at the time of 'liberation' or 'independence' (e.g. the rule of the ANC-SACP, Mugabe's dictatorship in Zimbabwe, the regime in Kenya, etc.). In northern Africa such a development is only in the future. Mubarak was overthrown by a mass revolt in Egypt, but thus far the victors in these early stages have been, first, the Muslim Brotherhood, who themselves were then overthrown by a section of the military, which daily inflicts executions and torture on them and on any dissenters. As is true for the many rebellions and protest movements worldwide (and the structural crisis of capital makes it certain that these will grow and intensify), the pressing needs that fuelled the massive protests of the 'Arab Spring' will begin to be met only when, through all these experiences, there grows the practical consciousness that the *source* of these needs – the exploitative capital system itself – must be directly organised against and overcome.

In introducing the examples of social and political struggle that follow, I am conscious, as are other authors of this book, of glaring omissions. The two major players in the world economy, China and the United States, are not dealt with, and neither is

Latin America, apart from a short section on Mexico. This, we hope, will be rectified in a companion volume now in preparation. At this point, it can be pointed out that the *interrelations* between these sectors are of great significance. A large proportion of the consumer goods on the market in the US (as in the UK and the other old 'advanced capitalist countries') are manufactured in China. They are made at a labour cost that is only a fraction of what the same labour would cost at home – a situation, a relationship, completely different from what was visible to Marx and his followers in the nineteenth century and much of the twentieth.

Marx wrote of the unemployed as a 'reserve army of labour' at the disposal of capital. China today provides for the 'Western' capitalists what might be called a 'reserve army' of *employed* workers. Work discipline, social control and low wages are imposed on these workers by the repressive autocracy formed by the ex-Maoist bureaucrats of the Chinese Communist Party, who have become finished personifications of capital. These new-born capitalists and the ruling class of the United States are thus mutually dependent. If this mutual dependence is in contradiction with their rivalry for global dominance geopolitically and economically, that should be no surprise. Contradictions of this sort are typical of the capital system at every level.

As for Latin America, US capitalism seeks, by means of all kinds of economic pressure – the latest of these being the North American Free Trade Association (NAFTA) – to incorporate and dominate the rest of the continent; and this must and will shape the social conflicts in these countries.

Southern Africa

Preface

by Cliff Slaughter

There can be no more compelling example of the questions raised in this book – the problems faced by the working class in establishing its political independence, the deadly dangers of domination of popular movements by nationalist leadership, the obstacles created by the treacherous role of the Stalinist rulers of the Soviet Union and its satellite parties, the need for a radical rethinking of Marxist politics – than the experiences of the working class of Southern Africa in the last half-century, experiences from which bitter lessons, it seems, are now being learned and acted upon. From his edited volume, *Revolutionary Times, Revolutionary Lives: personal accounts of the liberations struggles,* Robert Myers revisits some examples.

Southern Africa

by Robert Myers

In 1946 black miners and other workers in South Africa went on strike. The strike movement was defeated and for over two decades all attempts to organise in the black working class were unsuccessful. Then in 1973 a new revolt of industrial workers started. This is how it was seen by one young Durban worker in the Dunlop factory:

> It was the bad conditions that caused the men to come out of the factories. I think the struggle started at the Coronation factory. The workers there went on the rampage and demanded a wage increase. They went out in the street and

marched, shouting Zulu war slogans. Then everyone started to join in. Even the people who didn't want to strike came out when they saw them marching past. We went to the management and told them we wanted that money. They told us we must elect representatives. We said: 'No, give us the money.' Everywhere the police attacked the strikers but the situation was beyond their control: around Durban it had become a general strike. The management locked us out but soon agreed to give us what we wanted.

After the strike an old man in my factory started to tell me about this union, the Transport and General. I became interested. A few other people joined our discussions. Then we found out that the Metal and Allied Workers Union were trying to organise in our industry so some of us started going to their meetings. Even though some people in the ruling class wanted to allow unions most employers were fighting to stop them. Our meetings were clandestine and held at night.

I think the new unions were initiated by a few people who had come from the universities. Afterwards I found out that there had been the South African Congress of Trade Unions (SACTU) led by people from the ANC but I never came across it amongst the workers. From the start we said our unions must be independent from political parties. We concentrated on building the union. As the movement had started in our area we had to send people to other areas to organise. In my factory we started to give out recruitment forms. We had to get 50 per cent membership before we could get recognition. Most people were not easy to convince. They said 'You just want to take our money'. We explained that if we were to organise we needed money.

Our union targeted factories and sent people to leaflet early in the morning. One day my factory was targeted but as often happened the police came and arrested the activists. Then I heard groups of workers in the canteen discussing this and asking, 'What is this union that the management are so against?' Some said it was because the activists were telling the truth. So I gave them recruitment forms. Two days later we got the 50 per cent. My name was put as one of the representatives.

Now management tried to make an agreement that would have made the union weak. At a lunchtime mass meeting the workers decided to strike for recognition. It was 100 per cent for strike. The first day we stayed in the canteen. The next day we were all dismissed. So in order to maintain our unity we had to find meeting hall. We got a place and came together every day. A roll-call was taken, problems were discussed and people were given different jobs to do. It was illegal to picket and the management were trying to recruit new workers. So we formed a group called 'The Special Boys'. They went early each day to try to tell people why we were on strike. There were fights when people didn't listen. New workers were hired but management couldn't get production going as many jobs needed several months' training.

After three weeks management called us back and agreed to recognition. This was a big victory. We marched through the streets dancing and shouting. The police couldn't touch us. The foremen and some others who had scabbed were driven out of the factory. This went on for a week until our union told us to stop beating the men so they were let back in but they were never the same foremen again. This was one of the first battles for recognition and after we won it was an example to other workers.[4]

Workers organised unions across the country and in 1979 the Federation of South African Trade Unions (FOSATU) was formed. This is what Wikipedia says of FOSATU:

FOSATU's constitution enshrined the principles of workers'

> control of their trade unions, non-racialism, worker independence from party politics, international worker solidarity and trade union unity. It strove to build a tight national federation to work towards an industrial workers' bloc firmly based in strong grassroots organisation on the factory floor. It became the first truly national non-racial trade union federation in South African history, building unity and avoiding the regionalism which had pervaded earlier attempts at such an organisation. Its success here has been attributed to the fostering of a national leadership layer of 'organic intellectuals' through a strong focus on the political education of shop stewards, and tight integration of the national, provincial and local structures of the organisation.

FOSATU's founding documents made clear that while they would work with the ANC in the struggle against apartheid, the working class needed its independent organisations as it has its own goal: liberation not just from apartheid but from capitalism. And it was not just in workplaces that a new generation of working-class activists were making progress. In the townships the youth, the unemployed and community organisations were all organising against apartheid and poverty. Trade unionists often played important roles in this community organisation, helping unite disparate sections of the working class.

This emergence of a self-organised working-class movement threatened the claim of the ANC and its SACP affiliate to represent the black population through their South African Congress of Trade Unions (SACTU). While workers across the country were forming genuine trade unions, at the international level the ANC, the SACP and SACTU dominated the scene. Promoted by the Soviet Union and welcomed onto the platforms of trade union and anti-apartheid gatherings around the world, these people set about gaining control of the new union movement.

Here again is the Dunlop worker:

After the 1984 township revolt was crushed the only activity was in the unions. In the rubber industry the management's intransigence made us set about forming a shop stewards' combined committee to unite all the factories. The 1984 events had convinced us even more of the need for socialism. Joe Foster, one of the founders of FOSATU, had talked about the need to build a workers' party but we still thought that the unions would get us to socialism. I organised classes for our union shop stewards in the region. These meetings went from 7pm Saturday to 7am Sunday with a short break for refreshments. Because of our problems this was the only time it was possible to get people together.

We discussed socialism. Speakers were invited to tell us about things like the Russian Revolution. We had no books at all so we could only talk. The workers discussed the ANC's 'Freedom Charter' and we saw it was just minimum demands. It had no interest for us. We were interested in what had happened in Russia because we thought there was socialism there. Questions were raised about things like Solidarność in Poland but all we could understand was there was a lack of democracy in the socialist countries because of the 'command economy'. The stewards would report back these discussions to their workers. That was the way we always worked. Although we had these discussions we didn't get a clear picture of what was to be done. All we got from our speakers were history lessons. At that time some ANC supporters were talking with us, trying to convince us that the 'two-stage theory' was right [the policy of the SACP that a black democratic capitalist government would create the conditions for workers to fight for socialism]. As workers we said: 'No, we can't have that. Once you reach the first stage you never come to the second stage.' These people had no influence inside FOSATU. I was a delegate to our union's first national conference where everyone voted for socialism.

The exiled ANC was very influential in the United Democratic Front (UDF). It was trying to influence FOSATU but couldn't do so. So it started looking for other means to control FOSATU. There were unions outside FOSATU: the biggest was the National Union of Miners (NUM) but there were many small ones too. Years earlier the ANC had formed the SA Congress of Trade Unions but it had very few members, only organisers. The UDF had influence over these organisations. Of course we all wanted a single union federation, especially with the NUM in it. My union started talks with those little UDF unions in our industry. Their leaders saw their unions were crumbling. Everyone was joining FOSATU. So, before they vanished completely, they moved in to propose mergers. So their leaders got influence in our unions. Now there was a proposed merger of all the unions. This was done with the formation of the Confederation of South African Trade Unions (COSATU). When we formed our merged union we were urged to adopt the ANC's Freedom Charter. People from the UDF came to our conference to tell us it was impossible to go straight to socialism and that the only way to get our freedom was through the ANC. The workers didn't agree to this. The UDF people were shouting at the workers, but still they wouldn't adopt the Freedom Charter.

In 1987 we took our 'Workers' Charter' to the congress of the new federation, COSATU. There was a big battle. Now there was something new in our unions. The leadership saw it could not get agreement with the workers on this issue, so they just appointed some committees to investigate and decide. Finally the union leaders adopted the Freedom Charter but without ever going to the members. It wasn't the workers who adopted the Freedom Charter. This was the first time that decisions had not been democratically taken by the workers. Though the workers didn't agree with the Charter they didn't want to criticise the leaders because they felt that would split the unions.

Looking back I can see that in 1984 the ANC started having secret talks with the ruling class – with the Anglo-American Corporation, the biggest company in South Africa. Both sides in these talks were afraid of socialism. The only way to fulfil their aims was to take away democracy within the unions so that the workers could not question what was going on in the negotiations. So, in the same way as the Freedom Charter was adopted, now an alliance of the unions, the South African Communist Party and the ANC was agreed without any reference to the shop floor. We were just told there was an alliance. More and more decisions were reported back as having already been taken. In the past the workers were always consulted. Now union democracy was vanishing.

This Triple Alliance of the ANC, SACP and COSATU has been the indispensable tool that ensured ANC policies went largely unchallenged in the transition to black majority rule and throughout the subsequent years of ANC rule as it slavishly followed the diktats of global capital and the personal enrichment of its leading elite, including some former union leaders. While this process led to curtailing of democracy and militancy in the unions, in other organisations the results were even more terrible for those struggling against capitalism.

With the upsurge of community protest throughout the late 1970s and 1980s, many young people came to see the futility of confronting the apartheid state's armed forces with bottles and stones. They saw the need to arm the township uprising but no weapons were available. Word spread of ANC camps outside South Africa where people were receiving military training. Luvo Mbenga tells his story:

I am from Port Elizabeth [home of many big industries,

including car plants]. In 1978, after the events of the 16 June uprising, I was shot by the police. I was at secondary school. The same year I was arrested and charged. I got six lashes. In 1971 I joined the black consciousness movement in Port Elizabeth. In 1980 we organised a schools boycott and I was arrested for attending an illegal gathering.

In the same year I left with friends to join the ANC in Lesotho, in order to defend ourselves against the regime. In 1981 I was in ANC camps in Angola. In 1982 I was sent to the Soviet Union for special military training and security service training. I spent a year in the Soviet Union then returned to Angola. During this period there were complaints about the ANC security service: beatings, torture, arrests of those who wanted to go home to fight, and secret killings of members. I joined in these protests. I wanted to go home and fight.[5]

Luvo goes on to tell of being held for years in the notorious ANC prison camp called Quatro, and the same story is told by Bandile Ketelo:

I was born in 1957 in the Eastern Cape. I started to be active in politics in Hilltown High School which was run by whites and there one came into direct contact with the apartheid system. I participated in the black consciousness movement and helped set up the South African Students movement. I was an executive committee member.

Clashes between Hilltown and the authorities led to a strike in October 1975. As a result of the strike I was expelled. In February 1976 I was arrested by the South African security forces and detained at Fort Glamorgan. I was released after two weeks' interrogation. I continued my studies by post but as I knew the racist police would come for me again I decided to escape from South Africa.

We joined the ANC and went to camps in Angola. I trained

> in guerrilla warfare and had some introduction to the politics of the ANC and to Marxism. In 1979 some problems developed in the camps. Most of the cadres wanted to go home. We were engaged in training for war and felt we were ready to face the conditions back in South Africa. But we found we were given more and more training that was endless. We decide no, man, this was too much. We wanted to go back and fight. This led to an uprising in the camps. The ANC crushed the uprising. It was during that time that Quatro was built.[6]

In 1990 a group of MK soldiers, [Umkhonto we Sizwe, the ANC's armed wing], who had been held for years in Quatro, issued their account of the ANC's military activities in a document called 'A miscarriage of justice'. They described how soldiers in ANC camps across Angola, after years of 'training' and fighting in regional wars outside South Africa, mutinied.

> The guerrillas in Angola levelled their bitterest criticisms against three men in the NEC of the ANC, men who had a much more direct involvement in running our army. The first was Joe Modise, army commander of the ANC since 1969. He was looked down upon by the majority of combatants as a man responsible for the failures of our army to put up a strong fight against the racist regime, a man who had stifled its growth and expansion. He was above all seen as someone who engaged himself in corrupt money-making ventures, abusing his position in the army.
>
> The second was Mzwandile Piliso, the chief of security. He was the most notorious, the most feared, soulless ideologue of the suppression of dissent and democracy in the ANC. The last one was Andrew Masondo, freed from Robben Island after 12 years. In 1984 he was the national commissar of the ANC and was therefore responsible for supervision of the

> implementation of NEC decisions and political guidance of the ANC personnel. Masondo was to use this responsibility to defend corruption, and was himself involved in the abuse of his position to exploit young and ignorant women and girls. He was also a key figure in running the notorious ANC prison camp known to the cadres as Quatro. It was nicknamed after the Fort, the rough and notorious prison for blacks in Johannesburg, known to everyone as 'No. 4'.
>
> First the soldiers (involved in the armed mutiny) demanded an immediate end to the war by the MK forces (the ANC) against UNITA [the US-backed Angolan force] and the transfer of all manpower used in that war to our main theatre of war in South Africa. Second, they demanded the suspension of the ANC security apparatus as well as the investigation of its activities and of its prison camp Quatro, then called Buchenwald. Last they demanded that Oliver Tambo (ANC president) come and address the soldiers on the solution to these problems.[7]

The document goes on to give a history of repeated revolts and mutinies amongst the people who had left South Africa in order to get guns and training but who were never allowed to go back.

> In a bid to strengthen their repressive apparatus, Andrew Masondo created a security crack force in a camp known as Viana, near Luanda. This unit, known as the People's Defence Organisation, was composed mainly of very young men or boys. Its task was to guard the ANC leadership when they paid visits to different camps, to enforce discipline and quash any form of dissent and 'disloyalty'. By this time, after the Fazenda events [a revolt] the ANC leaders had begun to whip up an 'internal-enemy-danger psychosis' and whenever they visited the camps they had to be heavily guarded. Worse still, if it was Tambo who visited, the whole camp would be

disarmed and only the security personnel would be allowed to carry weapons.

The next hot spot for the ANC was in Zambia, where the HQ of the ANC was based and where most of the leadership was living. This was in 1980. MK cadres, who had been drilled for months in the 'communist ideology' of the Soviet-East European type to denounce all luxuries and accept the hazards of the struggle, here came into direct confrontation with the opposite way of life lived by the ANC leaders. It became clear that the financial support extended to the ANC was used to finance the lavish way of life of the ANC leadership. Corruption, involving rackets of cars, diamond and drug smuggling, was endemic.

There was also the burning problem of the insignificant progress made by our forces in South Africa, at a time when our people were alone locked into bitter mass struggles against the racists. This aspect was further complicated by the decision of the NEC to send back to Angola a batch of MK forces who had survived the war in Zimbabwe and were discovered by the provisional government in the assembly points disguised as ZAPU guerrillas. Those guerrillas, still itching to go back to South Africa and aware of the conditions in the camps in Angola, refused point blank the instructions to return to Angola.

Faced with these and many other related problems, a meeting was arranged between the leadership and representatives of three detachments. The June 16th Detachment advanced the proposal to hold a conference of the whole ANC membership where these issues could be settled democratically. This proposal, which had popular backing from the overwhelming majority of young cadres, was rejected by the ANC leadership, which never accepts any idea that puts in question its competence and credibility to lead.

It was in the process of these discussions that a discovery

> of a 'spy network' was disclosed and a clampdown on the 'ambitious young men who wanted to overthrow the leadership of Tambo' was put into operation. The ANC security went into full swing, detaining the so-called spies and the proponents of the conference. Many of these young men – Pharoah, Vusi Mayekiso, Kenneth Mahsmba, Oshkosh and others – were later known to have died under torture and beatings at Quatro prison camp.

Despite the repression the mutinies continued in different camps, suppressed not just by the ANC security forces but now also by Angolan government troops and Cuban troops, supposedly in Angola to help 'liberation'. In May, 1984, a revolt broke out at the Pango camp. The camp was encircled by a crack force of ANC loyalists.

> Some managed to break out of the encirclement and marched through the bush further up north. Those captured were subjected to beatings and tortures under investigation, with melting plastic dripped on their naked bodies and private parts, whipped while tied to trees and forced under torture to exhume bodies of ANC loyalists who had died several days before. A military tribunal was set up headed by Sizakhele Sigxashe, now head of ANC intelligence, and composed predominantly of security personnel such as Morris Seabelo, a former commander at Quatro. Seven men were summarily sentenced to death by public execution by firing squad. They were James Nkabinde, one of Tambo's former bodygaurds, Ronald Msomi, Bullet (Mbumbulu) Thembile Hobo, Mahero, Wandile Ondala and Stopper.
>
> Motivated by a genuine desire to democratise the ANC and push it forward to higher levels of armed confrontation for the people's freedom, they demonstrated a bravery and a spirit of sacrifice as they walked tall to the firing squad which shocked

even their executioners, not budging an inch from their demand for a national conference.

But how could the ANC allow a conference to discuss the fighters' demands to return to the townships in South Africa when the ANC leaders were negotiating a transition to black-ruled capitalism? The 'armed wing' of the ANC was a fraud, to give the ANC international status, and a trap to lure would-be young militants from the townships. The subsequent fate of people involved in the mutinies could not be more different. One of the leaders of the ANC's security apparatus was Jacob Zuma, now President of South Africa.

The ANC has always refused to acknowledge this history of mutinies in its armed wing or to give an account of the murders of hundreds of its own members in the camps. That the story has become known is down to the efforts of those who took part in the mutinies and especially to the unflinching work of a handful of courageous individuals, namely Paul Trewhela, Baruch Hirson and Bill McElroy, who published the survivors' accounts. They were denounced by 'left' and 'progressive' organisations around the world for allegedly damaging the liberation movement in the interests of the apartheid regime and its imperialist supporters.

In the trade unions the ANC's preparations for a negotiated end to apartheid, which would allow capital's continued rule over the people, necessitated a destruction of rank-and-file democracy, the elevation of a corrupt hierarchy and the imposition of the SACP's 'two-stage theory'. The 'armed struggle' led to the imprisonment, torture and death of the most militant volunteers.

This suppression of democracy in the liberation movements – and particularly the use of the 'spy' threat to silence potential critics – was not confined to the ANC. The same stories have been recorded by South African soldiers and activists about the struggles in Namibia, Angola and elsewhere. In Namibia, when the first independence elections were held, demonstrators in the capital demanded that the leaders of the liberation movement reveal what had happened in the military camps where so many young men and woman had been imprisoned and tortured and killed for allegedly being spies.

In neighbouring Angola a similar story emerges. A woman speaks of her struggle for freedom:

> In 1974 the workers of Portugal rose up and removed the despotic fascist regime in their country. By this act they also removed Portuguese imperialist rule from the backs of the Angolan working people. And so in 1975 we celebrated independence day.
>
> For many years before that the mass movement in Angola had been prepared by many underground groups and committees organised in the factories and in every sector of the population. I was a 16-year-old schoolgirl and active on a committee called Amilcar Cabral. Everyone was involved in one way or another. It was a massive movement. On Independence Day everybody came out in the open.
>
> Most Angolans thought the great Soviet Union would help their country overcome its economic and other problems, that there could now be a peaceful transition to democracy and socialism. But this was not the role played by the Soviet Union. Instead they exacerbated the differences in the MPLA [Movimento Popular de Libertaçao de Angola] and advised the government to clamp down on the people. Instead of encouraging the mass movement, and all committees that had been built throughout the country during the liberation struggle, they acted to behead the mass movement.
>
> First they stopped the right to strike. The first people to be put in prison were the leaders of the main textile factories in Luanda. Then the students were dealt with, their leaders

imprisoned. By 1976 the situation had become volatile.

We founded the Angolan Communist Organisation to organise opposition throughout the mass movement. We were very successful. The MPLA had one government-run newspaper but we had at least six. We were young and naïve. We were exhilarated by independence and we thought we could build a socialist future. We had no idea what would happen.

We came under attack. Our papers were closed down. Those who were not imprisoned continued the fight. There was revolt and unrest among the whole population. The people were looking for some alleviation of their hard lives. This put pressure on the warring factions in the MPLA leadership.

Nito was leader of one faction and those in the other, who were closest to President Neto, had been educated and trained by the Stalinist bureaucracy during their years of exile. Nito was much younger and he had been fighting inside the country, but neither of these factions had the interests of the working people at heart. Both were trying to prove to the leaders of the USSR that they were the most reliable allies to contain and defeat the mass movement.

Nito's forces took over the national radio and television stations and the main political prison and arrested members of the government. Thousands of people were already marching in the streets and on government buildings. The people thought they would get a government they really wanted – a government composed of people who had been in the forefront of the armed struggle. But the leaders of the armed forces had other ideas. They broke their agreement with Nito. On 27 May 1977, tanks, commanded by Cubans, were on the streets to defeat the coup. The masses around the national radio station were fired on and many were killed.

A clean-up operation started in the city. From then

onwards anyone who spoke against the MPLA was imprisoned and killed. It was impossible to speak. There was no free speech, no meetings. People were arrested on the spot. Many thousands died – it was worse than anything known under the old colonial rule. On the borders with Namibia people were thrown off mountains to be eaten by lions. Fear overtook everyone.

All opposition was eliminated. Anyone who showed the slightest opposition to the MPLA was taken away and killed. And all this was carried out under the supervision of the Soviet Union through the army, the government and the security forces. Advisers from the Soviet Union, East Germany, Cuba, Bulgaria and Romania ruled the country. Even methods of torture, of tracking down people and of making people speak were the methods and techniques perfected by the Soviet Intelligence – the KGB. The security forces were trained by Cuban intelligence and the KGB. We were all overwhelmed by the scale of oppression: none of us were prepared for this. My sister was arrested. Her husband was arrested and killed. My sister was not even political – she was a housewife and mother of two children who were one and two at the time. On the day they arrested my sister they left these two children completely on their own in the house.

And the state never acknowledged the deaths of the people they killed, they were just 'missing'. Many were incarcerated in the notorious Estrada de Catete, a prison near Luanda built by the Cubans. The cells are below ground so the prisoners feel they are buried alive. My sister was in Casa da Reclusao prison. When I visited her I saw South African and Namibian prisoners and we heard they were from the liberation movements in their own countries.[8]

These were the same South Africans who had demanded a conference of the ANC. However, imprisonment, torture and murder did not end the demands for democracy inside the mass movement. With the ANC unbanned and then becoming the government of South Africa, many of those who had led the repression in the camps became government ministers or commanders in the South African security forces.

The election of the ANC was greeted with great enthusiasm by the masses who hoped their lives would improve, but as years went past little changed apart from the emergence of a new black middle class and a black bourgeoisie. Ex-trade-union leaders became millionaires. Poor housing, unemployment, inadequate schools, everything people had fought against remained the same. At first the influence of the ANC, the popularity of Mandela, the co-option of all the mass organisations into mouth-pieces for the ANC, held back popular protest. But communities began to fight against electricity bills and disconnections, against the lack of sanitation etc. Wage struggles began to emerge again. Now they faced not the white apartheid regime but the ANC, 'their own people'. Police and troops used against the masses were now under control of a black government.

A massive turning point came with the massacre of 44 striking miners at the Marikana mine in August 2012. The ANC was now turning its guns on the working class in full view of the entire nation. And not just the ANC armed forces: some miners were injured when they were shot at by leaders of the mineworkers union (NUM) who had developed cosy relations with the mine owners. This act reverberated around the working class and the tensions that had been building for years are shown in the discussions inside COSATU's biggest affiliate, NUMSA, the National Union of Metalworkers, the union of the Dunlop worker quoted earlier. He explained how the ANC's Freedom Charter, rather than a Workers' Charter, was foisted on the union, and how COSATU was bureaucratically turned into a subservient partner of the ANC and the SACP. Now NUMSA called for the breaking of this alliance. This long process is best shown in NUMSA's own resolutions.

At its foundation in 1987, when the Metal and Allied Workers and other affiliates of COSATU merged to form the 140,000-strong National Union of Metalworkers of South Africa, they issued a declaration that tried to combine two opposed perspectives. On the one hand they talked of the working class's need to overthrow capitalism and on the other called for support for the ANC's freedom charter, a charter for capitalism. Twenty-six years later NUMSA had to reflect on this contradictory outlook. The union's special conference in November 2013 drew out the lessons of the years of the ANC's rule and the Alliance that subordinated the unions to government.

1. Resolution on challenges facing the alliance

1.1. The Alliance is dysfunctional, in crisis and paralysed. It is dominated by infighting and factionalism and fails to meet regularly.

1.2. Although there are protests everywhere and every day in the country, the Alliance is not an instrument in the hands of these struggling masses nor does it provide leadership to these struggles, which are largely leaderless struggles. The reality is that there is a political vacuum and the working class is on its own.

1.3. The Freedom Charter, which we understood as the minimum platform and programme of the Alliance, has been completely abandoned in favour of right-wing and neo-liberal policies such as the National Development Plan (NDP).

1.4. There exists little common understanding within the Alliance of the real objectives of the National Democratic Revolution (NDR).

1.5. The Alliance operates and works during election periods and it is our experience that the working class is being used by the leader of the Alliance – the African National Congress (ANC) – as voting fodder.

1.6. The Alliance has been captured and taken over by right-wing forces. Those who are perceived to be against neo-liberalism or to be advocates of policies in favour of the working class and the poor are seen as problematic, isolated or purged.
1.7. Dominant classes in society have swayed the Alliance in their favour.
1.8. The ANC has resisted the reconfiguration of the Alliance into a strategic political centre where issues of policy, deployments into government and programmes are jointly decided upon by all components of the Alliance.
1.9. The strategy of swelling the ranks has not worked and all resolutions of COSATU congresses in relation to how the Alliance should function have not been implemented by the leaders of the Alliance.
1.10. In practice the Alliance is still in the hands of one Alliance partner, the ANC. The ANC is the centre and implements government programmes and policies alone, with little or no consultation with other components of the Alliance.
1.11. There is strong opposition from the ANC to an Alliance agreement or pact. The movement has told us in no uncertain words that the ANC is the political centre.
1.12. As NUMSA we have been detecting an abuse by the ANC of other Alliance partners.
1.13. The Alliance is used to rubber-stamp neoliberal policies of the ANC and not as a centre of power that debates policy issues and implementation.
1.14. The treatment of labour as a junior partner within the Alliance is not uniquely a South African phenomenon. In many post-colonial and post-revolutionary situations, liberation and revolutionary movements have turned on labour movements that fought alongside them, suppressed them, marginalised them, split them, robbed them of their independence or denied them any meaningful role in politics and policy-making.

2. Further noting that:

2.1. There is no chance of winning back the Alliance to what it was originally formed for, which was to drive a revolutionary programme for fundamental transformation of the country, with the Freedom Charter as the minimum platform to transform the South African economy.

2.2. The South African Communist Party (SACP) leadership has become embedded in the state and is failing to act as the vanguard of the working class.

2.3. The chance of winning back the SACP onto the path of working-class struggle for working-class power is very remote.

2.4. In the struggle for socialism, the working class needs a political organisation committed in theory and practice to socialism.

3. Therefore we resolve that:

3.1. In light of the above as NUMSA, we should call on COSATU to break from the alliance. The time for looking for an alternative has arrived.

3.2. As NUMSA, we must lead in the establishment of a new UNITED FRONT that will coordinate struggles in the workplace and in communities, in a way similar to the UDF of the 1980s. The task of this front will be to fight for the implementation of the Freedom Charter and be an organisational weapon against neoliberal policies such as the NDP.

For this to happen it requires:

3.1.1. That our members and shop stewards must be active on all fronts and in all struggles against neo-liberal policies, whether these policies are being implemented in the workplace or in communities.

3.1.2. That in all our constitutional structures, there should be a standing agenda item on community struggles, their nature and NUMSA's attitude to these community struggles.

> 3.3. Side by side with the establishment of the new UNITED FRONT, we in NUMSA must explore the establishment of a MOVEMENT FOR SOCIALISM, as the working class needs a political organisation committed in its policies and actions to the establishment of a socialist South Africa.

Following this statement NUMSA placed a resolution in front of COSATU pointing out that its subordination to the government had led to a paralysis of the trade unions and an inability to campaign on the issues facing its members. NUMSA demanded it break from the alliance with the ANC and instead of being a conveyor belt for government neo-liberal policies become the leader of working-class struggle.

This resolution, which is reproduced on the NUMSA website, is cited at length because it is highly relevant to the themes of this book, and truly remarkable in more than one sense. It affirms the necessity of the political independence of the working class. It comes out of a long and bitter struggle against obstacles and enemies, not only the apartheid regime but also the ANC and the South African Communist Party. No less important is that NUMSA's declaration of intent comes not from some political group or party but from a trade union organising and representing a large section of the South African working class and with a proud record of struggle.

Above all, going beyond militant trade unionism, it is a call for socialism and for the building of a movement to achieve it. It will echo throughout the African continent and beyond. It has great significance for the theoretical and political questions that must be confronted by every movement that comes into conflict with the power of capital in today's world. The African National Congress, seen as the head of the movement to rid the country of the apartheid regime, had as its political and theoretical backbone the South African Communist Party, backed in every way by the Stalinist ruling group in the Soviet Union. The strategic line, persisted in till this day, has been that of 'first continue and complete the "national democratic revolution", and only then will it be possible for the working class to organise for the socialist revolution'. Only after the years of bitter struggle do we now see, in NUMSA's resolutions, a rejection of this policy and a break from the politics of the ANC and the SACP.

As we shall see in a later section of this book (on Lenin and Bolshevism), there is a striking parallel with the situation just preceding the October Revolution of 1917 in Russia. Lenin returned from exile in the April of that year to find the leaders of his Bolshevik Party adhering to the line of 'complete the bourgeois-democratic (read "national-democratic") revolution, and only then will the conditions exist for the working class to conduct its own struggle for socialism'. Lenin had to engage in a titanic struggle over seven months to defeat this 'old Bolshevism' and put his party at the head of the working-class revolution in October 1917. Could there be a more compelling example of the need for socialists to learn from history than the comparison between Russia 1917 and today's South Africa?

In January 2015 COSATU expelled NUMSA for its demand that the unions break from the Triple Alliance. Many organisations, community groups and environmental campaigns, as well as other unions, are coming to the support of NUMSA. NUMSA, quite rightly, is asking who the trade unions belong to, the working class or the government? Only with its independence can working-class democracy be restored and all the bitter experiences of the last two decades be seriously and honestly debated. The NUMSA initiative will open the door for many militants in the unions and those outside their ranks, like the guerrilla fighters, to work together free from the stifling control of the people who have so savagely repressed the workers' movement.

To appreciate the significance for all countries of these developments in South Africa, we note these extracts from István

Mészáros's article on *Historical Actuality of the Socialist Offensive*, which point the way forward:

> [T]he elementary condition of success of the socialist project is its inherent pluralism. It sets out from the acknowledgement of the existing differences and inequalities; not to preserve them (which is a necessary concomitant of all fictitious and arbitrarily enforced 'unity') but to supersede them in the only viable form: by securing the active involvement of all those concerned... [T]he socialist enterprise is *structurally unrealizable* without its full articulation in the manifold autonomous ('self-managing'), and thus irrepressibly pluralist projects of the ongoing *social revolution*... In reality, there can be no escape from Marx's programme of constituting a socialist mass consciousness through the practical enterprise of engaging in actually feasible and inherently pluralist common action... For the meaning of socialist pluralism – the active engagement in common action, without compromising but constantly renewing the socialist principles which inspire the overall concerns – arises precisely from the ability of the participating forces to *combine* into a coherent whole, with *ultimately* inescapable socialist implications, a great variety of demands and partial strategies which in and by themselves need not have anything *specifically socialist* about them at all.
>
> In this sense, the most urgent demands of our times ... – for jobs and education as well as for a decent health care and social services, together with the demands for women's liberation and against racial discrimination – are, without one single exception, such that, in principle, every genuine liberal could wholeheartedly embrace them. It is rather different, though, when we consider them not as single issues, in isolation, but jointly, as parts of the overall complex that constantly reproduces them as unrealized and systematically

> unrealizable demands.
>
> Thus, it is the condition of their realisation that ultimately decides the issue...[9]

Any attempt at imposing a direct political control on such movements, following the rather unhappy tradition of the not-so-distant past, is in danger of being counterproductive (even if for the best intentions of 'politicisation'), instead of helping to strengthen their autonomy and effectiveness.

Britain: A State of Disorder and a Disunited Kingdom

Preface

by Cliff Slaughter

After the Scottish Independence Referendum of September 2014 – when there was a 45-per-cent vote to leave the United Kingdom and a far higher level of political engagement notably in working-class areas than had been seen for decades – I was sceptical when a comrade suggested to me that 'things will never be the same again.' I was wrong, as the UK General Election held on 7 May 2015 was to show.

The Conservative Party, with a shameless programme of 'austerity', attacks on the living standards of ordinary people, privatisation and sweeping cuts in public services like the National Health Service and social housing, tax cuts for the rich and destruction of workers' rights, has been returned to power with an absolute (though small) majority of seats in Parliament. It will be able to rule even without the support of its opportunist Liberal-Democrat coalition partner of the last five years, the Lib-Dems having been virtually wiped out at the polls. How can it be that the voting capacity of the overwhelming majority, working people, could not prevent this result, with its obvious threat to their lives, their children, their future?

For many decades the working class of Britain was able, from time to time, to wrest reform concessions that tempered the rate of exploitation by capital and the imposition of conditions of poverty and deprivation. They were able to do this because British capitalism, historically sustained by its wealth derived from a colonial empire and the City of London's role in international finance, could afford to make those concessions to the strength of trade unions and the Labour Party. That strength and pre-eminence of British capitalism has been steadily undermined for almost a century. This means that its ability to concede significant reforms has severely diminished, to the point where, since the onset of the structural crisis of the capital system in the early 1970s, we have witnessed a consistent assault on the 'welfare state' and on the rights and power of trade unions. The policies of 'neo-liberalism', monetarism, Thatcherism, were the expression of this new stage in politics.

This new stage clearly demanded a new stage in the politics of the working class, but what happened? The working class remained at the level of being restricted to parliamentary party representation in the form of the Labour Party, and has remained so until today. But the Labour Party is no longer, as Lenin defined it in the early 1920s, a 'general association of the working class'; or even, as Trotsky said, a 'bourgeois workers' party'. Beginning with Tony Blair's insistence in the mid-1990s on removing the so-called 'Clause Four' (committing it, albeit in ambiguous terms, to the nationalisation of the means of production) from the Party's constitution, and on campaigning as 'New Labour', it has been reshaped into a self-styled 'business-friendly' party.

In the 2015 General Election, the overwhelming majority of the working class was still at the level, politically, of seeing (and indeed, of having) no alternative to voting for this rotting carcass. Despite the fact that Labour was no longer in any political sense a working-class party, the basic class loyalty of workers was expressed in the return of 232 Labour MPs, with all the main industrial and ex-industrial constituencies (except in Scotland) retaining their Labour majorities.

Why, then, such a shocking defeat at the hands of the Conservatives? The media pundits joyfully showed us Labour's failure to gain the 'swing' in votes needed to win seats they had targeted and even, in some cases, a swing from Labour to Conservative. But most of the votes Labour lost went, not to the Tories, but (except in Scotland) to the relative newcomers, the

United Kingdom Independence Party (Ukip). This far-right outfit, with close links to extreme right-wing groups in other European countries, and whipping up anti-immigrant prejudice, took 12 per cent of votes nationally. In a proportional representation electoral system, this would have given them nearly 80 parliamentary seats!

We are faced with what is a painful but inevitable and challenging contradiction. On the one hand we must surely welcome, rather than bemoan, the beginning of the breaking-up of the 'Labour' (social-democratic) hold on the working class, manifest in Labour's losses to Ukip in England and – in a very different way – to the Scottish National Party (SNP) in Scotland. This is a positive process rather than a negative one. But on the other hand, it brings real dangers.

Some hundreds of thousands of working people turn to the far right, to Ukip. This is because, seeing Labour offer no policies to deal with their real problems, they responded to the poisonous racism of Ukip's false idea that halting immigration will remove the threat to jobs and conditions, to their livelihoods. In Scotland, a different alternative to Labour presented itself: the SNP, having failed to win an independence referendum in September 2014, campaigned on its more immediate pledges to resist the ruling parties' 'austerity' attacks and to fight for 'progressive' policies. Therefore it is wrong, and dangerous, for the defeated Labour leader to equate his party's Scottish debacle – it lost all but one of its MPs north of the border – with the loss of Labour votes in England to Ukip, attributing both things to 'nationalism'.

Here then is the real contradiction: it must be recognised, confronted and resolved. Because it is a real and not just a logical contradiction, it must be resolved in a real struggle and not simply in some formula or argument. That the working class must break from the rotting corpse of Labour reformism, and is being compelled to begin to do so, is positive. But in the absence thus far of alternative forms of self-organisation and struggle there are imminent dangers, as the appeal of Ukip demonstrates. I very deliberately use the words 'self-organisation' and 'struggle', and not 'representation', because going beyond the trap of restriction to parliamentary politics is essential to any step forward. The next two essays were written before the general election. They are followed by their authors' joint post-election reflections.

A State of Disorder

by Tom Owen

The medieval church calendar had many feasts and saint days. For us, the most appropriate seems the 'Feast of Fools', which was presided over by the 'Lords of Misrule'. All known order and habits were overturned and anarchy ruled: the moral code was inverted for a day, and then the next morning, after the hangover, all resorted to normality. But the Feast of Fools, and the Lords of Misrule who now govern, will not vanish in the morning light while we return to our old normalities. They are now as dreams, and if we are to awake, we must make a better future.

In May 2010 a makeshift coalition of Tories and neo-conservative, 'Orange Book' (that is, neo-liberal) Liberal Democrats took power in the UK.[10] The leader of the Tory Party, David Cameron, had 'marketed' himself as a liberal, green, even Keynesian, 'one nation' Tory – in the tradition of Tory leaders like Benjamin Disraeli in the nineteenth century, and Harold Macmillan in the twentieth. What he failed to lay before the public was that he had been an office boy, like many of the frontline cabinet members of his generation, in Thatcher's war against the National Union of Mineworkers during the great strike of 1984–85 and the destruction of the coalfields in the aftermath. They had laid waste to the coal, steel and engineering industries as mass employers of labour in the industrial heartlands of the Midlands, the North of England, Wales and Scotland. The economies of mass production have been sold off or shipped off to the Far East.

It would be a mistake to read Cameron and his crew simply as a gang of posh-boy public-school louts. They are a class-war cadre, relentless in their persecution of the poor and distressed and vitriolic in their hatred of organised and political labour and their allies in the intellectual and cultural strata. Not only have they been allowed to indulge their class prejudices but have been introduced to a 'new' ideology that justifies their basic instincts: greed, the desire for power and superiority. The ideology goes under various labels – neo-conservatism, neo-liberalism, neo-Keynesianism and, by alchemy, neo-common sense. All this neo-newness celebrates the hollow victory of a very old, redundant and degenerately dangerous English ruling class. The aggressive ideology they have adopted in the last few decades was nurtured first in Vienna, then in Paris, then popularised in Chicago and taken to heart by the Reagan administration. It offered two self-serving advantages: the supremacy of competition in all human enterprise and the power of the market to determine the life and fate of humanity, down to the most trivial aspects of daily living. These combine to form a new Social Darwinism, elevating social status as a sign of competitive prowess and an inherited virtue from ancestors, feudal or bourgeois, concealing their past of pillage and exploitation behind the empty rituals of government, custom and privilege. 'New Labour' attempted to revive a fascination with modernity, which in reality continued the Thatcherite idealisation of the dirtiest forms of business, to the point of attempting, in Walter Benjamin's words, to 'aestheticise' the most alienated forms of life under the rule of capital. The worship of the 'new' in order to aggressively promote an old order is hardly novel; it is the rhetoric of fascism that we have seen before in the Europe of the 1920s and 1930s. Now the displacement of millions through the new technologies and chronic global instability has resulted in an enormous pool of 'redundant' human beings, surplus to the requirements of capital – to use Marx's words, a vast 'reserve army of labour'.[11]

One of the hardest-hit sectors of the structural crisis has been youth. Those who are going through the educational system in Britain are being burdened with enormous debts which they will carry well into middle age. When they do graduate they find it virtually impossible, without being 'well connected', to find work commensurate with their qualifications. Only a minority of young people are able to get skilled work with opportunities for training through the traditional apprenticeships and further technical education that earlier generations of the working class experienced as a 'rite of passage'. The 2010–15 coalition government's 'apprenticeship' schemes are short and superficial, providing none of the long-term professional formation needed in any advanced economy. However, a great number of working-class youths are outside the system, without education or training, left to their own devices on the streets and the estates, prey to petty criminals, drug dealers, police harassment, gangs and in some cases fascist gangs. This generation is attacked on all fronts: their welfare benefits are sanctioned and housing benefit has been withdrawn until they reach their mid-twenties, forcing them to live with their parents, with all the family tensions that inevitably follow.

There is much documentation of the social and economic impact of the past five years of government policy, from the data of the Institute of Fiscal Studies, Office of National Statistics, National Audit Office and the work of charities like the Joseph Rowntree Foundation, Christian Aid and the organisers of food banks, like the Trussell Trust. Whatever the Panglossian claims of government propaganda and its craven apologists and brazen ideologues in the mass media, the neo-con selective shock therapy and general austerity for the mass of the working class, the young and sections of the middle class have had a lasting effect on their lives and aspirations. They have dramatically widened the gap between the financial elites, the landowning classes, the remnants of the industrial bourgeoisie on the one hand and the working classes and the poor on the other. The middle class has collapsed, with the old professional classes and their associations forced into working-class forms of defensive action, or a small minority becoming 'financial advisors', stock-market gamblers and banking managers, rich beyond their dreams.

What we have witnessed in the UK is not as dramatic as the 'experiment' in Greece, or the complete collapse of the Spanish real estate and finance economy, but it has damaged and undermined the organisation and the political consciousness of the working class and has diminished its vanguard in terms of influence and numbers. A striking illustration of this can be seen in the drop in wage levels (figures published on the 30 January 2015 show that wages had fallen by seven per cent since 2003). Conditions of service and contracts including zero-hours contracts, part-time/under-employment and unpaid on-site standby practices are common even in some unionised plants where organisation and confidence are weak. The employers' offensive is comprehensive. In some companies, time off work for reasons of ill-health or injury is recorded as a breach of discipline and is subject to investigation, recorded and filed against the individuals concerned.

For those out of work, the regimes introduced by Cameron's Work and Pensions Secretary, Iain Duncan Smith, have brought a callous and zealous hounding of claimants and their portrayal in the right-wing media as scroungers at best or, at worst, criminals.

The question we have to ask is how this state of affairs has come to pass? How has a low-wage, poorer life been forced upon and apparently accepted by millions of ordinary families? Are there signs of resistance? Are there indications at the present period that the working class aspires to more than the security afforded in the past by a social-democratic welfare state? And, importantly, will right-wing populist and neo-fascist outfits like Ukip in the UK and the Front National in France attract enough sections of angry and demoralised workers and ruined middle-class people to cause serious divisions and facilitate a more open form of the dictatorship of capital?

On 4 August 2011, mass rioting instigated by the police killing of Mark Duggan erupted in London and rapidly spread across Britain to other cities like Birmingham and Manchester.[12] Unlike the aftermath of riots of a previous decade, nothing has really been done to assuage the frustration of black and poor white youth (then, the response was a series of inner-city programmes and the limited growth of a black middle class), and in March 2015 the police officer who fired the fatal shot at Duggan was cleared of any offence. Instead the state has militarised its policing capacity in dealing with civil disturbance, combining these provisions with anti-terrorist legislation and intelligence. Boris Johnson, populist buffoon mayor of London, has ordered water cannon and a range of weaponry not used before on mainland Britain. What this shows is that the ruling elites are more than aware of the chronic nature of the social crisis in the UK. We have not experienced any large-scale social disturbances in the last period and even some of the highest representatives of national and international capital are worried about the possible tipping points in face of protracted austerity. Mark Carney – the Cameron government's Canadian appointee as Governor of the Bank of England – and Christine Lagarde of the International Monetary Fund have made such noises. However, this does not seem to deter Osborne and Cameron from pursuing their 'Long Term Plan', which involves lopping off many billions of pounds more from government spending should they be returned to office after the May 2015 elections, which would return government expenditure to a similar percentage to that of the

1930s.

The loyal opposition, the Labourites and other 'social-democrat' observers like Will Hutton (an Oxford University college head and columnist for the London *Observer*) and Polly Toynbee (*grande dame* of London *Guardian* commentators) have a view that the Tories are making disastrously wrong choices, as if their responses had nothing to do with the needs and dilemmas of the forces of globalised capital. Both the Labourites and reformist social and economic pundits have programmes that are only nuanced versions of austerity they think can be sold to the masses. The ruling parties, however sure or arrogant they appear, are skating on thin ice. The society and 'culture' the Tories and Lib-Dems have brought into being in the last five years have changed aspects of UK life beyond recognition. The cry of many people that they 'don't recognise my own country' is very common and often linked to reaction to migration rather than to a complex of radical changes. It is the mechanisms and consequences of these changes that I wish now to examine.

At a political level this is a period where the ruling classes have swung to the right and in some cases to the far right. After the banking crisis of 2007–09, they have mounted a systematic onslaught on the working and middle classes to more than make good their losses. They have maintained their hegemonic power through a number of strategies. Referring back to an earlier period of reaction, may I summarise Lenin's characterisation of the years 1907–14 as ones of 'reaction', 'mysticism' and 'pornography'? I quote at greater length:

> All the revolutionary and opposition parties have been defeated. Depression, demoralisation, splits, discord, renegacy, pornography take the place of politics. There is an increased drift towards philosophical idealism; mysticism becomes the garb of counter-revolutionary sentiments.[13]

One epoch does not exactly replicate another, but there are striking parallels and similarities.

Contemporary philosophical idealism has many strands but the one form that has been seized upon is 'de-constructivism'. A branch of anthropology and linguistics has been popularised into the idea that everything can be reduced to subjective narratives and an assembly of half-recognisable signs. Allied to idealism is mysticism. Some years ago we would never have predicted the recrudescence of religion as a political force. The moribund Church of England still remains, with its diminishing congregations, the 'Tory party at prayer', in spite of the liberal-minded clergy tearing themselves to pieces over female bishops and homosexual priests. Many of them are genuinely repelled by the results of austerity and are prepared to criticise the state, of which they are an established arm. In fact the present Archbishop of Canterbury has had no qualms over worshipping both God and Mammon. His work for God was preceded by a career as an oil executive.[14]

But in the undergrowth of quasi-Christianity there is a growth of bizarre sects like Spiritualist Centres (some of them with enough capital to buy up old-established Adult Education Centres and shut-down schools). There is also Islam, the faith of ex-colonial peoples settled in Western European ex-imperial states. We know that these people are subject to a barrage of racist attacks, physical and cultural, down to the most personal aspects of their lifestyle practices. Their communities have been used as voting fodder in the UK, mainly by the Labour Party, but this hegemonic allegiance to Labour is crumbling, especially amongst a section of youth who are attracted to millenarian and apocalyptic strands of Islam. In the 1970s, when the National Front and fascist gangs were active, Asian youth organisations sprang up in many urban areas and were connected to far-left groups through anti-fascist alliances. The Labour Party and conservative community leaders were able to divert this kind of militancy into more conformist channels.

However, the most significant form of 'mystification' that has saturated the political culture has been the 'deification' of market forces. Not only have they been 'naturalised', they have been 'super-naturalised' and have now the status and powers of the old gods, omnipotent and omnipresent, capricious and vengeful. The function of the high priests is to worship and to divine the mysteries of their movement, to make the human sacrifices necessary to assuage their lusts.

In the new divine order, the sacred and the profane must become one, the trafficking of women and children for prostitution and its by-product, pornography, alongside the sales of narcotics, must be entered into the new 'Book of Numbers', the Treasury's Index of the Gross National Product.

If demoralisation, pornography and mysticism are aspects of the climate of this period, the active political practices that encourage and give rise to this are criminality, corruption and an aggressive 'cultural' and ideological war on any opposition to the naturalisation of the neo-liberal worldview in all its manifestations. The virtues are entrepreneurship, risk-taking, innovation and the accumulation of personal wealth; greed is good for you. The enemies of progress are socialism, trade unions, strikers and any form of collective resistance. Resistance to austerity that provokes a reaction from the state forces is met with a range of legislation drawn up for anti-terrorist purposes. Neoliberal libertarianism is backed by a strong authoritarian state.

But the increasing array of legislation has not been used to deter the criminal activities and 'irregularities' of the banking and finance sector responsible for the spectacular crashes of Wall Street and London in 2007–08, which started the recession that wrecked the lives of millions of people on the planet. Only one Wall Street fiddler and one petty French official of the BNP Paribas bank have faced any criminal charges. The laundering of drug money from Mexican and Central American gangsters by

HSBC, the fixing of the Libor rates, the RBS scandals etc., etc. are not aberrant examples of banking practices, they are the current *modus vivendi*. The collapse of traditional industry in the US and the UK and the sluggish tempo of manufacturing offer no attractive investments for the finance 'industry'. Indeed, manufacturing enterprises sit on large amounts of cash but claim that they lack the 'confidence' to invest in production. Instead wealth has to be realised in seeking profit not from surplus value produced by labour, but from gambling on more exotic 'financial products', involving packaging up debts, laundered money from arms and drugs, precarious mortgages, insurance policies and the future prices of metals and material commodities. These activities are risky and often illegal, but offer the punters enormous payoffs. This is the strange world of fictitious capital where nothing is tangible and 'all dissolves into air'.

In this world of fictive capital, of enormous wealth alongside enormous debt, one powerful impulse is to turn money assets into real assets; and so we have seen the rapid growth of what the early US sociologist Thorstein Veblen described as the 'conspicuous consumption' of the leisured classes. But the motive and need for the acquisition of 'conspicuous' material property is not that of aristocratic hauteur or a sign of prestige, but of finding more lasting, stable realisation of value in the form of personal property. Works of art, precious stones, jewellery, luxury yachts, hunting and fishing lodges and areas of moorland, stretches of rivers with fishing rights, football clubs, newspapers and most of all desirable property in cities like London, New York, Paris and Barcelona or on exclusive islands guarded by high security. Areas of cities become living and playground zones for the international global rich with fashion shops, restaurants, private clubs, gyms and schools. Often these apartments are left empty or only inhabited for a few days a year. They are there for investment, just as landmarks like the Shard in London are vehicles for Qatari investment. As in Victorian Britain, these centres of vast wealth are often not far away from the poverty their benefits engender.

The other side of the coin to this materialisation of value is the monetarisation of everything, however much things are valued in more displaced human categories like aesthetics and ethics. Art is a primary example. Since the 2008–09 collapse of Lehmann Brothers, Asian and other investors emerged unscathed, investing in fine art as well as bottles of Château Lafitte and Rolls Royce and Bentley cars. In 2014, global sales of fine art topped $16 billion. In 2015 Alberto Giacometti's sculpture *Pointing Man* sold for $126 million and Claude Monet's *Grand Canal in Venice* for more than $35 million. For the super-rich, the favoured painters are for the moment Monet, Van Gogh and Gerhard Richter, although Picasso and the New York Abstract Expressionists are still good bets.

The concept of justice has deep roots in the history of civilisation in philosophy, ethics and even religion. Nonetheless, the British government's Home Office has packaged 'British Justice' as a branded export commodity. One of its first customers is that great ally in the fight for Western Democratic interests, Saudi Arabia. Given our real economic restraints and the need to rationalise our armed forces, it seems more appropriate to export modules of justice than the old violence of the gunboat. At home, justice is becoming impossible to buy, not only for the poor but for average income-earners. Legal aid has been virtually abolished and industrial arbitration procedure is now available only by paying a fee.

However, these areas of the market are only titbits when compared with the lucrative areas of the socialised education, social welfare, health, municipal and state enterprises established in Western Europe since 1945. Take the proposed Transatlantic Trade and Investment Partnership (TTIP), a free-trade agreement between the USA and the EEC. Under this agreement, any US multinational corporation may bid for any enterprise, public or private, in the EEC, and no national government is allowed to protect any service or state-aided industry like the prestigious French cinema, for example, without being prosecuted in a TTIP court, for massive fines as compensation for loss of earnings. For those who had any illusions that the EEC would give us any social and legal protection from ultra-predatory, unbridled markets, shed them now, for the EEC, as we should have learned from the example of Greece, is a neo-liberal pact – with ambitions to be a neo-liberal super-state, happy to do business with the USA, as is excellently described by Tomas Fazi in his *The Battle for Europe: how an elite hijacked a continent*.[15] When this agreement came before the British House of Commons, the Tories enthusiastically voted for it, of course. And the Labourites – although lobbied by their members and constituents against support – after seeking some 'reassurances', voted with the Coalition government.

The Coalition that formed the government after the failure of either of the major parties to achieve a clear majority in 2010 initiated what can only be described as a Tory political coup, incorporating the Liberal-Democrats into their programme. What Thatcher started, and the Blairites continued, was escalated with a systematic department-by-department implementation of neo-liberal projects of outright privatisation, as with the Royal Mail and telecommunications services. Public ownership was eroded through a complex, often byzantine, system of forcing public services like the NHS to put out all their contracts to open 'competition' with the private sector; allowing Virgin to take over general practices, private operators to run MRI scans, private cleaning companies to take over hygiene provision. Large multi-national companies have taken over a multitude of functions from specialised public services with experienced staff. Capita, Serco, Veiola, Atos, Kier and others run everything from exam-marking and administration, employment and job-seeking and prisons, to highway maintenance. In each of these areas there have been multiple crises, breakdowns in service, failures to meet 'targets', scandals and outright frauds and fiddles. The scope for corrupt practices is multiplied by the endless distancing of accountability and ultimate responsibilities. One outstanding example was a Sheffield-based employment and training agency, much vaunted by the media and lavishly rewarded, whose records were found to be false or uncertain. The outfit was wound up and the CEO retired with £8m in the bank, a mansion on the edge of the city (Thornbridge Hall) and a real-ale brewery with a string of pubs.

The political processes of privatisation are worth examining, so that we can see the real role played by 'corruption'. At the centre of this are government and the whole political, legislative and parliamentary process. The corruption in the House of Commons does not involve merely the fiddling of expenses. MPs, ex-MPs and members of the House of Lords have access to possibly the most concentrated nexus of financial interests on the planet. Most Tory MPs have other interests, sit on company boards, and also act as lobbying agents for special interests. The Labourites are no different, especially after they have retired or moved on to the House of Lords. A good example of this is Alan Milburn, an ex-Health Minister under Blair, who now is a vocal critic of Labour's NHS policy, calling for more 'reforms'. And why not? He is chair of Price Waterhouse Insurance Company, and sits on the boards of a number of private health companies, some of them with American origins. And of course there is Tony Blair, one of the greatest criminals of our generation, who lied and conspired to wage a war in which an estimated one million people perished, going on to make himself a vast fortune.

Lobbying is a multi-million pound industry. A host of 'independent think tanks', mostly modelled on or even sponsored by right-wing Republican Party members, and others like the Institute of Economic Affairs, provide a constant drip of 'informed opinion' and expert talking heads on BBC current-affairs programmes like *Newsnight* and *The Daily* and *Sunday*

Politics, hosted by the veteran right-wing journalist and scab, Andrew Neill. There is a revolving door between think tanks, the right-wing popular and broadsheet press, lobbying companies and parliamentary consultants and PPIs (ministerial personal advisors) and researchers and large corporate interests. They are usually but not exclusively drawn from a similar social background and formation: public schools, Oxbridge, the City and the media. Entry into these circles at a young age is usually through family contacts or support through unpaid internships. So the middle and upper-middle classes have pretty well stitched up this career pool. (The most detailed recent research into, and account of, this world is Cave and Powell's excellent *A Quiet Word: lobbying, crony capitalism and broken politics in Britain*).[16]

These networks run deep into the establishment but are not protected from the pressures that build into explosive scandals like the one that engulfed the Murdoch press. This opened up the whole murky world of criminal practices, police corruption and networks that extended right into Cameron's prime-ministerial office. The dirty tricks used by the Murdoch press are repeated when it comes to softening up public opinion in preparation for the privatisation of a public service. The first step is to sow doubt in the public mind about the integrity, effectiveness and efficiency of a public service. Then use real injustices or create fictional outrages and moral panics with examples of money-wasting and featherbedding gross malpractices, in a service that is being starved of the necessary funding. Alongside this is the constant mantra of 'private good, public bad'.

This 'private good, public bad' is also used to label workers. Public-sector workers are 'good' when they are 'hardworking', but 'bad' when they want decent pay and even worse when they go on strike, and increasingly 'criminal' if they take some form of industrial action. Private-sector workers are 'good' because they are 'hardworking', have not had expensive pay rises, have had their pensions slashed and have not yet taken industrial action.

No one labels as 'bad' the hardworking hedge-fund managers and spivs and crooks in the finance industry who have made the City of London the greatest criminal enterprise in history.

This is the climate and the changed political world facing the working class, internationally and within its own nation states. It is not possible to look at the development of the British working class apart from the above processes. Its present levels of political and social consciousness carry the burden of its evolution from the post-war welfare consensus, a form of class-collaboration, which began to break up during the public-sector strikes at the end of the Callaghan administration and was shattered by the steel strike and then the miners' strike. These strikes were consciously prepared for by the ruling cadres of the Tories, the police and the military and intelligence agencies. The intention was to alter radically the relationship between the classes and eventually pave the way for a return to 'purer', uninhibited forms of capitalist 'enterprise' (read: unregulated exploitation), and the reduction of the state to its bare law-keeping function as 'armed bodies of men'. It was to be given another function as an extension of British financial interests. The Tory strategy had been prepared when in opposition. A blueprint called the Ridley document had been circulated among the shadow cabinet. It outlined a plan to privatise British Steel, British Petroleum, Rolls Royce, British Airways, British Leyland and the National Coal Board; break up the unions; suppress wages; and deregulate the financial markets. There was considerable opposition from workers in these industries to all the aspects of this project. It began immediately on 1 January, 1980 with the first national steelworkers' strike, which lasted thirteen weeks and was remarkable given the craven leadership of their union, the ISTC, headed by the odious Sir Bill Sirs. This opposition culminated in the year-long miners' strike, which ended with a return to work and a rapid closure of virtually every coalfield in the UK.

We are now living in the aftermath of these disputes, in a period of fallen trade-union membership, very few strikes other than in the public sector, low wages and unstable employment prospects. What happened to the thousands of active trade-union militants after the mass shedding of labour? Some of the branch officials and shop stewards were taken into the Labour local authorities as advice workers, some into the care services, and others used their experience as managers and supervisors. Many were taken onto retraining courses that usually led nowhere. An example was the ISERBS scheme where hot-metal workers from steel and heavy engineering were recruited by Communist Party members onto training courses in Further Education Colleges, as an alternative to occupations or to other forms of struggle. For the ordinary rank-and-file workers, redundancy pay offered a stopgap but many drifted into precarious jobs like taxi-driving or unskilled building work, or what are now referred to as 'white van jobs', subcontracted delivery driving with little or no protection. Some turned to semi-legal 'fiddle' jobs, others to outright criminal activity. There are pockets of some estates in Sheffield where heroin and guns are a source of rich pickings controlled by criminal gangsters. The only times when ordinary people get some knowledge of this underworld are when there are dramatic shoot-outs and murders. The Sheffield gangs of the twenty-first century are less flamboyant than their predecessors in the 1920s, but they represent the same acquisitive, individualist drive and 'ethic', a mirror image of the ruling classes.

In the period 1997–2010 there was nothing to stop New Labour from embracing neo-liberalism, as there was no longer a challenge from a militant organised left. In Sheffield – whose engineering workers, along with the South Wales miners and Clydeside shipyard workers, had formed the political vanguard of the working class – the British Communist Party had been built. In the 1960s and 1970s the Communist Party still had a relatively large presence. Its 'metal faction' controlled most of the engineering plants, and one factory in particular, Shardlows GKN, boasted over 100 members, selling 500 copies of the party's *Daily Worker* (from 1966, the *Morning Star*) a day. They had branch officials in the public sector and education unions. This considerable organisation's politics were unable to confront the onslaught of capital and it has now virtually ceased to exist.

A number of key historic events shook both the Stalinists and the Labour left to the core. The first was the implosion of the Soviet Union and its rapid mutation into a gangster-capitalist, secret-police, free-market state. The second was New Labour's continuation of neo-liberal economic policies and its love affair with the super-rich and the capitalist class. The third was the Iraq war and Blair's subservience to Bush's aggressive foreign policy. Labour could no longer hide behind Harold Wilson's refusal to commit to the war in Vietnam and Cambodia and present itself as having an 'ethical' foreign policy. The final nail in the coffin of New Labour's credibility for the old left leadership of the working class was the aftermath of the financial crisis of 2007–09. Neither Fabian reformism nor left-wing statist narratives could provide an adequate account or analysis, let alone a solution to the crisis.

The mass of working-class families were subjected to a regime of 'austerity'. Wages lost their value. Where it was possible all family members worked irrespective of age and gender, often at two or more low-paid jobs. Pensions were slashed so that older skilled workers went back to conditions that they would never have tolerated in their former lives. Those working-class people who were and are unfortunate enough to be ill, disabled or unemployed are subjected to a most vicious routine of interrogation, intimidation and surveillance. 'Austerity' is a raid, a massive pillaging of the minimal securities of the working class and the poor by the wealthy. The collapse of the traditional left meant that the working class was left to its own devices. The closure of the pits, steel mills, engineering factories, shipyards, the centres of mass socialisation of the working class, which had been the political universities of the class, became the memory of an earlier generation of the class now handed down to a new generation. The result of this 'memory' is hard to predict. Certainly the Tories have attempted to divide generations. David Willetts, between 2010 and 2014 the minister in charge of higher education, blamed the immediate post-war generation of pampered 'baby boomers' for having robbed future generations of their inheritance. One of his problems is that he forgot that the 'war babies', whose children and grandchildren are being blighted by Tory polices, remember the benefits of socialised health and welfare and, unlike their parents in the 1920s and 1930s, live longer to pass on their memories of poverty and struggle.

However, the Tories have been successful in their relentless campaign of divisive tactics. They have stigmatised the poor and unemployed as 'scroungers', lying in bed, boozing and procreating, whilst decent 'hardworking' people are grafting till they drop. Cameron and Osborne constantly push on TV their austerity propaganda, wearing safety helmets on building sites and lurid orange boiler suits in factories in front of handpicked audiences of silent workers.

When working-class youth from areas of high unemployment have been lured into the army and killed in wars of which they understand little, their corpses are flown back to England and paraded through some small southern town as 'heroes', rather than victims of criminal adventures.

The ultimate result of the trauma of de-industrialisation and the cultural offensive is the atomisation of layers of the working class. This has been reinforced by a radical shift in the representation of working-class life in the media, popular entertainment and the arts. One study that breaks from the academic sociology of the 'culture' of working-class life is Owen Jones's *Chavs*.[17] Jones shows how representations of the working class in the popular media constantly mock bad dress-sense, class varieties of speech, eating habits, and so on. He also looks at presentations of both 'fecklessness' and self-indulgence alongside cool criminal calculation of how to fiddle the benefits system. These themes are elaborated in the social pantomimes and melodramas of soap operas, the tabloids and now in the *Daily Express* television Channel Five. The working-class poor are under constant assault by all agencies of the state and media, the elite's paid hacks. The focus of popular arts and entertainment has shifted, and the profile of actors and professionals has changed. Leading British actors hail from the public schools – many of them, like Dominic West and Damien Lewis, old Etonians. Lavish costume dramas like *Downton Abbey* celebrate the lives of the aristocracy. The BBC has abandoned the tradition of film and drama that explored the lives of working-class people in the provinces and the industrial heartlands. There are very few equivalents now of TV dramas and films produced in the 1960s to mid-1970s like *This Sporting Life, Cathy Come Home, Kes* and *The Price of Coal.* Even the precarious and bizarre world of popular music has been colonised by the public-school brigade – as rueful rocker Neil Gallagher laments, 'Where are the scallies?' At this time the only exceptions are women writers from the working class like Jeanette Winterson, Hilary Mantel and Zadie Smith.

The physical environment of once-thriving working-class communities is now collapsing. Roads, pavements and public properties are in need of repair. In winter, there is minimal gritting of city streets so that older and disabled people become housebound, isolated and seriously ill. In Western European countries there are unprecedented levels of winter deaths through cold and summer deaths through heat strokes of the aged and frail. In a crumbling and dangerous environment, many older people – and some not so old – suffer from a nostalgic view of the past. In a world that is becoming increasingly de-familiarised, nostalgia and 'false memory' become intertwined and can become a substitute for rational thinking. For example, if 19 per cent of traditional high-street shops are shut down and boarded up, and the streets that had butchers, bakers, grocers and ironmongers are now made up of betting shops, booze shops, charity shops, and take-away fast-food outlets, it is the Asians who are seen to be thriving, not the blatant symbols of those who thrive on recession.

It is in this climate of resentment and disenchantment that the breaking-up of political alliances can lead to opportunities for the political advance of right-wing radicalism. The rise of Ukip in the UK is symptomatic of the dangers of a political vacuum which the Left has as-yet failed to fill. Ukip's Nigel Farage, a classic historic mixture of buffoon, political chameleon, trickster and demagogue, peddling the fool's gold of racism, nationalism and xenophobia, has gathered around him a 'party' that is an alliance of disaffected right-wing Tories, fascists, opportunists and disillusioned ex-Labour Party supporters. Although he casts a ludicrous image of a countrified city gent, he still can attract some working-class people. Even his blaming of traffic jams on the M4 motorway on immigration has not dented his credibility among people of a certain mind-set. However it is encouraging that he has not made much progress among the young. In fact 'a Ukip' or 'a kipper' has become a term of insult and of mental incapacity in some youth 'street talk'.

First Farage appealed to the disgruntled home-county Tories with his anti-immigrant and anti-EEC rhetoric and made big gains in the European elections. Then, in his words, we 'parked our tanks on Labour territory'. Ukip made some inroads into the Labour vote but at polls in early 2015 their predicted percentage of national vote was hovering around 15 per cent, more than the Liberals and Tories in industrial and post-industrial towns and cities. Then, in a cynical move, he attempted to profit from the scandal-torn Rotherham local council, implying that where the Labourites have large majorities there will lurk child-abuse scandals. When challenged by the journalist Andrew Neill for evidence, Farage did not produce any, but a Rotherham Ukip councillor repeated the same allegations. This linking of socialism with sexual deviance is a longstanding fascist practice with roots in Nazi Germany. It will also draw attention away from the rumours and leaks implicating high-level Tories, military and police figures in paedophile conspiracies.

At Ukip's spring conference in 2015 Farage spelled out his real political mission. He said that he was prepared to make an alliance with the Tories if Prime Minister Cameron and his Chancellor of the Exchequer (Finance Minister) George Osborne would rigidly keep to their promise to 'eliminate the deficit' and carry out the necessary cuts in welfare and social expenditure. Ukip's project at this stage is to regroup the far right in alliance with Ulster Unionists and the Tory Party's right. We must hope that this will be too bitter a pill to swallow for those ex-Labour voters who switched to Ukip.

Also alarming is that Ukip have the support of some ex-shop stewards and industrial militants who were either in, or on the periphery of, the Communist Party. It is not surprising that the talk of 'good patriots' that was current in the CP in the 1950s and 1960s, an extension of Stalin's 'socialism in one country', is now transvalued into a form of British nationalism. Racism and nationalism are divisive and corrosive. Both are complex phenomena that can morph into chimerical radicalism.

Scottish nationalism, once a form of romantic conservatism, has stolen the garb of a radical social democracy from under the noses of a moribund and corrupt Labour Party. The political activism we witnessed during the Scottish independence referendum was the result of an intense frustration with the political class and a hope that there could be a way out of the poverty and squalor of some of the poorest areas in Western Europe. But this form of radicalisation will not necessarily provide a spur to a movement to the left south of the border, especially if the SNP becomes enmeshed in coalition politics after the May elections.

In a period of fluidity and instability and rapid shifts in political relationships, an aggressive secular humanism without an understanding of the conditions that give rise to religious sentiment amongst the oppressed can turn into Islamophobia, and can echo the populism of the far right.

But it must be said that that however powerful and salient in the hands of a ruling class a conservative political ideology and its media channels may be, they can never be permanent under capitalism. The 'de-industrialisation' of the working class does not change the relation between labour and capital; in some ways it intensifies it, insofar as it delegates to the state and the legislature the task of extracting its pound of flesh from the working class, including even the most desperate and incapacitated. The levels of child poverty, homelessness and ill-health have grown exponentially as have the exhortations of the government to the feckless to eat responsibly, stop drinking and smoking, exercise more, etc. None of these prescriptions of course will change lives significantly. Put in grander economic terms, the main source of people's problems is debt.

The government has made its central myth the issue of public debt, through a tissue of lies about bloated welfare and social services. The main issue is private debt, most dramatically expressed through the banking collapses in 2007–08. Without the recourse to traditional trade-union methods of class struggle, working-class families had to spend savings and resort to debt companies who were like banks for those who had accounts, or to the notorious payday loan companies like Wonga and a multitude of others who alongside pawnbrokers have made their appearance on our streets. Others less fortunate were left in the hands of street-loan sharks. People who are weighed down by debt feel less confident in taking industrial action, especially when their contracts are insecure. This is a major factor in the decline in collective action but it does not guarantee a future of labour submissiveness. An indication of this is the determination of the Tories to legislate for further restrictions on the right to strike and other forms of action.

It is worth taking a closer look at the emerging structure and definition of the working class, not in the sociological sense of strata, but rather the relationship between labour and capital on a historical scale. The mass socialisation of labour in the form of the factory system and its necessary correlatives in transport, communication, urbanisation, energy, and forms of education, has shaped modern societies. The neo-con dream of atomised, free, competitive small enterprises is either a delusion or an ideological cover for global capital.

Despite the closure of steel mills, mines and quarries, factories, and a host of small traditional industries, mass socialised labour still exists but in a different form and with a different function. In the public sector, the hospitals and local health services, education, welfare, emergency, social and municipal services bring together in work contexts thousands of people who are indirectly supposed to serve the interests of the state and of the people. In the private sector again, there are thousands of workers in key industries: communications, transport, power and energy, the functioning of ports and shipping, the maintenance of the infrastructure, and in the retail industry. These workers do not produce surplus value at the point of production. They service capital indirectly by contributing to the maintenance of the total capital system.

The same applies to the finance sector, not at the top end, but at the level of the invisible thousands of workers who act as cleaners, canteen staff, call-centre operators, clerical and secretarial staff. The dream of escaping the socialisation of labour is like that of herding cats or plaiting sand. The Tories make a great deal of the medium and small enterprises that they consider to be the backbone of the economy. This sector has been particularly vulnerable to the crisis in the banking system because of its inability to secure loans or because it has fallen prey to predatory raids from banks like RBS. The idea that workers in these enterprises are biddable does not stand up to historical investigation. In the early periods of working-class development these crafts and trades were particularly volatile and the struggles very violent, as for example in the case of the Sheffield cutlery trade, or in the early period of the Catalan working class in Barcelona. There is no reason to believe that in a period of industrial decline history will not repeat itself.

Both in the US and the UK there have been movements against low pay in food outlets like McDonald's, Burger King, etc., and significantly in the supermarket chains. One important victory was that of Sheffield ASDA women workers who unionised a supermarket in Walkley and won equal pay with the warehouse staff.

This is significant on two levels, the first being that ASDA is owned by the US global company Walmart, which is notoriously anti-trade-union and has a history of ruthless intervention in the US agricultural industry. The second is that of the 'memory' of the working class. The women who unionised a Walmart outlet lived in families of engineers and steelworkers and also were socialised by and lived amongst unionised public-sector workers in what is often thought of as a 'relic' culture. What these conflicts demonstrate is that human response to hardship and humiliation is not predictable. The industrial and economic struggles of the working class are also expressed at a social, family and individual level. The housing problems of homelessness, rent arrears, evictions and poor maintenance in the public sector by outfits like Keir, who replaced Public Works Departments, create enormous tensions and struggles which are rarely mentioned in the press, until there are big demonstrations, occupations and resistance to evictions. At the social level we can see the development of both solidarity and creative independent forms of co-operative sustenance and support. These can give a glimmer of hope of an alternative to the capitalist rat race. There will be new forms of combination appropriate to our times that will involve not only unionisation but more generalised forms of social and political action, which are and will be far more difficult to control than are the traditional labour organisations.

We are now living through a period of violent reordering of the former post-World War Two settlement. Symptomatic of the instability and a chronic sense of crisis is the entry of war as an arm of foreign policy. What for three generations in the West has been the unthinkable on the land mass of Europe is now with us. War is also an extremely lucrative form of economy for arms producers and exporters as well as the mercenary military companies. It is the principal and most barbarous form of the capital system's now structurally necessary production of non-durable and waste goods. War was something Europeans were against, unless exported or out of view. Regional and proxy wars are now becoming a fact of life and are getting uncomfortably close to home. Once again warfare is being naturalised. The conflicts in the Balkans and now in the Ukraine are bringing back a sense of political fragility which is also heightened by fundamentalist terror. The threat of war or the descent into war will present a major challenge to the workers' movement. The root of this instability is the domination of capital. Instability, shock and the sense of heightened threat, real or manufactured, are not merely ruling-class conspiracies and the manipulative instruments of a degenerate media, they are an expression of the secret and hidden fears of the elites, the fear of the others they do not see in their world. As one city gent put it, it is the fear of the pitchforks. There is a sense that beneath the froth of the 'recovery' lurks a danger that is felt throughout society, whether it is expressed through economic insecurity or the loss of familiarity with a world held together with more or less common beliefs and feelings.

We will be coming to a realisation of what the ruling class has already seen: that they cannot rule in the old way and that subjugated classes find their way of life intolerable. At the moment we seem to be in a state of stasis in the relationship between the main contending classes. What the trigger for the oncoming conflict will be cannot be predicted, but the state forces are preparing for large-scale civil disturbances under the guise of anti-terrorist intelligence and legislation. Even some economic commentators far removed from revolutionary critical thought – and whose interests may lie primarily in proving that they were right and that the Lords of Misrule were truly fools – have a bleak view of the future. One asset manager, quoted in a Sunday newspaper recently, opined that '[t]his down cycle is likely to be remembered in a hundred years' and that it was going to create 'a great deal of damage', all the more so because of 'the efforts of central banks to thwart it.'

We can draw no satisfaction from being righteous: we have to play a part in righting the increasingly acute and dangerous crisis of human society. The playwright David Hare put the issue very clearly in his criticism of Ed Miliband, addressing that frustrated constituency who only wish that Miliband could make a killer speech that would expose and wipe out that glib, shabby fraud that is David Cameron: 'Why at a time when the public most needs it can he not shoot at Cameron's open goal? Why can he not take the whole thing on? Rhetoric is not an add-on, an extra facility or a gift. The truth is you can make a great speech if you can have a great analysis.'

David Hare is right, we need a great analysis, not for great speeches but for hope of a new world, something that has to be fought for tooth-and-nail as the working class and its allies take on the life-threatening consequences of capital's structural crisis and prepare the ground for a society of equality, freedom, collective ownership and care for the planet's resources.

A Disunited Kingdom: The Scottish Independence Referendum

by Terry Brotherstone

In his analysis of the state of Britain, Tom Owen alludes to Scottish nationalism as 'a form of romantic conservatism' that 'has stolen the garb of a radical social democracy from under the noses of a moribund and corrupt Labour Party'. The political activism seen during the campaign for the Scottish independence referendum on 18 September 2014, he writes above, 'was a result of an intense frustration with the political class and a hope that there could be a way out of the ... squalor of some of the poorest areas in Western Europe'. He is right to add the observation that the 'chimerical radicalism' of nationalism is unstable. It is historically contingent – a product of circumstance rather than ideological consistency – and it 'will not necessarily provide a spur to a movement to the left south of the border', especially if the Scottish National Party (SNP) becomes 'enmeshed' in UK coalition politics while remaining the main point of reference for the Scottish movement. But the real, if complex and contradictory, class movement that came into being in Scotland in the referendum campaign – while there is no guarantee (I write seven months later) that it is the harbinger of a decisive change in working-class consciousness – certainly provided a moment for new voices to make themselves heard and the opportunity for new thinking.[18]

At various times since World War One, Marxists have debated the part that should – or should not – be played in a revolutionary working-class programme in Britain by demands for national self-determination in Scotland. But that is not the main context in which to discuss the significance of the independence referendum. 'Every step of real movement is more important than a dozen programmes', wrote Marx in a different context.[19]

And there was 'real movement', especially, but far from exclusively, in the impoverished 'schemes' (housing estates) of Scotland's deindustrialised west-central belt. Socialists, including veterans of decades of campaigning, felt the political ground shifting beneath their feet.

In October 2012 some former members and associates of the Workers Revolutionary Party (WRP), which imploded in the aftermath of the 1984–85 miners' strike, met in London to set up a discussion on the idea of revolutionary working-class agency in the light of the transformational social changes in capitalism, the entrenchment of neo-liberal ideology and the collapse of Stalinism. The exchanges that follow have been extracted and edited from contributions to that discussion.[20] Two strands have been selected. The first highlights the referendum campaign on the ground and particularly the way it drew a new generation into left-wing politics; the second reflects on arguments amongst trade unionists, focusing on two thoughtful militants who played leading roles in the struggle against Thatcherism in the 1980s – one in North-East England in the miners' strike, the other in the North Sea oil-workers' industrial actions of 1989–90. The intention is not to comment on the general argument of this book, only to draw a range of activist opinion into it.

I.

Hilary Horrocks, born in London, came to Glasgow in 1979 as a full-time worker for the WRP. More recently she has been active in trade unions, in struggles such as the anti-Poll Tax movement, and in rethinking socialism. In early September 2014, an article on the independence referendum by the Keynesian, London *Observer* columnist Will Hutton – arguing that 'If Britain can't find a way of sticking together, it is the death of the liberal enlightenment before the atavistic forces of nationalism and ethnicity' – prompted her to write that while nationalism was important, she did not 'think most people voting "yes" in Scotland will be voting for nationalistic reasons'. That might once have been the case, but the determining factors now were 'the experience of a welfare-slashing coalition government and a warmongering Labour one' and 'the chance to rid yourself of a regime which doesn't represent you at all'. Having initially been put off by 'the saltire-waving brigade' (the saltire is the Scottish flag) with its assertions that 'that the Scottish working class is inherently more progressive than the English', she would vote 'yes'. In 'the last few months', she wrote, 'the debate has ... become very political, and ... reflects class issues [albeit] ... sometimes in an indirect way'.

Unlike the pro-Union English TUC leaders, the Scottish TUC did not take sides, rather promoting debate on its 'social justice' agenda. Horrocks was a delegate at its April 2014 congress. Fringe meetings saw 'veterans ... at each other's throats'. The 'no' camp tried to 'present Labour as a progressive party' when 'everyone ... knows ... this is long past'. They focused not on the class case for 'yes', but on the SNP and the idea that its then leader, Alex Salmond, was on an 'ego-trip'. Their mantra that the SNP were 'Tartan Tories' showed them 'out-of-touch'. The SNP had shifted to the left, appealing to 'disillusioned Labour voters' by taking over the welfare-statist political ground Labour had vacated.

The 'yes' campaigners were predominately lively, younger trade unionists – 'mainly not pro-SNP', and without illusions that independence was the answer in itself. The campaign for working-class demands would go on 'energetically ... whatever the Scottish government'. And 'a confidence has been generated during this campaign ... that will probably encourage this energy'. Horrocks saw similarities with the anti-poll tax movement 'which some left groups ... initially underestimated and labelled a non-working-class movement', but which 'saw off Thatcher' in 1990. She concluded: 'We must be sensitive to what is happening in Scotland now, even though it may not conform to the classic parameters of class action'.

Cathy Milligan, a community activist from the Castlemilk scheme on Glasgow's south side, as 'a citizen of the world', had wanted nothing to do with nationalism and was concerned about breaking up the British working-class movement and facilitating 'the rise of fascism, especially in England where Ukip have free range' in the media. But 'the young people of Scotland' had changed her mind:

> They are clearly saying that it is not about nationalism: it's about having a voice that can be heard – which they do not have now. They … hate the Tory and Lib-Dem [coalition] government that represents millionaires and the elite, and doesn't care that children are going without food. The increase in food banks, in a country that is relatively wealthy, is shameful. Young people in Scotland put the blame firmly on the unfair distribution of wealth. They state that it's … about us, the people, having our say in shaping our future. The talk is not about Scotland and Scottish people being superior, but about the opportunity for real people power …

Thousands were coming regularly 'to meetings to engage in the debate. [And the] meetings … have been about the ideas of socialism.' In 'poor and downtrodden' areas, previously disenfranchised people were registering to vote 'in huge numbers'. And these working-class, first-time voters were taking control of their own campaign, organising a 'Referenjam … [with] music, poems and self-expression … design[ing] their own leaflet … [making] sure that there was no flag waving and … [favouring] traditionally socialist colours' rather than the blue and white of the Scottish saltire. They had 'total contempt' for 'established politics'. Their enthusiasm was transcending Glasgow's traditional sectarian divide, with supporters of the Protestant

Glasgow Rangers Football Club rejecting attempts by the pro-Union Orange Order to divide them.

> [L]istening to them talk about unfairness, about the hypocrisy of the Tories and Lib Dems, about the downright betrayal of the Labour Party, and the need to fight for a better, fairer world where wealth is made for and by the people ... is inspirational. ... [T]he movement ... is strong, healthy and progressive ... not what the establishment, or even the SNP envisaged at all. The context is everything. The exposure of capitalism and its greed is so clear ... [to] these young people. The English people are not the enemies – and because of social media, they don't rely on the established media ... for information. ... [Whatever] the outcome of the referendum [they want to organise] against ... attacks on working-class people ... against austerity and neoliberal values, and against the whole capitalist state ... [and its] inhumane policies.

She thought that the 'whole point is that this debate on independence has taken on a life of its own' and that 'there is no going back'.

The result was announced in the early hours of 19 September. The voter turnout, at nearly 85 per cent of a registered electorate comprising 97 per cent of those eligible, was far higher than in any electoral exercise in Britain for decades. Much to the relief of the neo-liberal establishment, which had been in an undignified panic since opinion polls had begun to move towards 'yes' with one even putting it in the lead, the result was 55 per cent against independence. But major working-class areas voted 'yes'.

Hilary Horrocks spent referendum day with hopeful young voters in an Edinburgh scheme. She thought that – given the threats of economic ruin the electorate had been subjected to by government, banks, businesses, financial and retail corporations and almost all the mainstream media ('the political equivalent of carpet bombing', said one newspaper), the pro-independence vote had been remarkable. Over 70 per cent of the newly (and only for the referendum) enfranchised 16–17 year olds were for independence. There was a similar majority for 'no' amongst the over-65s.

Most significantly, the 'yes'-voting areas were not those with a 'nationalist' tradition but rather the traditional working-class, de-industrialised and poorer parts: Clydeside and Dundee. '"Red Clydeside" has become nationalist Clydeside', one analyst had snappily declared.[21] The scenes in Glasgow's George Square through referendum night evoked distant images of Cairo's Tahrir. A few reporters with an international range, notably Paul Mason, had heard echoes of Spain's Podemos and even Greece's Syriza in the Scottish campaign.[22] At a mass Radical Independence Campaign (RIC) rally several weeks after the Referendum both these movements were represented.[23]

The day after the Referendum, one young television interviewee, in tears, said 'that she would vote again for independence, but never in a general election', expressing the disgust of a generation with mainstream politicians and the remoteness – not only in geographical terms, but in class and cultural terms – of the UK government. People had queued up to cast this vote as 'a way of fighting against social injustice', not as an assertion of national identity.

The reckoning for the Labour Party would be stark, Horrocks predicted. They would be condemned for joining with the hated welfare-slashing coalition parties and, said one radio phone-in contributor, for 'splitting the progressive vote'. Some on the left had 'voted "no" for reasons of international solidarity' but 'for the Labour Party leadership it was a ... cynical exercise ... to try to keep their Scottish MPs in the UK parliament' because, without them, 'they would probably be stuffed' in the May 2015 Westminster General Election.

After the vote there were 'pious calls ... for "reconciliation"', led by church leaders and some Labour and Liberal Democrat supporters who had voted 'yes', but wanted to defuse any further threats to political stability. In Edinburgh's High Kirk of St. Giles, the 'no' and 'yes' party leaders came together in a spectacle of establishment hypocrisy to light candles.[24] But the grassroots campaign would not easily be damped down. Mason had commented on levels of passion reminiscent of what it was like when politics was still about ideology.

In two reflective post-Referendum contributions, Cathy Milligan pointed out that the 'margin was 383,937 ... so close' – despite the 'onslaught by the establishment' and threats to destroy 'our economy'. Some firms had even 'sent personal letters telling workers' that a 'yes' vote could lose them their jobs. Pensions, it was threatened, 'would be undermined'. Yet '1.6 million people voted "yes", against the Westminster elite and its austerity.'

There had been post-referendum violence in George Square, coordinated by the 'no'-voting Britain First campaign with its supporters 'singing Rule Britannia and spouting hatefulness' in 'a complete contrast to the previous evenings, when the square was full of hope'. But when 'some of the ... [right-wing] mob were seen wearing Glasgow Rangers shirts' it 'provoked ... angry Facebook posts from Rangers fans who were shamed by these people'. The campaign had seen 'the working class at its best and most powerful', people 'unified in defence of their interests' and against 'economic policies which ... have seen the number of billionaires in Britain rise ... while child poverty is increasing at an alarming rate'.

The extraordinary post-referendum surge in SNP membership Milligan saw as a 'reaction to the deflated feeling after the vote'; it was not based on illusions in the Nationalists as standing for the 'working-class interest'. The SNP seemed to many the quickest route to independence, which they had come to identify with ridding us of 'the Westminster elite'. This was understandable but 'very wrong'. The SNP had been in a majority government in Scotland for three years while '55,000 public service jobs [had been] lost', including 'carers for families with severely disabled members'. Their referendum campaign had been hampered when they couldn't answer the financial establishment's threats to leave Scotland without a recognised currency. 'They voted against a living wage' and wanted the right to reduce corporation tax, so that businesses could increase profits while workers endure 'zero-hours contracts' and school-leavers have a minimum wage of only £2.30 an hour.[25] There were no socialist grounds for voting for them.

The 'yes' campaign had 'channelled [the] anger of those who had no voice in the capitalist political arena. And, 'as Paul Mason had rightly pointed out, this energy and politicisation is emerging in a political void'. The Labour Party had been exposed; 'formed by the working class, [it] has long since abandoned it and become advocates for capital'. Milligan thought the movement was learning and 'growing arms and legs, in a way I have not witnessed in my lifetime'. As it gave voice to communities it was also making links throughout Britain on class issues. Having had 'the whole capitalist elite' from the US President to the Pope to the Queen scared of our unity', it would fight on, knowing that 'only us, the working class, [can] overthrow this barbaric system'.[26] The movement, Milligan added later, had 'brought to light the very undemocratic way our country is run [and has] created a vehicle ... for ideas on how to change it'.

What was happening in Scotland had to be seen in the light of 'many movements building throughout the world to ... fight for a more human society'. The time was ripe as, daily, 'more and more truths are being revealed about the corruption of governments as the capitalist economic crisis deepens throughout the world and people are uniting together and fighting for change'.

II.

The second strand in this discussion, equally important, can be more briefly summarised. It took place between trade unionists whose experience of struggles that had challenged Thatcherite neoliberalism had been made, symbolically, in the most important of the 'old' energy industries, coal, and in the one seen as opening the way for its replacement, oil. Without the 'windfall' revenues from North Sea oil and gas, which came fully on stream at the beginning of Thatcher's premiership and, in the early 1980s, were largely used to meet a burgeoning social-security bill as jobs were slashed, her government's socially destructive policies would have been even harder to implement. When offshore workers – in the aftermath of the 1988 Piper Alpha tragedy – launched action for trade-union recognition and a proper safety regime, they felt their economic importance could give them an advantage over the miners whose product was replaceable. But such victories as they won were short-term and pragmatic, leaving their strategic objectives unachieved.

Neil Rothnie, from North-East Scotland but now living in Glasgow, was the founder and first editor of the militant Offshore Industry Liaison Committee (OILC) – oil workers' – paper, Blowout, which helped lead the 1989–90 actions. He was later secretary of what became the OILC branch of the Rail Maritime and Transport union (RMT). He still works in the North Sea – in the Norwegian sector.

During the referendum, he expressed doubts, reporting workers' concerns for 'jobs and pensions'. They knew that 'another mob aren't going to be radically better than the old one' and did not 'see themselves (as part of the class – never mind as individuals) doing anything about building the New Jerusalem'. The campaign, from his vantage-point, seemed not to have 'raised ... the spectre of the working class acting as a class in its own interest', nor even to have really been about 'independence'

– certainly not from capitalism. It was 'more about a 1001 different reasons that people have for abandoning or keeping the status quo'. For him, the central question was whether a 'yes' vote would 'lead to the working class taking a step towards "governing ourselves"'; and whether it would 'have a knock-on effect in England, or in the English regions even, or throughout Europe?'

The result, Rothnie thought afterwards, was an '[i]nteresting call'. He predicted 'a complete implosion of the Labour party in Scotland'. The turnout on both sides showed how important everyone considered the decision. But:

> [as] there was no 'specific' ... class-based intervention, it's not really that surprising or necessarily ... negative that a big section of the working class ... decided not to take the chance. It would have been a very big step ... The Westminster establishment was looking particularly wild-eyed and acting extremely erratically in the last week (as far as I could see from my vantage point on a Norwegian oil rig).

Rothnie's experiences as secretary of the offshore workers' RMT branch had convinced him that workers were right to be cautious before entering a struggle trusting their leaders. His own 'yes' vote had been cast with an eye on the question 'who was going to lead us if the shit hits the fan'. Was a 'new' working-class leadership 'emerging' from the 'yes' campaign? Obviously, 'large sections of the working class' thought not. They feared being 'rudderless in giant seas.' With 'no discernible mass workers movement' in England, Wales and Northern Ireland, Scots could be isolated if the British establishment punished them for voting 'yes'.

Earlier in the campaign, in the spring of 2014, Dave Temple, a former Durham miner, a local leader in the great strike – and today the author of a number of books about the Durham miners

– had been invited to speak at a 30th-anniversary strike meeting in a former Scottish coalfield.[27] He had 'been asked to "say something against independence"', which, it was correctly assumed, he was. His audience included 'a mixture of Labour Party and former CP members' who all 'blamed the Labour Party for the rise of the SNP'. Knowing his political past in the Trotskyist movement, one asked 'why the far left groups were supporting the "yes" vote': commenting '"after all, aren't we all supposed to be internationalist?"'

The notes he had made for his speech showed Temple arguing about what the 'independence' on offer meant. It did not mean being independent of the banks, the hedge funds, the financial institutions – 'the real power in capitalist society'. The 'financial institutions ... dictate to the government of Britain what to do ... to the government of all countries which laws to pass ... which benefits to cut and how hard to cut them'. It was these 'institutions that created this crisis and now determine that we the working class have to pay for it'.

If you aren't 'independent of those parasites then you're not independent at all'. As a black American Civil rights leader once said, local government in the ghettoes merely afforded 'the right to administer your own misery'.

> We in the North-East of England share with you a proud history ... of struggle. We like you do not elect Tories to parliament. All our MPs ... are Labour MPs. The Durham County Council has never been a Tory council. It has been Labour for a hundred years and before that it was Liberal. I ask you, as comrades facing a common struggle, please do not abandon us to the Tories of the South. Because that is what Scottish independence will mean for us.
>
> We have suffered some setbacks since the great strike. Our backs are against the wall. We have no alternative but to fight. But, we are – first and foremost – the working class. Not a

> Scottish working class or an English working class but a working class. And as a working class our only strength is our unity as a class...

Rothnie responded by remembering 'the role played by the CP and Labour Party stalwarts in the coalfield in Scotland 30 years back' when the WRP attempted to assist young Fife miners to organise a march to a May Day rally in Glasgow – one aim of which was, symbolically at least, to unite the miners with steel-workers whose leaders, fearing closure of the Ravenscraig plant, had refused to call them out in solidarity. The Scottish NUM and CP leaders, George Bolton and Mick McGahey, had stopped the miners from participating in the march, which, they argued, breached the 'unity' of the class in action. 'Unity in that context [meant] subordinating all thought and action to the dogmas of "international" Stalinism [and] Social Democracy', wrote Rothnie, which is why he 'was never an "internationalist" as your ex-CP member understands the word'.

He drew attention to Cathy Milligan's accounts of how 'the youth in Castlemilk ... [had] been radicalised in this debate', and to the 'yes' arguments he had heard in Glasgow pubs. The fact that this working-class support for independence had created such a crisis for the Labour Party as well as the Coalition government, he saw as positive. 'However progressive the trades unions and their Labour Party have been in the past,' he said, 'they're pretty much a spent force now ... [They] hung the miners out to dry ... and have been degenerating at breakneck speed ever since.'

His own trade-union involvement was now largely in Norway – the 'last bastion of social democracy in Europe'. Talk of the 'Nordic model' had played a big part, certainly in middle-class circles, in the referendum debate, but, thought Rothnie, that is really 'all about the past rather than the future'. Despite their 'independence' and oil riches, the Norwegians are 'facing many of the same problems as the rest of us. It's just all taking a bit longer for them to feel the heat', in the same way as the working class in Europe 'has taken ... longer to begin to experience ... a little of what capitalism has been meting out to workers in the less developed world for ages'.

The SNP (today 'Tartan Social Democrats' rather than 'Tartan Tories', but that made them no less of a capitalist party), through their referendum, had unintentionally 'provided a focus for a new generation of young workers to open up a brilliant discussion centring on the completely broken nature of the Great British State and allowed these same forces to exercise their collective imagination about what a possible alternative future might be' – and to do so independently of the bureaucracies that have long constrained such collective discussions.

The former miners he had been talking to, Temple clarified, 'were at the time of the strike the young foot soldiers ... 20- to 30-year-olds trapped in an organisation and a mind-set, just like we were'. They, too, 'have moved on'. And 'their internationalism is ... very different from the old guard you remember – who are now mostly dead'. Certainly the Labour Party deserved 'a good kicking', but in Scotland, 'the alternative is the Nationalists, in Durham [it is] the reactionary Ukip'. Reluctantly, 'after many years of not voting', he would vote Labour – though he later emphasised that he saw this not as an endorsement the reactionary policies of Labour, only a tactical vote against Ukip.

The 'yes' campaign enthusiasm was understandable, an expression of hatred for 'the old parties ... [for] capitalism ... [for] the Tories in the south dictating to us'. It was great to see young people, long 'divorced from politics' joining in 'the passion of the debate'. But all the SNP were 'saying was that we, the Scottish nation, will be better off by ourselves' not that 'capitalism is in deep crisis'. Nor did they admit that when independent 'we will have to cut your benefits as hard if not harder than the coalition are doing now – which is the truth'. The question was that 'we should at least raise these questions and say we believe that we are stronger fighting capitalism united and together'.

III.

The discussion continued – and will continue. Even an interim conclusion here would be inappropriate. But perhaps the fact that it is happening may contribute to a wider understanding that the majority-'yes' areas in the Scottish independence referendum were looking for new ways of fighting for class justice, which elsewhere – for historical reasons – cannot find even temporary expression in 'nationalism' with all its reactionary implications, including what Temple fears could mean the abandonment of English workers to the Tories and Ukip. The May 2015 UK general election campaign showed that the newly apparent and energetic political intelligence of radicalised young Scottish workers and students was not ephemeral. But as Owen says, as long as its expression is cast in a nationalist cloak, it guarantees no positive, knock-on effect elsewhere. For this to be the outcome – as all four contributors to this discussion would, I think, agree – the Scottish movement must divest itself of that cloak.

It was and is, however, a 'real movement'– not a party, not a programme, but a movement for social transformation. And to grasp its significance, it has to be seen in the context of what is happening internationally – the rise (and crisis) of Syriza in Greece but also Podemos in Spain, and, more important, the pre-existing but still-in-formation social movements that lie behind these (for the moment at least) mainstream parties. The politics of the Scottish referendum have so far been contained within the processes of an electoral democracy which – although its manipulation to produce outcomes the ruling elites require becomes ever more obvious (particularly so in the UK since the parliamentary coup that put the coalition government in place in 2010)

– has just about delivered social control. And it is in Greece (in early 2015) that the ability of European 'democracy' to do this is under the greatest test. But grasping the significance of what happened in Glasgow's George Square on Referendum night can bring us closer to a practical analysis of the unresolved politically realities announced by the recent occupations of urban spaces everywhere from Cairo's Tahrir to Sýndagma in Athens. Therein, perhaps, lies Scotland's greatest significance.

The State of Disorder and its Scottish Question after the May 2015 UK General Election

by Terry Brotherstone and Tom Owen

'We can no longer be certain of anything about the future except that it will be unlike the past', wrote the Irish poet William Butler Yeats after the 1916 Easter Rising. 'All changed, changed utterly', he declared in his poem 'Easter 1916'. The 2015 general election involved no armed insurrection, no punitive executions: but it could prove to be the harbinger of political change in the UK even more profound than the Dublin Rising, of which Lenin insisted to some of his fellow revolutionaries that to dismiss it as a putsch led by outdated nationalist dreamers was to be incapable of understanding social revolution 'as a living thing'.[28]

Had it not been for the unprecedentedly unanimous failure of all the national opinion polls to predict the outcome – until the final 'exit polls', almost all commentary had presaged a no-overall-majority, 'hung' parliament and negotiations for a new coalition – the Tory victory and the comprehensive defeat of the Labour Party would not have come as such a shock. And it was Britain's antiquated and undemocratic (even in bourgeois-democratic terms) 'first-past-the-post' electoral system, which on this occasion awarded the Tories – with less than 37 per cent of the popular vote (about a quarter of the registered electorate) –

just over half the parliamentary seats contested. This has allowed the new government to claim a 'mandate' for its intention – masked with breathtaking hypocrisy behind Prime Minster Cameron's unctuous declarations of 'one-nation' Toryism and of leading the Conservatives as the 'real party of working people' – to wage ruthless class war. They think they can now implement viciously anti-social policies – including a further £12 billion of welfare cuts, a ratcheting-up of the UK's already draconian anti-union laws and new measures stigmatising and victimising immigrants – outlined in a Manifesto few had read and which was scarcely discussed during the campaign, not least because of the assumption that coalition negotiations would be the deciding factor.[29]

There was an underlying logic in the election result however. It was a confirmation that global capital could not, at this stage in its crisis, permit the crumbs of office to be thrown to even the most loyal and craven opposition. 'The owl of Minerva', wrote Hegel, 'takes its flight only when the shades of night are gathering': wisdom comes only when it can reflect on, rather than influence, what has passed.[30] But the wise owl flies not at all for Britain's Labour Party leaders, the most vocal of whom immediately pronounced their (in reality, in purely electoral terms, relatively marginal) defeat, a disaster that could only be overcome by even more open capitulations to capital. The Ed Miliband leadership was castigated not for its failure to seriously oppose the Coalition's austerity programme but for – it is hard to write this with a straight face – being 'too left-wing'. The aggressively neo-liberal former premier Tony Blair and his acolytes, including the main challengers to replace Miliband as leader, were quick to announce the need to abandon any policy that 'Business' says is not to its liking.[31]

The 'genuine catastrophe' for the Labour Party in electoral terms, wrote the political historian Ross McKibbin, was 'the loss of Scotland'.[32] Labour surrendered all but one of its 41 seats to the

SNP, which, with unprecedented swings, swept the country, also benefitting from an electoral system that delivered all but three of 59 Scottish seats in return for about 50 per cent of the popular vote. The SNP, as we have mentioned, is an ideologically unstable party that has filled the political vacuum left by the Labour Party – now associated with the Iraq War, capitulation to the basic tenets of neo-liberalism and a complete failure to fight the austerity agenda. Labour is finished as a living party of the masses, and it is in Scotland – where, it can be argued, the Party was born when the former coalminer James Keir Hardie ran in the 1888 Mid-Lanark by-election and helped form the Scottish Labour Party (a forerunner of the UK-wide Independent Labour Party and the national parliamentary Party itself) – that this has dramatically manifested itself.

The truth is out for what has become a rump of career politicians, who now stand frozen like rabbits in the headlights of the politically bankrupt but cynically ruthless reactionary forces that have defeated them. But for the working population and the unemployed at large, it is not just the duplicity of Labourism that has failed but the whole framework of institutional parliamentary representative democracy.

The vote for Labour in the election (despite the collapse in Scotland, slightly up on 2010) was largely defensive, based on a determination to stop the Tories by the only means available within the social-democratic framework, the ballot box. The strategy failed and now those workers, and others who defected to Ukip, will face the full Tory onslaught. Post-World-War-Two reformism and relative social peace is definitively at an end and, although the collapse of the Labour Party involves a bitter experience for many, this is no time for depression – which, in this case, can only mean mourning a lost cause. The Tories, the state, with backing of global capital, are bringing the fight to us. But it need not be an unequal fight since the working class still has immense socio-economic – indeed human – power when it can acquire the means, the organisation and the political will to exercise it. The question of mass economic, social and political democracy is now raised in its sharpest form.

This is what makes the positive step taken by many Scottish working-class voters in abandoning Labour for the SNP one that is richly but dangerously contradictory. As we argued above – writing after Scotland's Independence Referendum but before the election – the SNP's rise, and particularly the real political and campaigning enthusiasm amongst young people and socially deprived ex-Labour voters that underlies it, offers no guarantee of a parallel, related opposition movement in the rest of the UK. Even in the election campaign it was clear that the forces of reaction have been quickest to take advantage of the fact that the Scottish movement comes decorated with the insignia of nationalism.

While the SNP campaigned over-confidently on the assumption that it could reconcile English voters by insisting it would offer parliamentary support to a minority Labour government – even pushing it to the left in a way a cohort of Scottish Labour MPs had failed to do in the years of the Blair and Gordon Brown premierships – Lynton Crosby, the Australian hired gun determining the Tories' vote-winning strategy, evidently had some success portraying the Nationalists' leaders as pickpockets out to blackmail a weak Labour government and rob the English taxpayer ('the hard-working families' of Tory rhetoric) to fund Scotland's social services. Far from counteracting this, Labour effectively joined the Scotophobic chorus, ruling out any sort of parliamentary agreement with the SNP and thereby eliminating any practical likelihood that they would be able to form an effective minority government. This probably served to leak further support amongst English workers, who have long felt themselves unrepresented in parliament, from Labour to their only, but very different, 'nationalist' option – the odious Ukip.

The Crosby-led Tories, that is to say, exploited divisions in the working class not only (in their now customary manner) between immigrant and 'native' workers, but also amongst the English, Welsh and, particularly, Scots to capitalise on previously politically insignificant divisions. When, during the Scottish Independence Referendum campaign, the Pope cautioned his flock with chilling images of the aftermath of the break-up of the former Yugoslavia, his comments seemed absurdly alarmist – and the UK situation is certainly very different. But the possibility of 'collateral damage' from actions arising from the unmediated cynicism of a Tory party desperate to give a gloss of 'democratic', parliamentary legitimacy to its ruthless prosecution of class war should not be underestimated.

The radical social transformation now urgently needed, however, the transition 'beyond capital', to quote the title of István Mészáros's seminal work, is – as Lenin insisted in the very different circumstances in which the 1916 Irish Rising played its part in the international process culminating in the October Revolution – necessarily contradictory. It is 'a living thing'.[33] The task, to which the experiences recounted and the theoretical reflections reported in this book, seek to contribute, is both huge and complex: 'the mountain we must climb and conquer', writes Mészáros, 'is many Himalayas on top of one and other'.[34] But, yes, it must be conquered if humanity is to have a sustainable future.

Compared to this global task what happened in the 2015 UK general election, particularly in Scotland, represents only a small step in the foothills. If the significance of these events is wrestled with and grasped, however – if Scottish workers can find ways of shedding the nationalist cloak and uniting with all those in the rest of the UK who must now seek new, extra-parliamentary ways of defending themselves, their families and communities (their class) and of going on the offensive – then this moment of utter change in electoral politics could prove to have been a significant moment in the struggle for a truly human society.[35]

Spain

Personal Political Experiences

by Jonas Nilsson

At the time of the collapse of the Soviet Union and the Stalinist regimes in Eastern Europe, I had a discussion with the leadership of the Partido Socialista de los Trabajadores (PST – the Spanish section of the Ligua Internacional de los Trabajadores or LIT at that time) on whether this breakdown could offer revolutionary perspectives for the workers' movement.

LIT's slogan then was 'Now it's time for Trotskyism' (or words very similar). Many of the organisations claiming to be Trotskyist thought that the disintegration of the ruling bureaucratic caste, the usurper of socialism, made it clear to everyone that we were right, and so the way to revolution, power and glory was open for us. What few were able to see was that not only was a corrupt, repressive and murdering bureaucracy in decomposition, but also – and perhaps more important – the expectation of a socialist future without Stalinist repression and bureaucracy disappeared for millions of workers all over the planet. Workers in the West, though aware at least that much was failing in the so-called socialist countries, had still maintained until 1989 the hope of reform in these regimes, making it possible to overcome capitalism and achieve a life of socialism and dignity.

Until the beginning of the 1980s all workers' protests in Eastern Europe were directed against the Stalinist bureaucracy but never in favour of capitalism. In the middle of that decade the Polish working-class opposition in Solidarność was decisively defeated by the pro-capitalist intellectual wing and from there onward political perspectives changed in the working-class movement all over Eastern Europe. The breakdown of the Berlin Wall, in the way it was executed, produced a tremendous confusion rather than enthusiasm among workers in Western Europe and especially in the Communist parties. Capitalist forces knew how to take advantage of that confusion all over the globalised planet, and the neoliberal offensive started by Reagan and Thatcher advanced rapidly without consistent resistance from trade unions and other workers' organisations.

The working class in Spain, suffering a transformation of social relations at their workplaces into individualised working conditions and deprived of a socialist ideology, was gradually disarmed, and lost its place as the leading force in social struggles. The proud culmination of every general strike in Barcelona – the march of the SEAT workers from the industrial suburb where the factory was located into the Barcelona city centre – simply disappeared. And for the first time pickets had to be organised against scabs in the main industrial belts, rather than as previously in less important industrial areas. The workers as a social class of course continued to exist but, after the serious deterioration of their economic and social conditions, the class virtually disappeared as a movement, leaving workers' children without the identity and self-esteem of being members of the class of their parents.

For some years the expression 'the thousand-euro generation' was used to condemn the low wages offered to the younger generation – even those with academic qualifications. Today the wages of young people are considerably lower. In working-class districts youth unemployment is often considerably more than 50 per cent. This is a social time-bomb which sooner or later must explode, a time-bomb to which the ruling class tries to shut its eyes and ears.

In Spain a new generation of political actors began to fill the gaps left by the workers' movement. Some important international solidarity initiatives were inspired by Catholic youngsters, others by the ordinary left organisations (as in the formation of Workers Aid for Bosnia when the war exploded in the Balkans).

Then came the students and ecologists organising the anti-globalisation movement. What all these three had in common was the decisive role of young people, rejecting and resisting all attempts from the church, parties and trade unions to take control. They represented the first step in organising protests outside the old structures of social and political movements, breaking away from the organisational experiences of earlier generations. Reality had changed and many of the old formulae had expired. As a consequence of the confusion in the workers' movement, the social composition of these new movements was mainly middle-class and student-based.

One of the most important expressions of this new kind of organisation arose in Barcelona in the closing years of the last century, with the name Moviment de Resistència Global (MRG), embracing movements of international solidarity, radical trade unions and social and ecological protest movements. It had an important role in the preparation of the protests at the World Bank summit meeting in Barcelona in 2001, a strong mobilisation culminating in a videoconference, and in the demonstration against the invasion of Iraq in 2003, with a total of three million participants in Madrid and Barcelona. This organisation, MRG, like many others, had no real structure and no declared leaders or public faces, and it eventually decided to dissolve itself when different leftist organisations tried to take control of it and transform it into an organisation with a top-down structure. This anti-globalist or alter-globalist (global human activity) experience was the first expression of a young generation searching for new ways of organising against world capitalism's exploitation of humanity and natural resources, trying to break away from sectarian attitudes ('my organisation is right, the others are mistaken', a successor to 'my religion is right, the others are mistaken') and accept divergences as natural, positive and necessary within the movements. This change – understanding the necessary pluralism of opinions among the different organisations of the exploited – I consider to be an important development of social consciousness.

In 2007 the economic crisis began to change the social scene in Spain. Working-class organisations, mainly the trade unions, gradually lost their fighting spirit, and the Socialist Party, PSOE, won its second mandate in 2008. The consequence of the crisis was a strong increase in unemployment and housing evictions affecting working-class families. A new protest movement, Plataforma de Afectados por la Hipoteca (PAH), started in defence of citizens affected by mortgage foreclosures, which has grown into a considerable force. Since the start of the financial crisis there have been half a million foreclosures and 184 evictions a day, and the situation of hundreds of thousands of families is critical. Politicians currently in power are all discredited by the extensive corruption that even affects the two dominant trade unions, Comisiones Obreras and Unión General de Trabajadores (UGT). Given this new situation, with the traditional political and social leaders losing their support from below, and the masses lacking a solid revolutionary alternative, the social movements have understood the necessity of constructing their own political options, and are organising in an improvised way new alternatives at both local and national level. In the municipal elections in May 2015 many social and independent movements will be present with important possibilities in several big cities.

The young formation called Podemos ('Yes we can') is for the moment the party with the biggest chance of winning the next general election at the end of 2015. It appeared only four months before the European elections in May 2014 and won five seats, presenting itself as an alternative to 'the old regime', meaning the one that had been in power from the death of Franco in 1975. Its leader, Pablo Iglesias (not to be confused with his namesake, the founder of the socialist party, PSOE, in 1879), had an extensive presence in the mass media and internet, and the leadership is dominated by people from universities and with academic professions. It is growing rapidly to the extent of becoming the target of the fear and fury of the main parties, who see their privileges threatened. The United Left (Izquierda Unida, former Communist Party) is divided on the question of how to avoid the desertion of its members to Podemos. In recent months the influence of Podemos in working-class areas has become clearly visible, due to effects of the crisis, the loss of trust in the old working-class organisations and the extensive corruption scandals in all institutions and organisations linked to 'the old regime'. Podemos has succeeded in constructing a real threat – even though not a clear alternative – from the opposition arising from the global crisis, even though this has been mainly organised by the social movements. Its structure combines very open 'circles' at base level (many decisions taken by internet) with a tendency to centralise programmatic decisions and with a general secretary (Iglesias) and a broad top leadership.

In this respect Podemos has a different structure from that of the social movements and the Catalan independence organisation, Candidatura d'Unitat Popular (CUP), which has a more assembly-based structure, without clear leaders. The explanation given was that demands cannot be diluted in an interminable reflection on its own methods of functioning. And in the course of its spectacular growth, some of Podemos's principles as set out during the European elections have been modified and deliberately leave significant gaps in order to gain more influence and avoid intimidating accusations from the decadent existing parties. For example, in their recent documents and speeches much has disappeared, such as the necessity to renegotiate the debt imposed by the IMF and European Union, the necessity of an economic policy which takes into consideration the ecological needs of the planet instead of Keynesian recipes of eternal growth, and the right to self-determination of the nationalities in the Spanish state.

In December 2014 the CUP (with three deputies in the Catalan parliament) asked Podemos to support the right of the Catalan population to decide its own future, but received no answer, which probably should be understood as one of their calculated omissions, to avoid losing votes in other parts of Spain. That is only one example of how the question of national self-determination is misunderstood and underestimated outside Catalonia and Euskadi (the Basque country). In its nearly 30 years of existence the CUP has learned to present the right to national separation as a fundamental democratic right situated within the class struggle and social conflicts. It brings together a strong sector of activists in the social movements which cannot be ignored in the struggle to break up the old rotten and corrupted social structures.

In order to achieve the possible and absolutely necessary bringing-together of the social movements, local electoral candidates inspired and promoted by them, anti-capitalist movements for national independence like the CUP, and broader political alternatives like Podemos, it is important to introduce a more global alternative, where all inputs and contributions can be treated in common. Greece and Spain have in common that the popular mobilisation against the EU squeezing the poor in favour of the rich is dominated by anti-capitalist alternatives instead of the extreme right. With enough patience and generosity from the participants in this new and fresh experience in both countries, they can probably play an important role in breaking away from the rotten structure of capitalism upheld by the European Union. In Spain it is easy to unify on the basis of what we reject but, as always, it is more complicated to define a common positive perspective. The writer and former political prisoner Manuel Vázquez Montalbán described this reality with the phrase, '*Contra Franco vivíamos mejor*' ('We lived better against Franco'), a variation on '*Con Franco vivíamos mejor*' ('We lived better under Franco').

Here it would be worth taking into account the contribution of the new social consciousness brought in by the anti-globalisation movement and the *indignados*, trying to break away from former working-class political structures. This search for direct participation – without transmission through 'representatives' – is present in most of the popular protest movements, especially in neighbourhood mobilisations. Politically and organisationally, from the middle class and working class, there is a very strong opposition to the old regime, but what is missing is a programme to confront the EU and an economic programme that excludes the unsustainable mantra of eternal economic growth. These are crucial questions not defined or clarified by the new alternatives. The import-export proportion for Spain vis-à-vis Europe is four to one, something to be explained only through the shameful fact that the poor always sell cheap.

When the alternative movements treat this as a universal question, without exclusions and accepting the differences while advancing towards a society controlled by its citizens, able to reanimate the working-class areas which for too long have been absent, knowing that no real break with capitalism and no solid results are possible without their active participation ... then it will be possible to enter into a process of revolutionary change in Europe. It would probably be a mistake to advance one of the diverse alternatives on the political scene of anti-capitalism without support from the others, especially in such a complex political situation as the one in which we now find ourselves. I think that even strategically this method is preferable in order to avoid repeating sectarian experiences from the past.

Theses on Podemos and the 'Democratic Revolution'

by Raul Zelik[36]

Crisis of Representation

Even more remarkable than Podemos's surge in opinion polls, and its successes in the 2014 European elections and the regional Spanish elections of May 2015, is the social mobilisation that set the new party (founded in January 2014) in motion. It is the expression of a crisis of representation that has gripped many countries with neo-liberal regimes since the 1990s: it appears to have emerged out of a political vacuum and is expanding in an explosive manner. No existing political structures (such as trade unions, the larger NGOs or the media) have supported the project; the party activists – most of them under 35 – belong to the generation characterised as apolitical; and its immense popularity is not easily explained. In the Spanish mainstream, left positions were decidedly marginal until 2011.

But of course Podemos did not come out of nowhere. Its bases are the new anti-institutional protest movements that have repeatedly filled public squares and streets in the Iberian Peninsula. That Podemos is more than a fleeting protest party like the Pirates in Germany has mainly to do with the 15M Movement and the *mareas* ('tides'). The 15M Movement (public-square occupations with the demand for 'real democracy now'), which many on the left at first regarded with suspicion and at the very least saw as naïve and tending to apoliticism, has brought forth a new generation of activists and new forms of politics and made possible a tremendous repoliticisation – both internally and externally.

The crucial factor in the 15M Movement is its intuitive linking of criticism of capitalism with democratic demands. Starting with the concrete European experience, in which there is no longer a distinction between the economic and social policy of socialists and conservatives, the movement has identified the systemic limits to democracy in the bourgeois state. The democratic process ends where the interests of big capital, that is especially the banks, begins. Before the outbreak of the financial crisis, Spain's debt ratio was 40 per cent below Germany's. Only when Madrid was forced by the EU to bail out private Spanish banks (and thus also German investors), did the state deficit explode. The cuts in healthcare and social services already made by the PSOE governments showed that in an emergency government executives have the function of carrying out underlying power interests. However, political parties also seem to be increasingly standing in the way of democracy. With the 'political class', distinguished by professional politics and closed decision-making circuits, a specific social group has emerged with its own strategies of power and self-enrichment. In Spain, the political apparatuses are strongly shaped by the real-estate boom of recent decades. The awarding of building permits and construction contracts, as well as state oversight of public-savings banks (which have flourished in conjunction with the construction industry) guaranteed the 'political class' lucrative (mostly illegal) sources of income.

In contrast to what media reports suggest, the 15M Movement has in no way dissolved itself after the ebbing of the 2011 street protests but has spread throughout society. Thus we have seen the emergence, among other things, of the so-called *mareas* protest movement for the defence of the public education and healthcare systems, in which public-service employees come together through patients' initiatives and patient and refugee groups, or the movement against forced evictions – the Plataforma de Afectados por la Hipoteca (PAH), a coalition of base groups, which connect direct action, solidarity and case-oriented self-help in a remarkable way. There has also been a revival of labour organisations: in Andalusia, for example, activists of the trade union Sindicato Andaluz de Trabajadores (SAT) organised the non-violent redistribution of food purloined from supermarkets. The *mareas* in the healthcare and education sectors are supported by local groups of various smaller and larger trade unions. And, finally, the Marchas de la Dignidad, nationwide protest marches on Madrid, mobilised a million people in 2014 once again.

These movements made it clear that there is a social majority beyond the political apparatuses. But it also became clear – and this in turn led to thinking processes among the anti-institutional left – that the neo-liberal regime has no difficulty in sitting out social protests (as Germany's red-green government did with the Hartz IV protest at the beginning of the 2000s). Since the use of force is no longer an option, as it was for the labour movement of the twentieth century, a central means of pressure in adversarial politics is missing. 'Citizens' protests', which duly request permits from the authorities and do not disturb capitalist 'business as usual', do not affect the neo-liberal regime. It is not prohibited to have a different opinion because in the end it has no practical consequences.

Transforming Political Power

Against this background, the social movements in Spain faced the question of how these constant mobilisations could be transformed into real power from below, into *poder popular.* The Podemos and Guanyem initiatives – and this distinguishes these phenomena from other organisations of the European left – aim not simply at the founding of a new party but at the redefinition of political space. What is at issue is thus not simply new parliamentary political majorities but a transformation of the institutional framework.

The danger of accommodation to the institutions (as in the case of the German Greens, who in the end transformed themselves more than they did politics) has up to now been held at bay through the sheer speed of the movement's growth. The anti-institutional resistance is permeating the institutions with such vehemence that the institutions cannot hedge and absorb the dissidence – at least this is the project's manifest hope.

In this Podemos can certainly be accused of being itself a result of 'alienated' politics. The comparison with the Guanyem initiative in Barcelona makes it clear what this means. The latter is committed – completely within the logic of grassroots movements – to local processes of change from below. Guanyem Barcelona, which will very likely present ex-squatter Ada Colau as a candidate for the mayoral elections there, arose from the Plataforma de Afectados por la Hipoteca (PAH). The declared goal of Guanyem is to set into motion a municipal grassroots movement via municipal district assemblies, which will work out a platform for an alternative city government. It is thus expressly not aiming at welding together left groups through negotiations to form a coalition but at circumventing the existing (fragmented) left and at the same time incorporating them through the emergence of a grassroots movement. In terms of method, a path is being consciously taken here that is an alternative to the extant forms of representation.

Podemos is proceeding completely differently in this respect and has had great success – although in so doing it is in conflict with the radical-democratic postulates of 15M. Podemos' founding group – Pablo Iglesias, Juan Carlos Monedero, Carolina Bescansa, Luís Alegre and Íñigo Errejón – are Madrid political scientists, most of whom have worked for extended periods in Venezuela or in Bolivia. Its central figure is the 36-year-old Iglesias, who has made a name for himself on radio and television talk shows as a critic of the neo-liberal regime.

The rise of Podemos thus does not completely conform to the grassroots criteria of the 15M Movement. The initiative is carried by a small group, which to be sure intends to subject itself to democratic contestation processes but at the same time has formulated a clear claim to leadership. And it is doubtless also a product of the mass media; without television Podemos would probably be a marginal phenomenon. The grassroots participatory process unfolding with Podemos was thus originally set in motion in a more vertical way.

Podemos' founding group is pursuing a strategy overtly based on Latin American experiences. The central objective is to transform the general social discontent into an alternative political hegemony and thus launch a mobilisation that in turn will open up perspectives going beyond a classic reform policy. In this context we should remember that the political change in Venezuela, Ecuador, and Bolivia was neither the simple result of electoral victories nor the result of revolutions but emerged from the combination of radical rupture, continuity and transformation. The anti-neo-liberal revolts and mass uprising have blocked the neo-liberal regime in these countries for almost a decade, but the regime change took place within the existing political system. The opening up of larger transformational perspectives after this was in the last analysis due to the constitutional processes that gave form to the underlying constituent processes (the emergence of alternative popular power). These constitutional processes resulted from the fact that in these countries there was broad popular participation in the discussion of a new social contract. Podemos appears to be pursuing a similar project: it is formulating, at least implicitly, the problem of a democratic revolution that bursts the existing institutions...

Long-term transformation project?

But the central question is a different one: does Podemos actually have a transformation project that goes beyond the removal of the Partido Popular (PP) government? I think it does. For what would have to be done has been obvious after the mobilisations since 2011 and the ongoing conflicts with the other nations in the Spanish state: the notorious corruption has to be fought against, for example by establishing mechanisms of the social control of public projects and administration, introducing salary limits for functionaries, and legally anchoring radical democratic forms of participation. The privatisation of basic social services and the policy of forced evictions have to be stopped: no economic logic can justify the socialisation of speculative losses and their being shifted onto the shoulders of the population. The repressive policy against social and independence movements has to be ended and the anti-democratic exceptional laws annulled.

But most of all Spain needs a constitutional process similar to the process in Latin America. The 1978 constitution was the result of an elite pact of Francoist, regionalist, social-democratic and Eurocommunist party leaderships and it is therefore the expression of a fundamental democratic deficit. It is true that this constitutional pact made possible an opening in Spain after forty years of dictatorship, but it impeded a real break with the power of Francoist elites in the state and economy. A constituent process – that is, not just a meeting of constitutional jurists and politicians but a fundamental social debate as the form of development of a new popular hegemony – could finally bring to a close the unfinished democratisation process. In this the *derecho a decidir* (the right to decide), defended by both social as well as independence movements, could be given a key role as an instrument for the re-democratisation of all social spheres.

Finally, there is the question of why IU (Izquierda Unida – the United Left) was not able to articulate these wishes for change, although it shares many of Podemos' demands and in some cases formulates them more clearly. The answer seems obvious to me: IU could not articulate the revolt against the political system because it was itself an integral part of this system in many respects. The Communist Party (CP) – as the most important part of IU – actively backed the 1978 constitutional pact and also participated, via the trade union Comisiones Obreras, in the social partnership, established by the PSOE, with all its corporatist practices. IU, as a broad electoral alliance, has repeatedly formed coalition governments with the PSOE and in so doing also reproduced the usual corrupt practices. It participated – as, for example, in the case of the Caja Madrid savings bank – in the plundering of public financial institutions.

But even apart from the question of individual cases of corruption, IU's organisational structures stand in contradiction to the radical democratic ambitions emerging from society. The political practice of the CP and IU was always marked by the classical logic of representation in which priority is given to the strengthening of one's own organisation and its electoral successes over social (self-empowerment) processes. Even if thousands of party members are active in movements, the institutional logic dominates. Radical attempts at reorganisation come too late.

Podemos has – up to now – been different: the organisation is presently the instrument of a social process that is progressing too rapidly for the party to turn around the relation between the democratic revolt and the institutional form.

This of course does not mean that everything that happened in IU or was done by it in the last thirty years was wrong. Podemos will probably soon be confronted by many of the problems that characterise the IU today. For example, how can a balance be found between the emerging political tendencies without internal organisational considerations determining the politics of the organisation? But this is probably the central insight of the political process in Spain today: the intervention of the organised left was not at all irrelevant; without the experience of left activists, the 15M Movement would have fallen apart sooner, the PAH would never have emerged, and Podemos would probably have been a diffuse liberal internet party like

Germany's Pirates. However, a social process is sweeping aside even the organisational forms of the left. The revolutionary-democratic awakening, longed for by a part of Spanish society, cannot be articulated through the bureaucratic corset of the IU. How long Podemos remains the appropriate space for this is to be seen. However, today it is one of the spaces of the democratic revolution in Spain and probably the most important one.

Afterword Following the Spanish Municipal Elections of 24 May 2015

by Jonas Nilsson

The results of the local elections confirm that the social movements organised by the young people who have broken away from the traditional party structures – whether from the right or the left – have worked seriously and successfully over the years since, first, the anti-globalisation movement of the 1990s, and then, in 2012, the 15M occupations of public squares in the main cities. These protests against the rescue of the banks after 2008 at the expense of ordinary people – against housing evictions, unemployment and police repression – have now seen their first substantial result. The fact that most of the big cities in Spain have transferred their political allegiance to various alternative social and political combinations means a confrontation with the old state structures and with the supra-national masters of the world of global capital. Several of the new town councils, for example, have pronounced themselves against the Translatlantic Trade and Investment Partnership (TTIP). Who knows what the future holds, whether this movement can continue to develop. But the very fact that it has reached this point shows that the mystique of capitalist power has been seriously injured and that social consciousness has taken an important step forward.

Bosnia-Herzegovina

Report of a Workers' Aid Delegation

by Robert Myers

Early in 2014, two small protest demonstrations in the town of Tuzla were brutally attacked by police. The next day 10,000 people took to the streets. They demonstrated against the police actions and against privatisation, impoverishment and the corruption of politicians. Government buildings were set alight, the Tuzla governing body resigned and fled, and on the same day a large meeting of people set up a 'plenum', an open forum, in an attempt to give a coherent voice to the protests. Very soon, plenums emerged in other towns. The plenums tried to coordinate their activities and to develop social policies on a range of issues.

As in South Africa, we were seeing here the working class fighting to overcome great historical obstacles and repression, to recognise its own role and to find its own voice. It goes without saying that what we see is only the beginning of a new stage in a long historical process, with many problems, confusions and enemies to overcome. The historical background is important and complex, from the break-up of the Ottoman Empire to the 'Balkan Wars' and the late Yugoslavia, and of course it differs from that of the South African working class. A brief outline of the more recent history is contained in what follows, which consists of extracts from a report by comrades on their visit to Tuzla shortly after the recent events, unedited, in order to preserve its immediacy.

Our delegation consisted of two people who were active in the Workers Aid for Bosnia campaign in the 1990s and one person from the London region of the British trade union Unite. The Workers Aid campaign was first proposed by the Serbian socialist Radé Pavlovič. Groups of people in the UK and then across Europe responded to his appeal for the workers' movement to come to the aid of the multi-ethnic miners of Tuzla who were fighting to defend the city against the ethnic division and the land-grab plans of the Serbian and Croatian governments. For three years volunteers took convoys of food into the besieged city and speakers from Tuzla were helped to come to speak to trade unions and other gatherings in the West to counter the lie – pedalled by all Western media, politicians and the UN – that the three groups in Bosnia wanted to kill each other.

During the present visit we held meetings with various trade unionists and with people active in the Plenum. As far as possible this report summarises what people told us, with my own observations confined to a final section.

But first some background information. Before the 1992–95 Yugoslav wars the population of Bosnia was roughly one-third Serb, one-third Croat and one-third Bosniak – that is descendants of people who had converted to Islam under the 400-year Ottoman rule. Nationalist political parties based on the different ethnic groups came to dominate the country prior to the war, except in Tuzla. The 1995 Dayton peace agreement, forced through by the US, mirrored the aims of the Serb and Croat nationalists and rewarded their war efforts by formalising the country's division into three parts. The Croat and Bosniak entities have to some extent merged into the 'Federation' while the Serb territory remains separate. A so-called national government covering all the country has been almost totally paralysed by the squabbling between the nationalist politicians. The country is further divided up into cantons, each with their own local governments also mostly ruled by nationalist parties. The whole mess is overseen by a governor, the EU's High Representative.

During the war Tuzla and the surrounding region, with its century-long tradition of working-class solidarity, held out against ethnic division. That resistance is key to the present protests. Nationalism was used to divide the working class of Yugoslavia in order to carry out privatisation. Tuzla's resistance to ethnic cleansing, its support for the right of all people to live and work together, is the bedrock on which this upsurge of activity and debate takes shape.

Yugoslav pre-war property ownership was different from the rest of Eastern Europe. All factories and companies were worker-owned and self-managed. At least that was the legal status. In reality the Communist Party exercised a total top-down control system that emptied the legal framework of any real working-class input. The 'trade unions' were really more like a personnel department and operated as part of management. And this has really continued in many unions till today, and their top-down structure has been made worse because most industries ceased to function during the war so some of the 'unions' are largely devoid of working members.

Meeting with the Tuzla District TU committee

We were met by the president of the committee and representatives of some of the unions the committee embraces. Tuzla district president, Fahrudin Sahovic, said:

> Tuzla, with its huge coal and salt deposits, was the centre of the Yugoslav chemical industry. It also had furniture and wood-processing industries as well as large metal-working industries. Many enterprises had over 1,500 employees. During the war workers' ownership was ended by the state taking control of all property. This was done under the influence of the IMF in order to make privatisation easier.
>
> Privatisation began straight after the war. Workers were given vouchers giving them the right to buy shares. Many workers had to immediately sell these vouchers at knock-down prices because of destitution (most people had not

earned anything for the four years of the war). In some of the big factories workers took out loans from the banks to buy shares in their own company but in most cases nearly half the company shares were sold on the open market and bought by war profiteers and foreign buyers. These newly privatised companies were supposed to honour the conditions of all existing employees for three years, but sackings and asset stripping began right away. Sacked workers or workers who had no pay were unable to keep up the repayments on loans they had taken to buy shares and were forced to sell them to the private owners.

All this has been a catastrophe. For example, there were 25,000 metal workers in Tuzla pre-war, and now there are 2,500. A few individuals, all connected to political parties, have grown rich while workers are impoverished.

Despite endless worker complaints to the legal authorities no action was ever taken against the new owners who failed to pay workers, paid no National Insurance (NI) payments or taxes and who used their new assets as collateral to raise loans from the banks, loading the companies with debts, then departed with the borrowed money leaving the company bankrupt. Over 100 enterprises had suffered this fate. Because of non-payment of NI contributions 3,500 workers are unable to receive any pension. Of 80,000 people working only a third get regular wages and many have not been paid for nearly two years.

Meanwhile the government at national and cantonal level is a huge institution, divided three ways by the Dayton agreement and divided again at canton level, all with ministers and staff. In the Federation (Croat and Bosniak entities) there are ten cantons and 300 ministers. Tuzla canton (the size of Lincolnshire) has a staff of 526 serving ten ministers. Politics is the only profitable business in the country. On top of their regular pay, which is five times what a pensioner gets, the ministers claim huge expenses, extra monies for sitting on various boards and are entitled to 'white bread', the rule which allows them to receive a year's pay after they leave office. Their political allies are also enriching themselves via the 'golden helicopter', which sees them all given jobs running different state companies and activities like health and education. Everybody in any position of authority is directly tied to one of the political parties. The average government monthly income is 10,000 kmarks a month while the average worker's pay, if he is lucky enough to get paid, is 500-600 kmarks (£250) a month.

The government borrows from the IMF and the World Bank but all of this goes into the pockets of politicians and their cronies, none goes to industrial development. The health service is in crisis and the unions fear a national bankruptcy.

In 2012 the unions organised a demonstration and told the government that if they didn't make changes there would be trouble. In 2013 the Tuzla canton government organised tripartite talks with unions and employers on the state of the economy, and there was a limited, warning strike in the education sector, but nothing changed. No one in government is willing to listen to the unions. Strikes and demonstrations were all ignored. The unions do not support violence but the recent demonstrations have made government take notice.

A representative of the Education Union said:

We need a globalisation of the workers' movement to oppose globalisation. We didn't organise the recent demonstrations nor did the student union or war veterans, we don't know who organised them but they did grow out of protest by frustrated workers in the big five companies destroyed by privatisation. Although not in support of violence, we want to thank those responsible for setting up the Plenum. We agree with 90 per cent of what the plenum demands. In fact we think the big demonstration was started by people with a political agenda, tied to one of the parties. We participated individually but could not do so as an organisation because the law prohibits us. Our worry is that the demonstration took place just when the anti-union laws inspired by the IMF were being discussed. Now the unions are blamed for everything. Allegedly we have failed our members so they spontaneously took to the streets. Now we have a schism in the unions which weakens us. But the unions were not responsible for the violence. We need education and exchange of views with unions internationally

A short meeting with people active in the Tuzla canton plenum

Protests developed around workers' dissatisfaction with privatisation and asset stripping. These have been going on since 2006. Now there is 50 per cent unemployment and for the under 35s it is 75 per cent.

The idea of the plenum was to give a voice to this dissatisfaction. In the plenum anyone can speak freely, whereas previously the oligarchs occupied all public space and the political parties dominated all debate. The plenum is outside all previous political institutions and outside the ethnicity which has been used by political parties to keep people in fear.

On 5 and 6 February there were protests that the police attacked with CS gas and batons, beating youngsters and women indiscriminately. The government refused to meet the protesters. On the 7th there was a massive demonstration as well as protests in other cities. At that demonstration we read out a list of public demands covering health care, payment of wages and taxes etc. We asked people to come to a meeting and the plenum was born. For the first week it met every day but that was too exhausting. Workers were very involved in the protests but the trade unions seem to follow political lines and don't seem to want to work in a public, democratic way.

Of course the plenum contains people from political parties because it is an open forum but it is not tied to any party and many people are critical of all the parties. We know about the people who want to form a Solidarity-type union but some of these people just want to be a new Lech Wałęsa. Many of the union representatives are old and all they really want is for somebody to pay their NI contributions so they can get a pension and retire. Also several union leaders have been heavily involved in promoting the privatisations.

A meeting of the plenum

The meeting started at 6pm in a cultural centre. There were about 250 people present, fewer than previous meetings. First there was a call for two people to act as moderators for the meeting. One man was nominated who we later found out was an ex-soldier with political ambitions and a great ego. It also seems he has some support from a Croatian group who are connected to the right-wing group in Europe headed by Nigel Farage. Another man nominated himself saying he was an ex-Ditta worker. In practice the first moderator took sole charge of conducting business.

Various working groups had been meeting and there was a report from the group that had met with the canton government. They had agreed to abolish 'white bread', the year's salary paid to people when they left office. The demand of the plenum that the chief of police be sacked for authorising the violent attack on demonstrators was not agreed to. Also the demand that all people arrested on the demonstrations should have their charges dropped was also not agreed to (in fact while we were there several of the trade unionists we met said they had just been pulled in for questioning by the police and many people were being fined or imprisoned by the courts).

The plenum legal team is trying to defend people picked up by the police, but many people were pleading guilty or being tried without the plenum being able to get to see them for lack of any information from the police/courts/government of who was being held etc. From the floor someone questioned when would the legal team have an office so they could be contacted easily. The speaker replied that they had no money for offices but they were always contactable by email. A voice from the floor called out that many people did not have email. A suggestion was made that more young people should be admitted to the police to reduce corruption. A meeting had taken place with the head of the courts to request access to all documents relating to the privatisation of the big five companies. The legal team had met with 27 young people beaten by the police.

A young man from Serbia received great applause for his speech praising the actions in Tuzla and hoped that similar actions would spread to other parts of former Yugoslavia as problems were the same everywhere. A speaker said, 'Tuzla is a workers' town, and yet the unions aren't here. We need the trade unions at the plenum.' A war veteran called for special treatment to be given to veterans as they were suffering. (The meeting then became increasingly hard to follow via our translator as the first moderator became increasingly autocratic, wanting to reply personally to every contribution from the floor with more and more people shouting against him. People began to leave in frustration, the first to go being a whole row of teenagers. Others followed, shouting out as they left.)

Meeting with another group of trade unions

We met with trade unionists who had separated themselves from the Tuzla District Committee (the schism referred to above).

Ditta washing powder and chemical factory

Pre-war we had 760 workers and produced 760,000 tonnes of washing powder for all Yugoslavia. All production stopped in the war. We resumed with 360 employees in 1996. The state took 51 per cent ownership which was sold off and employees got loans to buy 49 per cent. In the year 2000 problems started. Seven directors tried to get full ownership. Workers had not been paid and were forced to sell their shares as they could not repay their loans. The directors were able to get control of a company worth 20 million kmarks for 650,000 kmarks (£1 = 2.3 kmarks). They were able to remove 3 million kmarks worth of stored materials so actually they got the company for nothing. We went to the prosecutor's office to demand the arrest of the robbers, and delivered documents, but nothing happened. The President of the Federation of Trade Unions was complicit in the privatisation and signed privatisation agreements. In 2008 contractual obligations expired, and pay ceased. In 2009 the strike started. For 52 months pension and insurance payments have not been made. We have had no wages for 27 months.

Hotel Tuzla

Amira was the only woman we had met so far. She felt she was not welcome at the meeting and had not been invited but she was fighting like a woman against illegal privatisations. Hotel Tuzla (the biggest hotel in town) had been privatised in

2002 with 67 per cent of shares going to the workers and the rest sold on the open market. This privatisation was done with union approval. The privatisation agency imposed the sell-off to 'help' them as the workers could not run the hotel in compliance with the law, but the workers didn't elect the new company or the union that agreed with it. Everything was imposed on us. Out of 138 employees 117 took out loans to buy shares but were soon unable to repay them because of sackings and non-payment of wages.

In 2007 the hotel was resold to a new company who were supposed to take over payment of unpaid wages but didn't. They did nothing except refurbish the hotel so in 2007 we created a new union as the old one was tied into privatisation and had done nothing for us in 20 years (at this point other people began shouting at the woman and demanding to know why she hadn't gone on the big demonstration. She broke into tears but then continued). We want to preserve the hotel but it is a disaster. People with 35 years' service are being sacked without compensation. They replace them with young compliant people. The restaurants are sub-contracted with new non-union staff. Many of us have not been paid for 14 months.

Sacked workers from the chlorine plant

In the war socially-owned property was converted to state property and then the bandits planned their robbery. They gave us shares or vouchers, then made us hungry so we would have to sell them. They took control of the unions and turned them into their postmen. So the unions ceased to exist in the private companies. So we as individuals formed our links across companies and tried to achieve our rights. The leadership of our branch unions in the Tuzla District Committee have money and waste it on travel etc. We want to start setting up a 'Solidarity' union amongst the whole community then we will pressure government to meet our demands – to restart production, pay wages, pay NI. We also want free health care for all and unemployment benefits. We need assistance to set up this solidarity union.

Polychem chlorine factory

The workers at Polychem defended and saved the factory during the war but have been unable to defend it from our own bandits. Pre-war we had 11,000 employees and good conditions. After the wartime shutdown production restarted but in 1998 the director took a 2.5 million kmark loan on behalf of the workers at a high rate of interest and in two years it had become a 5 million debt. We forced him to resign. In 2001 we were privatised in a public sale. The new owner was responsible to no-one. When we went to the privatisation agency to ask why he allowed such a bad kind of privatisation they said 'because that's what the new owner wanted'. Valuable assets were sold off despite court cases brought by workers. Then electricity was cut off to the factory and we started hunger strikes. On 4 March 2002 the director took revenge by bringing bankruptcy procedures and sacking all workers. But our strike forced the resumption of production in 2004 with a grant of 1.5 kmarks from the government.

Then in 2007, on April Fool's day, the company was sold for 10 million kmarks to yet another criminal from Poland. He promised to restart production in all areas but parts of the company were hived off and asset-stripped. Nothing was invested in production and all the non-organic things were destroyed. This new company employed 250 people, which was cut to 200 in 2008 and in 2010 everyone was sacked, even security and the firemen, so the place was left in a dangerous state with many explosive and poisonous materials stored on site. We found the 13.8 hectares of land had been used as collateral to take out bank loans. We won a court case for 3 million kmarks but got nothing as the courts are in league with the robbers. So now there is no production.

Konjuh

The president of the Konjuh branch thanked Workers Aid for their solidarity during the war. The factory was started in 1885 as a sawmill taking timber from the surrounding forests, and the town of Zivinice had grown up all around it. Workers had defended the factory and their livelihoods through both world wars and through the recent war, but 'our nationalist politicians have destroyed it'.

The factory produces high-quality furniture and other wood products which were exported worldwide and the factory is still capable of doing this, but there is no working capital and all the factory bank accounts have been frozen. The tycoons only want to get their hands on the huge area of land that the company owns as it is in the town centre. Three times the workers have marched the 110 km to Sarajevo to protest. We marched in the 40-degree heat of summer and in the minus 20-degree depth of winter. But the marchers were met with silence apart from being accused of being politically motivated. We also camped outside the municipal headquarters in Tuzla for a month but no result. We met with the head of the unions in Sarajevo and with the High Representative (the UN's overall governor of Bosnia), warning that there might be an explosive reaction, but nothing came from it.

Now we have all been discussing what kind of a union we need in this situation. On 28 February we invited all the different branches in the Tuzla region to a discussion about this. We proposed that we end the branch division between crafts since we all now face one common problem and individual strikes, sector by sector were ineffective. The heads of the unions opposed this idea. The Tuzla committee president you met yesterday is opposed to this. But we are going to start collecting signatures from all workers demanding a new united union for the Tuzla region. We will also spread this idea to other regions.

The plenum is a problem as we don't know who the leaders are. The moderator at the meeting last night wants to be the new Tito.

Asking about the miners, the backbone of the Tuzla workers' movement, we were told that the miners were being bought off by government. Their wages are paid regularly and the mines are being subsidised by government by being allowed to run up huge non-payment of NI contributions. The leader of the miners' union is imposed by the mine management.

A family

I visited old friends. The father is a retired engineering worker, the mother still works in the office of a small private company. Their son is a teacher in Sarajevo and their daughter is an unemployed law graduate who does voluntary work for one of the unions. They had all been on the big demonstration but left when the violence broke out. Then they went to a meeting of the plenum but couldn't get in because there were too many people. They were following what the plenum was doing and saying but felt that the problems of ordinary people were not being spoken about there. The politicians are crooks but most of the union leaders are also not representing us, especially the head of the union in Sarajevo who is just a government servant.

Summary

I had not been in Bosnia for nearly four years. I don't speak the language and given the shortness of the visit I cannot really know what is going on but a few things are clear. The generation gap is significant. Many of the trade unionists are older people, predominantly men. A new generation is now entering the scene with women as prominent as men. They were children during the war and because many of them could speak English they got jobs with the postwar circus of NATO, UN, NGOs, etc. and learned at first hand the real agenda of the 'international community', which was not to help Bosnians determine their own future but to impose a predecided policy on them.

Some of these people have studied abroad and have been active in student protests elsewhere, for example in the student fees protests in the UK. They use Facebook and the internet to communicate with each other, with the Bosnian diaspora and with radical thinkers around the world. They are also part of that movement which has developed all over the world over the last twenty years, often independent of the unions and healthily suspicious of hierarchical structures and 'leaderships'. Some could clearly leave and get academic positions abroad. The fact that they don't, and that they are putting in huge hours to sustain the plenums, shows how different they are from the nepotists associated with the political parties. All this gives them a great advantage. But it seems that some of them are inclined to see things in terms of right ideas against bad ones, clean politicians against corrupt ones. But right ideas will not abolish the coalition of robbers, both national and international, politicians, national and international, all of them acting on behalf of capital. Indeed after a moment's retreat in the face of the demonstrations, the ruling elite have regained their composure and are preparing to clamp down on further protest and resist making any significant concessions.

The mass demonstrations which frightened the politicians gave birth to the plenums but the plenums do not yet seem to be able to galvanise that mass movement. This is almost inevitable. Apart from a brief period of mass demonstrations before the war, this is the first opportunity in most people's lives to take independent action free of political parties, trade union bureaucracies etc. Everyone is suspicious of one another and used to political patronage determining everything. There is also clearly a conservative layer, i.e. in the trade union leadership, with many ties to parts of the regime that resist any independent action. Their warm praise for the old 'workers control' and 'planned economy' is misplaced. The non-payment of wages and collapse of industry began long ago. The economy of pre-war Yugoslavia was in crisis and it was this crisis that fuelled the nationalists' drive to war.

Some of the people from the plenum that we met were very aware of the plenum's shortcomings but thought that even if the plenums failed to develop it was an important first step, that the social protest would continue and that new ways would be found to enable people to organise themselves. They were adamant that a new kind of social movement which did away with 'leaders' and 'led' was necessary.

Not long after this report was made, terrible floods in Bosnia led to thousands of people being made homeless. Despite this, the protests of workers in the destroyed industries continued. At the end of 2014, two hundred workers marched three days from Tuzla to the Croatian border (the EU border). They said that since the EU's 'High Representative' had overseen the destruction of Bosnia's industry and they could no longer feed their families they demanded the right to go and seek work in the EU. The police blocked their way, but their protests continue and their voice is being heard throughout the region, gaining support from trade unions in Croatia.

Ukraine

War as a Means of Social Control

by Gabriel Levy[37]

In Ukraine the tumultuous social movement of last winter has been overtaken, divided, and almost silenced, by military conflict. It is a sobering contrast to those times in history, for example at the end of the first and second world wars, when military conflict produced social revolts. This article attempts to consider the historical parallels and what they mean for socialists.

Expressions of discontent around social issues continued to spread across Ukraine – including in the eastern regions – after the overthrow of the government of Viktor Yanukovich in Kyiv in February 2014. Some of these protests fed into the so-called 'anti-Maidan' movement, which actually mirrored the Maidan movement in many ways. But on both sides, corrosive nationalism took its toll.

In the midst of all this, the armed separatist movement appeared in eastern Ukraine and grew rapidly. The main factor that helped it was the support of the Russian government, which (i) annexed Crimea in March, (ii) gave strong political support to the separatist leaders (who include activists from Russian fascist and extreme nationalist organisations, and mercenaries accused of war crimes in Chechnya) and (iii) allowed large numbers of mercenaries, weapons up to and including tanks, and money across the border.

Although Russia has always denied that its army is participating in the conflict, by the end of August a huge amount of evidence had been collected that not only Russian weaponry but Russian soldiers were present. The role of the Russian army was exposed in particular by journalists and human-rights organisations in Russia who helped to identify Russians killed in the conflict – whose existence the military authorities tried desperately to hide. The Committee of Soldiers' Mothers, who had also stood up to the Yeltsin and Putin governments in protest at the use of young men as cannon fodder in the Chechnya wars, played a prominent part in exposing the undercover military operation in Ukraine.

In September a ceasefire was worked out between Ukraine and the separatists, with Russian participation. It has quietened the conflict down but not stopped it; at least 300 people have died since then. It is possible that this peace process will continue, but it seems inevitable that the separatist 'republics' will remain – with their arbitrary and violent form of military rule and their extreme right-wing politics – indefinitely.

In the language of international politics, this may become a 'frozen conflict' used by the Russian elite to destabilise and put pressure on the Ukrainian government – similar to, but on a much larger scale than, that in the Pridnestrovye region of Moldova. In class terms, it means that people in Ukraine's largest industrial centre will live under something like a military occupation potentially for a long time into the future. In west and central Ukraine, militarism and fascism may also gain ground. And divisions have opened up between working-class people.

The causes

The separatist movement was only able to mount an armed conflict with the Ukrainian state on this scale because of support from the Russian state. The main reason this support was, and is, given is the Russian state's fear of the movements that developed in Ukraine prior to Yanukovich's overthrow – the demonstrations on Maidan and the high level of social protest right across Ukraine that accompanied them.

I am not glamourising the Maidan movement. Alongside

progressive and democratic ideas there were many reactionary and nationalist ideas among those who took part. *But* I am saying that the Kremlin looked on these demonstrations with horror, because it showed that collective actions by large numbers of people in the former Soviet space could create situations it could not control. Fear of social movements, whether in Russia or other former Soviet countries, is a hallmark of Putin's government.

As a result of direct Russian military involvement in the conflict, NATO countries have introduced economic sanctions against Russia and there is now a real conflict between Russia and some of the western powers. But it is a tension within limits. It is a mistake to believe that a new 'Cold War' is in progress – or that there is somehow something progressive, 'anti-imperialist' or 'anti-fascist' in the Kremlin's actions. The next section argues that more fully.

A century-long perspective

This year (2014) is the centenary of the start of World War One. That war ended in revolution: the mutiny in the German fleet; in these islands, big movements in Ireland and Scotland; but, above all, the Russian Revolution. A central feature of the revolution was the mass desertion from the front by Russian soldiers. They took the slogan of peace, constantly referred to by so many Russian politicians at the time, literally: they picked up their rifles and went home.

It was the willingness of the Bolsheviks to endorse this mass desertion, over which they had little control – just as they endorsed the peasant land seizures, over which they also had little control – that enabled them to take, and hold on to, state power, at the end of 1917.

Very often, discussions by twenty-first-century activists tend to focus on the retreat, defeat and reversal of the revolution –

Kronstadt, the rise of Stalinism and all the rest – and we forget what a tremendous step forward the revolution itself was, what a huge release of creative energy took place, what a turning-point was marked by the active participation of millions of people in trying to remake the world in a new way.

I think it's possible to interpret the decades that came after, very briefly and sketchily, as follows. The revolutionary wave at the end of World War One was proceeded by the 1930s slump, the rise of fascism and World War Two – and that again ended with a huge wave of social struggles. That post-war wave was, generally speaking, contained via the domination of the workers' movement in the richest countries by social democracy and Stalinism, and by the arrangements that evolved between the Soviet Union and the capitalist powers to divide Europe, divide the working class and contain and control it on each side of the 'Iron Curtain'.

This Cold War system evolved – with its two 'great powers': the threat of nuclear war, and a social compromise with workers on each side – as a system of social control, not only in the Soviet Union and the USA, but also in other countries, for example those in the Middle East whose leaders manoeuvred between the Western and Eastern blocs. This system broke down in 1989–91 with the collapse of the Stalinist bloc. In Eastern Europe and the former Soviet countries, new forms of social control had to be put together – and it is the continuation of that process that is now unfolding in eastern Ukraine.

It is important to keep in mind the position of the Russian elite. Russia is being integrated into the world capitalist economy as an exporter of raw materials, i.e. in a role subordinate to the most developed capitalist economies. Its economy, its exports and its state finances are completely dominated by revenues from the sale of oil, gas and various metals. Manufacturing and processing industries have progressed in a very patchy way in post-Soviet times, and the elite has concentrated on dividing up the spoils from commodities exports.

To make up for its economically subordinate position, for its failure to regain status as the second superpower, the Russian elite has desperately tried to compensate by strengthening its hold on the former Soviet space by political and military means. This is not only about controlling the elites of Ukraine and other former Soviet republics, but also about disciplining the working class. The Russian elite's role has very fittingly been described as that of a gendarme. This is to my mind the best way of understanding its prosecution of its murderous wars *against* separatism in Chechnya, and *for* separatism in eastern Ukraine – in both cases, with the full complement of torture and savagery undertaken not only by uniformed soldiers, but also by irregular armed formations.

The breakdown of the Cold War system of social control has also meant that social and labour struggles of the last quarter of a century, both in former Soviet countries and elsewhere, have taken place under very different conditions from those of the 1960s and 1970s. In the last five years, since the economic crisis of 2008–09, we have seen an enormous wave of social struggles and national conflicts – I am thinking particularly of the 'north African spring' and Syria, as well as Ukraine – that seem to be different from the movements I have mentioned during and after the two world wars.

These movements of recent years have *not* resulted in deep-going social change. We have *not* seen a release of creative energy, and a development of radical ideas and ways of organising, such as that experienced by Russia in the first few years after the 1917 revolution ... not even in Egypt, where the largest popular revolt took place. On the other hand, the mechanisms of social control imposed after World War Two – through social democracy and the welfare state in Western Europe, and through the Stalinist bureaucratic system in Eastern Europe and the USSR – are not operating in the way that they operated at that time.

One horrible consequence of this has been that in the face of social movements, elites have resorted to much cruder and more violent methods of social control. This is at least part of the explanation for what has happened both in eastern Ukraine and in Syria. Huge amounts of weapons and money have poured into so-called civil wars that in many respects are proxy wars between capitalist states. The heaviest price in terms of deaths and injuries is paid by the civilian population.

But another side to this is that social and labour movements of today are developing under conditions where the mechanisms of social control operated by Stalinism and social democracy are severely weakened. This is not automatically good news, but for communists and socialists it opens up different kinds of potential, and different kinds of problems.

For a start, the social movements of today are often influenced by different ideologies and different organisations, and use different symbols, from those of 30 or 40 years ago. This is inevitable, given the historical crisis of Stalinism and social democracy. The dangers for communists are to think *either* that we need simply to re-hash those slogans and policies from previous generations *or* that we can simply throw historical experience in the bin and start again. Neither of those approaches work, in my view. I think communist organisations will successfully develop by working over the experience of the past but finding ways of advancing our ideas in the present changed conditions.

I don't claim to have answers to the question of how we do this, but here are some ideas about how war shapes that question.

Social movements at a time of war: three points

1. One consequence of the war in Ukraine is that some so-called 'lefts' have openly supported the separatist regimes established by gangs of armed fascists and other thugs. To my mind, this is a turning-point in the politics of these Stalinist (and some Trotskyist) groups. The logic is that if people have guns and they are on the opposite side from the USA, they deserve support. The fact that this is done in the name of 'anti-fascism' – an argument that dovetails completely with Kremlin propaganda that the Ukrainian government is fascist – makes it all the more obscene.

What events in Ukraine have reminded us is that, once working-class people are armed with baseball bats and revolvers – let alone heavy artillery – and are turned against each other, it's already very, very late to start thinking of ways to promote social struggles. It is bad enough that some so-called socialists participate in this. It is worse that other so-called socialists sit in other countries, far away from the violence and the hurt that it brings to working-class people, and not only applaud this activity but also use it to justify political alignment with the Kremlin.

2. Recognising war and military conflict as a form of social control means acknowledging its disastrous impact on social and labour movements. The widespread availability of lethal weapons in society amounts to a new type of hierarchy – of the armed against the unarmed – that reinforces the hierarchies of state against civilian population, capitalist class against working class and men against women.

News from eastern Ukraine – where protesters face shooting into demonstrations by unidentified thugs, and grenade attacks on their homes – confirms this. So does the situation in western Ukraine, according to friends and comrades there who say that many households now have guns and that there is mounting pressure on young men, from both the state and extreme nationalists, to join the military conflict in the east.

War inevitably deepens splits in the workers' movement. A depressing recent example was that of the independent miners' union, one of the first unions to emerge during the collapse of the Soviet dictatorship in 1989–90 and still one of the best organised. In June the branch of the union in Donetsk – where most of the mines are closed, and many have been flooded and ruined in the course of the military conflict – issued a statement supporting the Kyiv government's 'anti-terrorist operation' against the 'Donetsk People's Republic'. What made the statement especially problematic in my view was that it denounced trade unionists in Kyiv who had protested against the government's plans to take austerity measures including a public-sector wage freeze, on the grounds that the funds were needed for military action.

What a classic victory for our enemies: an organisation representing workers under siege by the pro-Russian military dictators turning against those representing workers in central and western Ukraine. Even workers' organisations built up over long periods of time can very quickly be divided, and solidarity between them wrecked, in war conditions.

There are some examples of community and worker organisation independently of the state and armed formations: the protesters who took to the streets of several eastern Ukrainian towns in the summer of 2014, the miners at Kriviy Rih who called for the formation of working-class self-defence units, and others. Unfortunately these remain few and far between. But this, and only this, can be the place to start to build social movements.

3. For communists and socialists (however more exactly defined), anti-militarism needs to be at the centre of our activity. In Russia and Ukraine this is a very concrete issue: socialist organisations there are thinking about how to support not only community mobilisations mentioned above but also, for example, soldiers who refuse to serve, and the families of those wounded or killed in conflict who are then denied support from the state.

A heartening step forward was taken by a wide array of socialist and anarchist groups in Moscow, who joined the huge anti-war march on 21 September in an 'anti-militarist coalition'.

Their slogans included 'Capitalism causes all wars. This one too', and 'Profit for the oligarchs; medals for the generals; bodies for soldiers' mothers'. The coalition called for the release of Aleksandr Kolchenko, the anti-fascist activist imprisoned by the Russian authorities in Crimea, as well as anti-fascists jailed in Moscow following the protest movement of 2011–12.

Every step of the real movement is more important than a dozen programmes, Karl Marx once said. In Ukraine, the real movement is now trying to break the shackles of war and militarism with which its feet have been chained to the floor.

Voices from Ukraine and Russia

In the early months of 2014, the workers of Ukraine found themselves caught up in a conflict of interest between European and US capitalists on the one hand and the 'greater Russia' nationalism of the ex-Soviet, ex-Stalinist bureaucrats led by Putin on the other, both employing mercenaries, provocateurs and ultra-right gangs. This situation was the immediate outcome of the popular uprising that had driven out the pro-Russian government of Yanukovich. Governmental power in Kiev then fell to the factions acting on behalf of Western capital, their function being to implement the severe 'austerity' measures essential to capital's control of the economic and strategic assets of Ukraine. In order to do this it was necessary to suppress all opposition, and the new government could do this only by deploying the most reactionary and murderous elements with ultra-right and neo-Nazi groups to the fore. Putin was able to take advantage of the hopes of the Russian-speaking majority of Eastern Ukraine, many of whom took action to seek autonomy from the Kiev regime. Important sectors of the working-class movement there sought to organise against the Kiev government's rule, but how was an independent voice of the working class to take form in a situation where rival nationalisms, each of which were prey to rival outside interests (Putin's 'greater Russia' and Western imperialism), were in open conflict? The following declarations give some indication of the early reactions to this dilemma.

Appeal of the Kryviy Rih Basin miners to the workers of Europe, 11 May 2014

The attention of the world community is currently focused on the confrontation between pro-government and anti-government forces in Ukraine. This confrontation is becoming all the more tenacious and bloody. It is being turned into interethnic confrontation that is stoking up a hysterical mutual hatred between workers of different nationalities.

What remains beyond people's attention at this moment is the sharpening social and economic situation, and not only in the regions where the fighting is taking place. The rapid devaluation of the hryvnia [Ukrainian currency], the steep rise in prices of consumer goods, transport and basic services, as well as the cutbacks in production in many enterprises – all this has led to a sharp fall of 30–50 per cent in workers' real wages.

The announcement by the governor of Dnipropetrovsk province of an increase in pay for April 2014 was actually turned into an insulting handout to workers of 300–700 hryvnia (£25–£58). Miners received only 15 per cent of the actual rate, which often makes up less than half their actual income.

As a result we have no option but to demand an immediate doubling of the real wage in the interests of preserving social peace in this country. We are deeply convinced that the main cause of the destabilised situation in the country is the greed of Ukrainian and Russian oligarchs, who pay a beggar's wage to workers, send all their profits off-shore and don't pay taxes in Ukraine.

We turn to you with a call to support our struggle against the oligarchs, who have brought Ukraine into the current crisis and who continue to destabilise it further, threatening to provoke a fratricidal war in Ukraine which without any doubt will have catastrophic consequences for all of Europe. It is necessary to put pressure on the corporations of the Ukrainian and Russian oligarchs, many of whom have their shares placed on the London Stock Exchange.

At the same time we are demanding that the authorities officially recognise the miners' self-defence and the arming of miners' brigades. Organised workers and workers' self defence are precisely that stabilising factor which can effectively prevent the escalation of violence in Ukraine. In those places where organised workers are controlling the situation mass actions never turn into mass killings.

We call upon the workers of Britain for solidarity. In particular we will be grateful for any information and humanitarian support, but the biggest need we feel right now is for personal protective clothing for members of the self defence brigades (body armour and the like) and mobile radio communications equipment.

Long live international workers' solidarity! By preserving the peace in Ukraine we will preserve the peace of Europe!

[Oleksandr Bondar, head of the Independent Union of Miners of Ukraine branch at EVRAZ Sukha Balka plc, and Yuri Samoilov, coordinator of the Confederation of Free Trade Unions of Ukraine in Kryviy Rih, head of the Independent Union of Miners of Ukraine in Kryviy Rih.]

For an independent social movement! For a free Ukraine! Left Opposition statement, 7 May 2014

The mass killing of people in Odessa on 2 May cannot be

justified in any way. The socialist union Left Opposition is convinced that whoever the deceased people on both sides are, the force used against the majority of them clearly exceeded any self-defence. It is necessary to undertake a full investigation of these events and to expose the provocateurs and the killers, more than likely from all sides of the confrontation.

We are unable at the present time to name the people responsible for these murders, their organisations or groups. However, we can see the political consequences of the Odessa massacre and we cannot but see that left-wing political organisations are among those that carry political responsibility for it.

Without a doubt the violence was directed and organised in the first instance by ultranationalist and chauvinist groups who quite consciously kill people and try to exploit the blood of the deceased to whip up bestial nationalist hysteria in society. However, there appeared in Odessa on 2 May on opposing sides of the barricades people, including activists of left-wing organisations, who only a year ago were taking part in common protests against restrictions on the freedom to assemble peacefully and against the introduction of an enslaving Labour Code. Activists of the 'Borot'ba' (Struggle) union appeared on the side led by the right-wing chauvinists of the 'Odesa druzhina' (Odessa Guard). On the other side anarchists and anti-fascists took part in actions that were actually directed by their opponents, in particular the right-wing football ultras. The latter group distinguished themselves by their particular brutality against opponents.

The left organisations were unable to put forward an independent, distinct working-class programme. They did not distance themselves, nor even manage to restrain the masses of people from fratricidal violence under nationalist slogans. For the protesters in Odessa the right of the Ukrainian state to exist unfortunately carries more weight than the labour rights of the Ukrainian working class of all nationalities. Instead of a strategy to remove the capitalist oligarchies from power in Ukraine and Russia there is a discussion under way as to whether the creation of a Ukrainian state was a 'misunderstanding' or 'a historical mistake'.

It is no surprise that by and large the workers of the big factories in eastern and central Ukraine are not taking part in mass protest actions. Anti-Maidan and pro-Maidan actions are on the whole poorly attended and in no way can they be compared to the 100,000-strong mobilisations of Kievans during the Euro-Maidan in January and February this year. Armed radicals remain a small group of adventurists even in Sloviansk, where they have seized power and clearly are holding on only by intimidating the local population who quite logically don't want to become the victims of the Anti-Terrorist Operation of the Government.

It is very doubtful whether a majority of the residents of Sloviansk support the monarchist idea of resurrecting 'the one and indivisible' [Russia], which is openly proclaimed by the Russian officer Strelkov-Hirkin, 'commander-in-chief' of the Donetsk People's Republic. At the same time it is clear that neither do they want to see in Sloviansk the 'little green men' of Strelkov nor any other soldiers. After all, they understand only too well that with the continuation of the Anti-Terrorist Operation fighting will start sooner or later in the inhabited homes of the town and they will be the first to suffer – the peaceful local inhabitants.

The workers of Sloviansk and Kramatorsk by and large are not taking part in the stand-off, but continue each day to drive through the checkpoints to work. The question of a general strike has not even been raised here. Local lumpen-criminal gangs and old people who dimwittedly pine with nostalgia for the USSR are the main supporters of the

'Sloviansk junta'.

At the same time a mass organised workers' movement is present without a doubt in Ukraine. It has appeared in Kryviy Rih when the miners' self-defence brigade prevented the escalation of violence in that city during the attempts by 'titushky' [thugs hired by the authorities and employers] to attack the local Maidan. The workers showed themselves also in Chervonohrad, Lviv oblast, where they intervened in the political process and then de-facto nationalised the local electricity power station, which belongs to Rinat Akhmetov, the oligarch.

The workers' movement has shown itself even more powerfully in Krasnodon, Luhansk oblast. During a general strike here the miners took the city under their control. It is significant that they did not want to ally themselves with the Luhansk separatist 'anti-Maidan', nor did they declare support for the bourgeois oligarchic leaders of the Kyiv Maidan. They had their own Maidan, of the workers, armed with slogans for social justice and seriously intent on realising these slogans, unlike the Kyiv Maidan. The workers were demanding not only an increase in their wages, but also an end to outsourcing for supplementary workers in the mines. Thus it was not a narrowly economic strike, but a movement that raised the need for solidarity between workers of different skills, a movement sufficiently powerful to take the whole city under its control. And in doing that there was no violence, there were no casualties or victims! The city was taken not only without a single shot fired, but without anyone offering even half-hearted resistance.

Understandably, a workers' movement organised on a national scale is still very weak. Truly active, class-conscious workers' unions are concentrated in a few centres of the mining industry. However, it is also the case only where the workers really intervene in a confrontation that it becomes possible to avoid mass casualties and to calm down chauvinistic hysteria.

Indeed, the emergence into the political arena of an independent, class workers' movement remains perhaps the last chance for the survival of today's Ukrainian state and the prevention of a civil war which is unfolding before our very eyes. If the scenarios of dismemberment of Ukraine come to pass we will not be able to avert an explosion of violence and massive casualties. Alongside that the confrontation will assume more and more an international and inter-ethnic character, not at all a class one. When the war in Yugoslavia was only just beginning the ultra-right forces were also very weak and marginalised. They had no more support in society than Yarosh and Tiahnybok, with their microscopic ratings, have today. However, less than a year into the war Serb and Croat Nazis started to dominate in the Yugoslav political arena and turned themselves into big mass organisations.

If the miners of Luhansk, Donetsk, Lviv and Dnipropetrovsk regions cannot by their joint efforts stop this war we will all be dragged into its meat grinder. In that event a left movement in Ukraine will truly be destroyed for many years to come. It is doubtful whether it will survive in Russia either.

Workers of Krasnodon and Kryviy Rih urgently need your solidarity and support! The Krasnodon strike has not ended, but only been suspended during negotiations. In Kryvyj Rih the miners are also preparing to strike in the event their demands are not met.

No support to chauvinists regardless of the flags under which they stand!

For an independent and united workers' Ukraine!

For an independent workers' and social movement!

To citizens of Ukraine and the world: No war in Ukraine! Letter by Oleg Yasinsky, a Ukrainian socialist, published 6 May 2014 in Russian on the website of Spil'ne (Commons), a journal based in Kyiv

Suddenly our country, Ukraine, has been turned into an unknown planet. At the start of all this I thought that at least I understood the language. But then, when I listened carefully, not even the language was comprehensible. The very same words turned out to have no permanent meaning: what they meant yesterday was completely different from what they mean today.

Apart from the problem of government, and of the forces that support it, Ukraine has also changed because its people have changed. My love for friends and family alike has not changed, but I already have no idea how to express it. Yesterday, we could laugh together at our political differences. Today, I cannot even gather my closest friends around a single table to talk to each other. And I would never have dreamed that I could hear from them the things I hear now. What has happened to us?

Looking at our country from outside, I see it broken into pieces by big imperialist predators in the course of their endless geopolitical struggle for power. Ukraine has been turned into a theatre of military operations between the decadent and arrogant US-EU empire and the cynical, calculating and equally arrogant capitalist Russia. With all that in mind, I know that the real power in Ukraine – where we are constantly reminded of loyalty and independence – actually lies with oligarchical groups who were, are and always will be collaborators with one of the foreign great powers.

There is no justification for the military and economic pressure being put on Ukraine by Russia, and no justification either for the forthcoming loan programme of the IMF, which will become a 'kill shot' in the head of our already mortally wounded national independence. All that will be left of that independence will be the national anthem and little flags with ribbons of the right colours.

In all the conflicts in Ukraine, we feel the presence of a hidden hand, pushing one part of the population into conflict with the other, to divert attention and energy from the fight against those who are really guilty of taking the country into this tragedy. By sowing death, they provoke the most awful emotions, and by controlling our indignation they push it in the directions that profit them. The next step is civil war – for which the people will pay with their lives, as usual, and those who are responsible will be awarded with new political appointments and with the trophy of a stolen country, as usual.

Maybe now – while tomorrow's victims are still breathing, and smiling ironically at these 'naïve' words that 'don't reflect Ukrainian realities' – maybe there is still a little time to do something. Notwithstanding all the gloomy prophecies and all the professional lies of the official press, maybe we are able to do something together. Before we are Ukrainians, Russians, Australians, left, right, Christians, Muslims, atheists, men, women, etc., etc., we are all people. And so we can never, not under any 'exceptional' circumstances, justify either the right to murder or the shameful celebration of people's deaths.

The fate of Ukraine must be decided by its own people, not by the governments of the foreign great powers. The authorities in Ukraine, and the traditional political parties – before, during and after the government of Viktor Yanukovich – continue to demonstrate their helplessness and shortsightedness. While the foreign great powers interfere, the current Ukrainian government has done nothing but redivide power between old and new economic groups – without touching the essence of the system against which the people rose up. If we talk about our homeland, or about independence, the first and basic condition to achieve that is the real power of the people – the democratic election of all authorities and the reimposition of national control over the fundamental natural wealth of the country. All flags, hymns and words are secondary.

The popular uprising against the Yanukovich government was aimed against lies, corruption and the overwhelming cynicism of an authority that was controlled by oligarchical groups. I was thrilled by the civic wisdom of those who went peacefully into the streets at that time. I think that people who have risen up today in the south-east regions did so for the sake of the same ideals – and when they came to understand that the new authorities in Kiev do not represent their interests.

On both sides of our divided society are armed groups, who are setting out violently to compel the rest of the country to do what they consider to be right. These armed groups, on both sides of the conflict, have committed crimes. Both sides are being manipulated – politically and militarily – by Russian and Western imperialism, who pursue interests that are very far from the interests of the Ukrainian people. But on both sides of our artificially divided population, the absolute majority are honest and decent people, who love their country and are honestly striving for aims the justice of which they believe in. And these people, real Ukrainian people, need to wake up, to unite, and to put a stop to the fratricidal nightmare that is being forced upon them.

The crisis in Ukraine is of course part of the legacy of Stalinism and the collapse of the USSR in 1989–90. Putin's regime serves to exercise political and social control over the Russian gangster-capitalism in which Stalinist ex-bureaucrats have appropriated the wealth of the country. The following account by Alexei

Gusev[38] tells what happened to opponents of Putin's 'Greater Russia' intervention in Crimea and the Donetsk region who demonstrated in protest in Moscow, and goes on to give an invaluable insight into the position of Russian socialists on the events in Ukraine.

Alexei Gusev

The left democratic wing of the University Solidarity Union issued a statement of solidarity with our brothers and sisters in Ukraine universities, students, free labour unions and civil society which in a day collected 35 signatures from professors working in eight Russian cities.

But the situation in Russia, in the context of the Ukrainian events, is getting quite dangerous. The ruling regime is very frightened by the victory of the Ukrainian revolution and is ready to launch new repression against dissidents. Today seven victims of the Bolotnaya case (participants in the mass pro-democracy demonstration in Moscow on 6 May 2012) were sentenced to prison terms of from two-and-a-half to four years. Pro-government writers comment that now, after Ukraine, riot police are justified not only to beat but to shoot protestors. We narrowly escaped arrest when policemen in full ammunition brutally dispersed a 1,000-strong picket near the court building protesting against the shameful Putin's 'justice'. At the same time, leading propaganda officers of the regime (like the Orthodox fundamentalist Milonov, member of Putin's party and of the Municipal Council of Petersburg, and notorious TV figure Boloviev) initiated a witch-hunt against an 'anti-patriotic underground' consisting of Ukrainian revolution supporters who have to be 'unmasked' among university professors and students.

Anti-revolutionary and anti-Western hysteria is on TV screens every day. The population is being prepared to accept harsh measures against an opposition which is now associated with 'traitors of the Motherland'. In the propaganda state-sponsored film *Biochemistry of Treason,* shown at prime time on the main federal TV channel, dissidents of today who 'betray' the Putin regime were presented as a link in the chain of treason – from the revolutionaries of 1917 (who betrayed Tsar Nicolas) to General Vlassov's ROA [Russian Liberation Army, who fought on side of Germany during World War Two] (who betrayed Stalin) and opponents of Brezhnev. It is announced that the next part of this film will cover in particular the treacherous activities of Bronstein-Trotsky, enemy of the people and spy, who betrayed Russia to Nazi Germany. Who could imagine in the early 1990s that these things would happen in Russia in 2014?! We are really worrying about possibilities of a purge in universities and other forms of crackdown on the opposition.

An additional complexity of the situation is that the massive media propaganda against the Ukrainian revolution combined with great-power, imperialist sentiments and Stalinist rudiments in social consciousness led to confusion even among some members of independent unions. Heated debate is going on there on the Ukrainian question, with some people taking the anti-revolutionary side.

The tiny Russian and Ukrainian left (I am not speaking about various kinds of Stalinists, of course) is divided too. Some tend to see in the revolution only rightist political forces and even talk about a 'Nazi and imperialist coup', rhetoric close to that of the Kremlin. Others are interested only in 'social and economic slogans', but to raise slogans like 'lower cost of public transport' when there is fighting and people are dying on the streets is not a very effective line (this could be said mostly about the anarchists who, as usual, tend to ignore the importance of politics, state power and the national question). And only a small part of the left, including supporters of various libertarian, democratic and socialist ideas, openly joined the Maidan movement and the structures of self-organisation and self-management created by it. Some of them were killed in action by Yanukovich's troops. RIP. Ukrainian free trade unions, which at our November conference declared their left democratic orientation, of course actively participated in Maidan from the beginning.

Among the Western left I see the same confusion. I am not talking about people like Stephen Cohen, whose pro-Putin position has been clear long before. Other people too turned their backs on Maidan because of the role played there by rightist Ukrainian nationalists. But, on the one hand, the role of the right is very overestimated by them (not without the influence of *Russia Today*, etc)… On the other hand, this part of the left seems to forget or ignore the fact that throughout history nationalists have been involved in all revolutions on the imperial periphery. And in spite of that, the socialist left never refused to give full support to the Polish uprising of 1863 or the Hungarian uprising of 1956, where nationalists participated with other political forces, etc. To counter their influence is possible only by participating in the mass popular movement.

Again, Putin's politics

The French weekly *Le Nouvel Observateur* reported in October 2014 on a 'close relationship' between the Le Pen family and the Russian Embassy in Paris. The far-right National Front leader Marine Le Pen confirmed after a media leak that her party had borrowed nine million euros from the Russian-owned First Czech-Russian Bank, to be used to finance the party's election campaigns. The owner of this bank, Roman Popov, is well known to be close to the centre of power in Moscow. The London *Times* newspaper, reporting on this matter, wrote on 25 November

2014:

> The National Front, like its EU counterparts, admires Mr Putin as a strongman who stands up for his country ... He proposes a patriotic economic model, radically different from what the Americans are imposing on us, Ms Le Pen said last month.
>
> Mr Putin's stand against homosexuality and in favour of religion and conservative moral values also goes down well with the National Front ... Ms Le Pen's fondness for Russia is partly shared by Nigel Farage and Ukip. He recently named Mr Putin as the world leader he most admired 'as an operator but not as a human being'.

The National Front is not the only European extreme-right organisation to be cultivated by Moscow. Again the *Times* report:

> Reports have emerged of Kremlin support for Belgium's Vlaams Belang, Greece's neo-fascist Golden Dawn, Hungary's Jobbik, Italy's Northern League and the Freedom Party of Austria. All except Golden Dawn were invited, along with the National Front, to observe Crimea's vote to join Russia last month and all approved the annexation. Jobbik, one of Europe's most right-wing and pro-Kremlin parties, has been under investigation in Hungary over allegations that it has received secret funding from Russia.
>
> Germany's anti-euro Alternative for Germany (AfD) party was also reported yesterday to be in the Kremlin's sights. The Moscow-based Centre for Strategic Communications, a think-tank, set out in a report for the Kremlin how it could finance the German anti-euro party via gold sales as part of a campaign to influence key EU member states, according to German media.

Nothing could say more about the reactionary, counter-revolutionary role of Putin than the following story. In February 2015, Putin visited Hungary. He took time to visit a monument that had been illegally erected by extreme right-wing elements and laid a wreath in honour of the 5000 'brave Russian soldiers' who in 1956 'defeated the counter-revolutionary regime' established by the Hungarian revolution against the Kadar government.

Comment on Ukraine

by Cliff Slaughter

The situation in Ukraine suggests the outlines of a methodological framework for understanding present and future developments. *Observer Ukraine* reported in January 2015:

> The government and employers now face growing labour unrest. The most common cause of labour disputes throughout 2014 was the widespread practice of employers to withhold wages from their workers for months on end. While wage arrears continue to grow, protests over this and other issues are now taking to the streets and starting to focus on a broader programme: the coalition government's austerity programme.
>
> Workers' protests picked up noticeably in mid-December when the Verkhov na Rada (parliament) made public the 2015 state budget Bill. It contains far-reaching cuts in health, education and social security and threatens workers' legal rights.
>
> The 2015 budget was denounced by two trade union centres, the Federation of Trade Unions and the Confederation of Independent Trade Unions, by five provincial trade union councils and by local meetings of miners, teachers, industrial and public service workers.

Four demonstrations were mounted in the last two weeks of the year. One thousand teachers and other public service workers rallied in Ivano-Trankivsk on 18 December. Over 10,000 workers gathered outside the Cabinet of Ministers in Kyiv on 23 December in a demonstration called by the Federation of Trade Unions. In Novovolinsk hundreds of miners held a one-day strike on 24 December, demonstrated in the town and blocked the interstate highway. And on 25 December workers at the state gunpowder plant in Zirka protested in Kyiv outside the Cabinet building demanding increased security for their workplace and an end to state managers' efforts to bankrupt the plant and sell its equipment off for scrap.

Meanwhile Kyiv tram drivers struck twice in December to secure payment of their wages, withheld since October. They won only part of their back pay. There are many such unresolved disputes over wage arrears across the country – they are concentrated in the most profitable private enterprises and in public sector occupations. They demonstrate the extent to which workers' contractual and legal rights are routinely ignored.

The rising protests come against the backdrop of a deepening crisis and haemorrhaging public finances. The incomes of the tiny middle class, the workers, pensioners and students were decimated in 2014 by inflation (23.9 per cent, the highest since 2000), wage cuts, and a currency devaluation of 50 per cent. The real level of unemployment is far higher than the official figures contend (nine per cent), and would be even higher were it not for the ongoing war, which consumes its own share of working people. *Then there are over 850,000 internally displaced people in the country, many destitute and dependent on relatives and neighbours for their survival.* [Emphasis added.]

We can view this situation in Ukraine (as anywhere) as a particular unity and conflict of opposites. It is, also, of course, a situation in motion, a process, in which there are always quantitative changes, at determinate times leading to qualitative changes. At the same time, any such particular (in this case national) situation is always part of, and interconnected in many ways with, a wider reality – in this case, the world of capital's interconnections. This world is also in process of change, development, and is a unity and conflict of opposites.

Thus, in Ukraine, rising from the ashes in 2014–15 we see the beginning of a revival of the working-class movement. It is in unity and conflict with its immediate opposite, the blows struck against the working class: unemployment, dispersal of communities resulting from war, itself the product of the conflict of interest between US/Western European imperialism and the 'Greater Russia' project of Putin and the class of ex-bureaucrat mafia capitalists he represents.

The immediate stimulus to this revival is the ruling class's response to the exigencies of the pressure of the ongoing unfolding of world capital's structural crisis – necessitating 'austerity' and vicious attacks on the existence of workers and their families. The revival is taking place despite the blows struck – mass unemployment, necessity of a daily fight for individual survival, and dispersal of communities (nearly a million people displaced).

Significant are particular aspects of the historical process of which the capital system in its structural crisis consists, namely, the geopolitical, strategic and economic results of the collapse of the Soviet system, in this case resulting in Putin's role directly impacting on Ukraine.

All this has of course wider significance for the class struggle. The unfolding and deepening of the capital system's structural crisis is *bound to* stimulate resistance and possibility of revival of the workers' movement and resistance to all manner of attacks (on health services, social security, legal rights, etc.). Clearly, then, what is said here about Ukraine is in principle true for all other countries.

In the light of these and other struggles and experiences, is it possible to reconcile the 1848 *Communist Manifesto*'s ringing call to arms, 'Workers of the world, unite! You have nothing to lose but your chains!' with our situation today: the vastly contrasting conditions of life of workers in Western Europe, North America and Japan and the toiling masses of Asia, Africa and Latin America; the emerging ex-Stalinist, new capitalist powers Russia and China, the latter with a growing mass of industrial workers, in contrast to the de-industrialisation of the older capitalist countries?

At the risk of some repetition, we can bring together important aspects of the examples dealt with in this section (noting in the first place that in the 1840s Marx and Engels were considering a capitalist system in its early stages of industrial development, with conditions in England foreshadowing those in only a few other countries).

'Nothing to lose but your chains'? In terms of living standards and rights gained in struggle, millions of workers in the 'advanced capitalist countries' see themselves as having a good deal to lose. 'Having nothing to lose but their chains', by contrast, rings even more true than it did for English workers in Marx's day for countless millions in the rest of the world. Along with mass poverty and high mortality rates, they are subject to the destruction of their communities by wars and civil wars at the instigation of imperialist powers (cf Gabriel Levy's 'Ukraine: war as a means of social control', above), added to the long-imposed super-exploitation by the capitalists of those same imperialists powers. These conditions are brutally imposed and perpetuated by the oppressive regimes and puppet governments and by forces of reaction such as religious fundamentalism.

With widely varying degrees of conscious intention and

planning, the ruling classes of the 'advanced countries' are daily spending billions to murder, scatter, and make life and self-organisation impossible for these people (recent examples are Ukraine, Syria, Yemen and the rest of the Middle East).

However, at the same time the structural crisis of capital, which unfolded in the last quarter of the twentieth century, will inevitably bring the workers of Europe, North America and Japan to a 'nothing to lose but your chains' situation. That process is still in its very early stages. Only when it is much more developed can we expect the emergence of what Marx called the necessary mass communist consciousness. The same goes, in principle, for the workers of China and Russia. What kind of struggles will take place, and how soon and at what tempo, on the road to this change? We cannot know in advance. But we will get to know by engaging as closely as we can with every manifestation of resistance, protest and defence, contributing to the best of our ability and resources to their success, interconnection and continuity – and not by preaching or criticising their inadequacy.

Wherever the 'great powers' in this virtual conspiracy of global social control cannot, or need not, impose their direct military control, they work through and pay to sustain the oppressive regimes of 'independent' nations, as in Pakistan, Egypt, Libya, Saudi Arabia, etc., but at the same time find ways to ensure that it is they (the US, UK, Russia) who successfully compete with rivals for geopolitical strategic control (in the South China Sea versus China, in Ukraine versus Russia, and potentially in Europe versus Russia, perhaps beginning with Greece).

Paradoxically, at the same time the whole (global) process is beyond their control. They are like the man with a bucket with eleven holes but with only ten fingers. The utterly confused but deadly interventions in the Middle East and the 'war on terror' are obvious examples.

Mexico

Mexican Workers in the Continental Crucible

by Richard Roman and Edur Velasco Arregui[39]

In addition to its investments in industry in China and the Far East, with cheap labour available and repressed by the state machine manned by the Chinese Communist Party – a new-born gangster-capitalist class hatched out of the old Maoist 'socialist' dictatorship – US capital has a millions-strong source of cheap labour on its doorstep. The North American Free Trade Agreement, established in 1994, places Mexican workers at the disposal of US and Canadian capitalists, under political circumstances where independent working-class organisation and action are extremely difficult to achieve. The comparison with China is very apt, the unions being for the most part led by members of the ruling party and virtually integrated into the one-party state. The central purpose of the North American Free Trade Agreement (NAFTA), which celebrated its twentieth anniversary on January 1, was the consolidation of the neo-liberal domestic agendas of the three member countries (Canada, United States and Mexico). Private corporate interests and the governing bodies of the three countries systematically sought to decrease labour costs and militancy, erect barriers against economic nationalism, and push the public sector and common goods into the profit streams of private capital. By incorporating low-wage, low-rights Mexico into the continental production system, a process that was well underway before NAFTA, big business sought both to discourage labour militancy as well as to harmonise labour costs downward in Canada, the United States, and in the older industrialised and unionised regions of Mexico. NAFTA 'constitutionalised' these transformations by treaty, seeking to make them near impossible to change. As Jaime

Zabludovsky, the coordinator of Mexico's negotiating team for NAFTA, put it: 'By consolidating the opening of its economy in an international treaty with its powerful neighbour, Mexico made economic reforms permanent and, thus, extended the planning horizons for domestic and foreign investors.'

And now, 20 years later, the roadblock of the nationalised Mexican oil company PEMEX, already permeated by disguised and partial policies of privatisation, has largely been removed by the energy reforms recently passed in Mexico.

State power has not declined in Mexico's transition from a one-party state to a regime of constrained electoral competition and an imagined 'free market'. The Mexican state continues to play a central role in shaping the economy and repressing resistance. Its coercive role is greater than ever as shown in the rise of human-rights abuses throughout the country. The liberalisation of the electoral system has taken place within the straitjacket of growing corporate hegemony and the increasing fusion of state and big business. Public assets continue to be sold to private capital at very low prices; workers' rights continue to be violated by business and the regime; and those workers who challenge these violations face brutal repression through state and private violence.

The growth of privatisation and 'free market'

The publicly owned goods (natural resources, especially mines and energy) won in the Mexican revolutionary process are all being transferred to the hands of the rich and powerful. And the drug war, a real conflict between rival factions of the state-drug cartel complex, is being fought out in the very regions of recent industrialisation, such as the northern border, and in the key regions of transport of global commodities, such as the state of Michoacán. The brutal drug war is a powerful, if unintended, force of intimidation against attempts at collective organisation and public protest.

The ongoing war of big business against workers in Mexico, as well as the continuing transfer of the national patrimony to corporate hands, has been sped up in the first year of the presidency of Enrique Peña Nieto. One of Peña Nieto's first actions in office was to arrest Elba Esther Gordillo, the corrupt, authoritarian head of the national teachers' union who had once been a powerful force in Peña Nieto's own party. It was clear to all Mexicans that Gordillo was arrested not for her well-known and officially tolerated self- enrichment, but for her opposition to the new president's neo-liberal agenda in the field of public education. This was a clear message to teachers and to all unionists that any resistance to neo-liberal transformation of education was hopeless, a message modelled on a similar action at the beginning of the presidency of Carlos Salinas, Peña Nieto's mentor, against the head of the oil-workers' union.

Peña Nieto, as Salinas before him, has shown a willingness to authorise ferocious repression. Mexico's electoral liberalisation has been accompanied by a deepening repressiveness of the regime: space for electoral competition has been opened up within limits at the same time that space for workers' struggles has been sharply narrowed by state, private, and corporatist union repression and now by labour law changes designed to undermine if not completely destroy workers' rights and unions.

The state of Mexican workers

The working class constitutes the vast majority of the Mexican population, a population that is overwhelmingly urban. Sixty-three per cent of Mexicans live in cities or municipal centres of over 100,000 people – that is, 75 million of a total population of 120 million as of mid-2014. Official statistics in 2013 show that there were 52 million people in the economically active population as of the last quarter of that year, of which 20 million were women, the highest share in Mexico's history. If we add the eight million workers born in Mexico who work in the United States, we arrive at a grand total of 60 million people in the Mexican labour force. The average wage of workers covered by the Mexican Social Security system is $2.60 per hour as compared to $12.50 per hour of foreign-born Latino workers within the United States. If we only looked at blue-collar workers within Mexico's formal sector, the hourly wage would decrease to $1.30 per hour. But the vast majority of wageworkers are actually in the informal sector where wages and working conditions are even worse.

The neo-liberal reorganisation of the Mexican economy and its integration into a continental production system has involved a massive geographical relocation of industry and a restructuring of the labour market and labour processes. Just as factories left the US mid-west and north-east in the 1980s and early 1990s to head for the anti-union south and south-west, so factories left central Mexico and re-established themselves near the northern border both to escape areas of strong union traditions as well as to take part in the continentalisation of North American production. As the north was sparsely populated, new workers, from a variety of regions and backgrounds, were recruited for the then-expanding sector of assembly plants known as *maquilas* or *maquiladoras*.

The first wave of *maquilas* – electronics and textiles – mainly recruited young women for their plants. But in later waves of *maquila* development, especially in auto parts, men were the main recruits. The recent character of migrations to the border, along with extremely repressive corporate and government policies, has made collective organisation and resistance very difficult, though there have been recurrent attempts to organise genuine unions.

The decline in unionisation rates in the country has been a decisive factor in the decline in real wages in recent decades. The rate of unionisation of the working population decreased from 22.4 per cent between the first half of the 1990s and 2012. Having said that, however, we must add that Mexican unions – excluding the very large number that are phantom unions with only a paper existence – are hybrid institutions that blend features of a state institution, a party machine, and an authoritarian union. Their leaders have been part of a state-linked elite whose career paths often flowed from their role in authoritarian unions to important positions in the ruling party, the government, state enterprise, and even the private sector. Their personal advancement depended on controlling their members. They were the 'labour lieutenants' of Mexico's one-party, state-guided capitalism and continue to play that role for Mexico's neo-liberal capitalism. In the past, a challenge to a corporatist union in any important sector was seen as a challenge to the state. Now, it is seen as a challenge to the new regime of neo-liberal authoritarianism and its fluid and fragile system of labour control.

There are very few independent unions, and even fewer that are both independent and democratic. And all, whatever their ideology and structure, have to function within the iron cage of Mexico's sophisticated system of labour exploitation. Mexican workers face the challenge of gaining democratic control of existing state-linked unions and building new ones, two aspects of the same struggle.

A common thread in the struggles of electrical workers, *maquila* workers and miners alike is over the right to choose their own union. A second common thread is the right to dignity, including safe working conditions, respect for labour rights, funding for the school system (in the case of teachers), and freedom from harassment and arbitrary management practices.

The task of navigating between the immediate and short-term interests of the members and the long-term goals and necessity of transformation is a terribly difficult one for unions, whatever the strategy, structure, and politics of the union. It is all the more complex and difficult in Mexico's situation of multiple crises (economic, political legitimacy, drug war, violence). And the complexity is deepened by the trans-border character of the Mexican working-class and of integrated continental production, which would make major conflicts in Mexico resonate almost immediately throughout much of North America.

The Mexican working class has been formed and has formed itself in the shifting cauldron of class dynamics within two nations that have become more and more economically integrated. Mexican industrial workers, on both sides of the border, are often part of an increasingly continental system of production. And all Mexican workers in the United States, whether in the industrial or the service sector, are linked, through their own lives, their families, their collective organisations, and their experiences, to the working classes both in Mexico and the United States. Developments in either society, especially developments in the struggles for labour, democratic, and social rights, are likely to have important ramifications for their consciousness and politics. There are the beginnings of formal transnational organisations of Mexican workers as well as a variety of formal and informal links within bi-national Mexican communities.

Mexican workers provide a vast reservoir of cheap and vulnerable labour to US capitalism, both in Mexico and in the United States. Over 58 per cent of Mexicans who are employed in the formal economy are employed continentally – either in the United States itself or in activities that are part of a continental production process, such as *maquilas*, auto assembly, trucking, export agriculture, and mining. One in four industrial workers in Mexico is employed in a *maquila* and as many as one in three employed Mexican nationals are working in the United States. One in six workers in the United States in 2010 was Latino and it is estimated that Mexicans make up 63 per cent of the 50 million Latinos in the United States.

A continental labour response?

The deep integration of the continent makes a continental labour response necessary and possible. However, the prospects of such a response depend on the political evolution in the Mexican working class on both sides of the border, the political evolution of unions in North America, and more general developments in the politics and economy of each country. A continental movement will have to struggle in the framework of each of the three NAFTA states. The attempt to lock in neo-liberal domestic changes, as articulated by Jaime Zabludovsky, has to be challenged at the level of each national state. But because of the very integration of the continent and the pre-eminent power and ambition of the US capitalist class and state, the struggles, to be successful, have to be both national and continental at the same time. The transformation of the continent could well start in its politically weakest, albeit most repressive, link, Mexico, but to be successful it would have to extend well beyond Mexico.

There are many important local struggles taking place in Mexico as well as in Canada and the United States. The challenge is to help these movements grow and coalesce with each other into larger regional, national, and continental movements. But to have any hope of halting and challenging the neo-liberal juggernaut, they will eventually have to challenge capitalist power at the national and continental level. The building of such a movement will necessarily require an inspiring vision of transformation and major organisational resources sooner or later, whether the movement starts as actions from below or a strategy from the major organised unions of North America. These unions can only play this role if they themselves transform their vision, their strategies, and their politics, and propose a continental economic strategy that facilitates solidarity and not competition. Such a strategy could be built around a set of immediate, concrete demands that directly challenge *Mexico's low-wage, low-rights regime* and the neo-liberal transformation of all of North America. These demands could include the right to freely choose a union, the right to a job, *the right to migrate or stay home,* the right to a living wage, and the right to safe working conditions. Such a movement would, of course, face great repression in Mexico, and continental and international workers' solidarity would be crucial to its survival. *La lucha sigue.*

PART III

The History and Politics of the Crises in the Middle East

by Yassamine Mather

[This essay was completed before the deal on nuclear power concluded with Iran by the P5 + 1 countries (the permanent members of the United Nations Security Council – China, France, Russia, the UK and the USA – plus Germany) was signed, after prolonged negotiations, on 14 July 2015. The essay that follows makes it clear that the deal came as no surprise: I have added a short comment about it at the end.]

I: Introductory: the origins, politics and economics of Islamic State

Every day – I write in early June 2015 – news of new atrocities committed by Islamic State, the al-Nusra Front in Syria, as well as by the Assad regime, makes headlines. From the beheading of young journalists to the mass extermination of religious and national minorities in Iraq and Syria, there seems no end to the barbarism and brutality of the latest brands of Islamist jihadism. US air strikes might have slowed down the military progress of Islamic State (IS); but IS is clearly far from defeated. The US-sponsored coalition to defeat it includes the very states which until recently sponsored, financed and armed this latest group of jihadists: Qatar, Saudi Arabia and the United Arab Emirates.

Ironic to think that only two years ago the debate was about US military intervention on the side of Syrian opposition forces – even then dominated by the very jihadists who later chose the Arabic name 'Daesh', or Isis, and now IS – against which the US is conducting air raids. The mass media portray these raids and drone attacks as yet another humanitarian intervention, downplaying the extent of the change in US policy. Is it justified by regime change, the relinquishing of power by the Syrian dictator the imperialists were so keen to see removed? Is this government more democratic than a year ago? Of course not! Bashar al-Assad has held phoney elections, but only to consolidate his power; and his army – supported by another 'rogue state', Iran – is as repressive as ever. What *has* changed are the priorities of the imperialist powers: there is now an urgent need to maintain control over the country they ruined in a previous 'humanitarian' intervention in 2003 – Iraq. So as far as the United States is concerned, Shia Iran is no longer the main enemy, even though its ascendancy as a regional power must be contained. Iran's support in Iraq is welcomed, while its backing for Assad is not to be tolerated.

Islamic State (IS) – one offshoot of al-Qaeda and fighting the Shia occupation government in Iraq – is an enemy; al-Nusra – another al-Qaeda offshoot but fighting Assad – is an ally, supported openly by Qatar, Saudi Arabia, Turkey and, according to some reports, Israel.

The US legacy

Ten years after de-Ba'athification in Iraq – and 'Year Zero', when neoliberal economics was supposed to bring about a flourishing, democratic civil society and, according to some on the left, trade-union rights for workers – the country remains devastated. Contrary to the US vision, it soon became obvious that the regional power benefiting from the political vacuum was Iran's Islamic Republic. With a friendly, at times obedient, Shia-led state in Baghdad, relative influence in Syria and growing links with Hezbollah in Lebanon, the clerics in Tehran and Qom could not believe their luck: the neoconservatives in Washington had handed them the Shia belt, stretching from Tehran (some would say Kabul) to the Mediterranean coast. Yet Iran's influence and at times direct interventions in Iraq and Syria – not to mention Hezbollah's political success in Lebanon – increased sectarian tension, fuelled by Saudi and Qatari financial support for Sunni militias in Syria and Iraq, as well as for political opponents of Hezbollah in Lebanon.

US threats against Iran and the hysteria about Iran's nuclear programme since 2007, as well as subsequent crippling sanctions, were inevitable consequences of attempts by US presidents, first Bush and then Obama, to address the increasing geopolitical strength of Iran. The 'Arab Spring' in 2011–12 only reinforced this position, as the US now had to consider the coming-to-power of the Muslim Brotherhood in Cairo. Ironically it was the defeat of the 'Arab Spring' and the rising power of fundamentalist jihadists, especially in Syria, that changed US foreign policy. Obama's recent statement to the effect that the administration had (as yet) no strategy started new debates. A level of disorientation in Washington was now apparent. For all the claims of Israel's supporters that the 'strategy' is appeasement of nuclear Iran (according to Israeli Prime Minister Binyamin Netanyahu, the biggest threat to world peace since Hitler), the reality is that last year's enemies (the Iranian rulers) are today's allies. Israel and Saudi Arabia, however, remain influential, and they consider Iran (if a nuclear deal is signed) a major threat to their regional status, as the main US allies in the region. It is a complicated and contradictory situation, in which the Obama administration is pursuing a dual policy: seeking a nuclear deal with Iran while reassuring Israel and the Saudis of their position as close allies. I can see no other explanation for the US's ongoing support for regime change in Syria (contemplating the possibility of a jihadist group – IS or al-Nusra – coming to power) while negotiating with Iran's Islamic Republic.

On 18 May 2015, a US conservative group, Judicial Watch,

published a selection of formerly classified documents obtained through a federal lawsuit. A document from 2012, issued by the Defence Intelligence Agency, talks of support from the West, Gulf countries and Turkey for the Syrian opposition: 'There is the possibility of establishing a declared or undeclared Salafist principality in eastern Syria ... and this is exactly what the supporting powers to the opposition want, in order to isolate the Syrian regime.'[1] The blog, Levant Report, comments:

> Overall, what we can see in the document clearly states that a Salafist principality is not desired by the West in terms of the Iraqi situation, but may or may not suggest that this principality is desired in terms of isolating Assad, which is a stated goal of the West and its allies (not just isolating, but removing).[2]

Recent developments suggest that the US agency's predictions have come true – except that now we have a Salafist/Wahhabi region in Iraq as well as in Syria. The fall of Ramadi, capital of Anbar province, in the spring of 2015 was the worst military setback suffered by the Iraqi government since 2014, when IS took control of the north. According to US military sources, the Iraqi army left behind artillery, tanks, armoured personnel carriers, etc. No doubt there is little willingness in the Iraqi army to fight IS, as a US general recently claimed, but he omitted to mention the following reasons for its collapse: first, US regional policy until 2014, which helped the rise of IS in the region; second, continued US support for al-Nusra and other Islamist groups in Syria, which also strengthened IS; third, the fact that the US turned a blind eye to IS financial transactions in the Gulf states, including the obtaining of funds from the sale of oil, and ongoing financial support from Arab princes and emirs; fourth, the 'de-Ba'athification' and complete destruction of the Iraqi army after the 2003 war, which was crucial in strengthening the grip of a corrupt military command associated with a failing government in Baghdad; and, fifth, the alienation of the Sunni population when post-war carpet-bombing of cities such as Fallujah created a breeding ground for new jihadists within and beyond Iraq.

Now IS's overall territorial control is far greater than the US predicted in 2012: the jihadist group rules a third of Iraq and around 50 per cent of Syria. The continuation of Bashar al-Assad's rule is in doubt and, although many in the Middle East and elsewhere would celebrate the fall of his dynasty, Syria's future remains bleak. As summer approaches, IS is marching on Damascus, and, in addition to Palmyra, the group has captured part of the industrial city of Sheikh Najjar in the northern Aleppo province and Al-Waleed on the Iraqi-Syrian border.

IS, then, controls the east of the country, while in the north a new coalition of rebel forces is led by an affiliate of al-Qaeda! As the Syrian military loses territory, the two jihadist armies are approaching each other and, whether there is war or peace between them, the possible scenarios are horrific. The predicted civil war will extend throughout the whole region; but if some agreement is reached, it could provide the foundations of a Salafist caliphate encompassing large parts of Syria and Iraq.

Given what is happening in Syria and Iraq, not to mention the resumption of air raids by Saudi Arabia against Houthis in Yemen, it is not surprising that Iran's supreme leader, Ali Khamenei, has entered the debate about the threats posed by IS, accusing the US and 'some idiotic leaders' in the Persian Gulf of trying to start proxy wars on Iran's borders – a clear reference to IS and al-Nusra military advances in Syria and Iraq. And, according to Iranian general Qasem Suleimani, the US has no will to fight IS:

> The US didn't do a damn thing to stop the extremists' advance on Ramadi, while their air base is only a few kilometres away

> ... Does it mean anything else than being an accomplice in the plot? Today, there is nobody in confrontation with IS except the Islamic Republic of Iran, as well as nations who are next to Iran or supported by Iran.[3]

Although the governments in Iran and Iraq have publicly accused Saudi Arabia of funding the jihadi movement, the main concern of the Saudis, together with Jordan and Morocco, is that their own rule might be endangered. They fear the monster they have created is out of control. Nothing else would explain the rapprochement during the first half of 2015 between Iran and Saudi Arabia, which included talk of a possible visit to Riyadh by the chairman of Iran's Expediency Council, Ayatollah Hashemi Rafsanjani, who said that '[t]o fight extremism ... a collective effort should be made by all Muslim countries, particularly Iran and Saudi Arabia, in order to prevent a perception that Islamic nations and governments depend on foreign powers to maintain their stability and security.'[4]

Confusion

The confusion in imperialist foreign policy has added to the pre-existing disorientation amongst anti-war activists and the left. Writing in *Socialist Review*, Sam Hamad is right to criticise the simplistic arguments of those who, in the reductionist style of Press TV (a part of the English-language media of Iran's Islamic Republic), avoid the real complexities in the current situation by putting all the blame on the US and its allies. On Iraq, Hamad is correct in describing the disastrous policies of the former Iraqi prime minister Nouri al-Maliki and pointing out Iran's involvement. But his arguments have grave shortcomings, because they imply support for US air raids in 'defence' of Iraqi Yazidis:

> If anybody, revolutionary socialist or not, wants to see Daesh defeated or weakened without relying on or appealing to imperialism, then we must deal with the realities and complexities of the balance of forces of Iraq since the invasion and occupation by the US and its 'coalition of the willing'. Narratives that advertise the identification of 'new fault lines' in the Middle East, but that then end up relying on old formulations, such as advocating 'working-class independence' against Daesh, are usually those which necessarily stay as far away as possible from reality. Perhaps, following on from the usual line of regional Revolutionary Socialists, we ought to conclude that the only solution to Daesh is revolutionary socialism?[5]

Against this, it has to be made clear that the choice is not between the abstract claim that only 'revolutionary socialism will do' and a descent into the 'realistic' politics of supporting 'humanitarian' interventions by the US and its allies. Even in the current Middle-Eastern mess, it is possible to maintain the principled position of opposing foreign military intervention, while resisting the temptation to support one or the other reactionary state, one or the other hopeless, 'moderate' Islamic group, simply because they oppose the local dictator. Why should we do so?

The answer, first, is that the origins of many of these jihadists go back to Saudi Arabia and other US allies, and because, as I shall show, it was colonialism that created the underlying problems of the region – arbitrary borders, deliberate imposition of ruling elites from religious minorities (Sunni rulers in Shia countries and vice versa). This history determines that imperialism can play no part in the solution. If the US were serious about stopping the massacres, it would impose sanctions on Saudi Arabia and other Gulf states; it would take action against the Arab billionaires who finance these dubious organisations. In reality it does no such thing: indeed, it continues to arm the states that are fuelling the flames. Second, all imperialist 'humanitarian interventions' are political, with the single aim of advancing the geopolitical hegemony of US imperialism. Otherwise we would have witnessed, if not US military action against, at least forthright condemnation of, Israel as it massacred over 2,000 Palestinians in Gaza. Third, as Obama has admitted, the US has no clear strategy and the left that tails the latest 'humanitarian' intervention ends up supporting the bombing of pro-Assad forces, including Iranian Revolutionary guards, one day, and the bombing of Assad's opponents the next, as ground troops supported by Iranian Revolutionary Guards help Iraqi forces to recapture Shia or Sunni towns. Fourth, every military intervention, 'humanitarian' or otherwise, brings new recruits into the ranks of the jihadists. Anyone in doubt should look at events in Afghanistan and how US bombing increased support for the Taliban.

One of the revolutionary left's most important tasks in the current situation is to point to the fallacy of 'humanitarian intervention'. It is the short-sighted, opportunistic politics of falling behind this or that Arab/Middle Eastern state or Islamic opposition ('moderate' or jihadist, from the Muslim Brotherhood in Egypt to al-Nusra in Syria) that continues to discredit the international left in the Middle East, and play into the hands of the religious fundamentalists.

Rise of Islamic State

Iraq's political problems were compounded after the 2010 elections, when the more or less non-sectarian, mainly Sunni Iraqi coalition gained the largest number of parliamentary seats. Prime Minister Maliki used the courts to block its attempts to form a government, following this with attacks on non-Shia ministers and officials.

The destruction of Iraq started with the 2003 invasion. The current wars in the Middle East are a direct consequence of the gap created by the fall of Saddam Hussein. Iran's Islamic Republic's rise to a regional power dates back to this period and Saudi and Israeli hysteria about a powerful Shia state in power in Tehran, with allies in Baghdad, Damascus and Beirut, is the source of many of the current civil wars in the region. But it is true also that Maliki's sectarianism – his refusal to incorporate Sunni militias in the regular army, his intolerance of tribal leaders in northern Iraq – also contributed to the ensuing chaos. Iraq, where religious and national minorities had lived in relative peace side by side for centuries, has become the scene of vicious battles between Sunni jihadists and Shia military sects, and of Kurdish peshmergas driven out of their homes, refugees in no man's land, and victims of 'humanitarian' air strikes aimed at stopping IS's advance. According to the most conservative estimates, there are three million internally displaced persons in Iraq.

Anyone who fostered illusions in the potential of air raids to halt Assad's atrocities, just like anyone who is fooled by US air attacks today, should be ashamed. Nothing could be further from the minds of American and British politicians, whose concern is with their own interests in the region.

And what of IS itself? Who has been financing it over the last few years? How did it achieve such prominence? According to Charles Lister of the Brookings Doha Center in Qatar: 'There is no publicly accessible proof that the government of a state has been involved in the creation or financing of Isis as an organisation.'[6] But the Iraqi government, Iran's Islamic Republic and a number of independent observers have accused the governments of Qatar, Saudi Arabia and other Persian states of financing IS in 2013 and early 2014; and there is credible information about wealthy members of ruling families from the Persian Gulf countries funding it over the last two years. For all the Saudi and Qatari denials, there is little doubt that, before it gained access to oilfields in north Syria and, later, banks in Mosul, IS was the recipient of financial support from states in the Gulf region.

Michael Stephens, director of the Royal United Services Institute in Qatar, asks:

> So has Qatar funded the Islamic State? Directly, the answer is no. Indirectly, a combination of shoddy policy and naivety has led to Qatar-funded weapons and money making their way into the hands of IS. Saudi Arabia likewise is innocent of a direct state policy to fund the group, but, as with Qatar, its determination to remove Mr Assad has led to serious mistakes in its choice of allies ... many taking bags of cash to Turkey and simply handing over millions of dollars at a time.[7]

Some of this money was originally destined for al-Nusra (al-Qaeda's wing in Syria). However, IS also benefited from money smuggled via a Turkish border left deliberately unchecked. This has made the organisation one of the richest jihadist groups in the world, now also in control of oilfields in Syria – indeed selling oil back to the Assad regime – and the conquerors of Iraqi cities: 'During its conquest of the northern Iraqi city of Mosul, Isis fighters looted more than 500 billion Iraqi dinar, worth about $420 million ... Iraqi officials estimate that the group now has about $2 billion in its war chest.'[8]

IS leader Al Baghdadi has established a military command including officers from Saddam Hussein's military. In the Middle East it is widely reported that former Iraqi officers like Fadel al-Hayali, one of the Ba'athist regime's top commanders, and Adnan al-Sweidawi, a colonel of the Saddam Hussein era, hold key positions in the IS military leadership. These men fought the US occupation in the mid-2000s. Other Sunnis, linked to northern Iraqi tribes – groups which fought al-Qaeda in the 2000s – felt so isolated and betrayed by Baghdad that they sided with IS. The Iraqi government of Maliki broke its promise to integrate over 90,000 Sunnis who fought al-Qaeda into the security system and thus give them a proper income. Instead, incompetent, corrupt Shias were promoted to the highest ranks of the army, and were among the first to abandon their posts as IS advanced.

Kurds

There have been many stories in the Western media about the role of Kurdish fighters in the current battles in Iraq. Former Liberal Democrat leader Paddy Ashdown has encouraged the government to 'arm Kurdish forces' and called on Britain and the US to act as 'handmaidens to Kurdish independence'.[9]

Those familiar with the region, however, tell a different story. Fighters from the Kurdistan Democratic Party (KDP) and Patriotic Union of Kurdistan (PUK) have not been as brave as reports suggest, nor were they in the forefront of recent battles. Those who survived the IS's onslaught in Sinjar province last month claim that the peshmergas and the political parties of the Kurdish Regional Authority abandoned them. Throughout the last few years, the KDP has recruited members and supporters from among Yazidis in the Sinjar province, promising them protection. In Sinjar province, the KDP assured the residents, both Christians and Yazidis, that they would be safe from Sunni and Shia extremists. Sarbast Baiperi, head of the local KDP in Sinjar province, appeared on KDP radio and TV and on Facebook claiming: 'Until the last drop of blood we will defend Sinjar'.[10] In return the KDP expected the population to vote for its deputies. Yet in the first test of this pact, the local population claims that when the IS advanced, KDP peshmergas fled.

Other Kurdish fighters, of course, mainly from the YPG (Syrian Kurdish People's Protection Units), members of the Syrian wing of the Kurdistan Workers' Party (PKK), and Iranian peshmergas based in Iraqi Kurdistan, did fight against IS. As the refugees approached a checkpoint where Kurdish Regional Government authorities were confiscating weapons, the Yazidis and the Christians sent word back down the convoy behind them: 'Give your guns to the YPG!'[11]

The Western mass media might confuse the heroism of left-wing Kurdish fighters with the cowardice of Barzani, Talabani and their useless armies, but the peoples of the region know better.

Principles

It is inevitable that, faced with the horrors inflicted by IS, the left in the imperialist countries is confused. But there are straightforward answers. For example, in 2007 Hands Off the People of Iran (HOPI) pointed out – in opposition to the line of the Stop the War Coalition leadership – that threats of war against Iran should not cause us to side with a reactionary religious state that intervenes in the affairs of other countries in the region. In 2012, during the 'Arab Spring', HOPI said that, while in Egypt the departure of Hosni Mubarak was a cause for celebration, we should remember that, in the absence of any viable left-wing alternative, the adherence of the Muslim Brotherhood (MB) to neo-liberal economics, accompanied by the imposition of aspects of Sharia law, would be a recipe for disaster, a point examined in more detail below. HOPI rejected claims about the allegedly progressive and anti-imperialist nature of the MB and warned against calling for a vote for it. It was also against the military coup in Egypt in the summer of 2013 – initially giddily supported by, for example, the Socialist Workers Party. It opposed US military intervention in Syria, where foreign interventions from Iran and Russia on the side of the Syrian dictator, and from Saudi Arabia and Qatar in support of al-Nusra, IS and the Free Syrian army, paved the way for subsequent disasters.

The same warnings must be repeated. The Middle East has a complicated history, compounded by arbitrary borders drawn up by the colonial powers and the imperialist interventions of the last century. For the left there is only one position that has stood the test of time: we refuse to echo social-imperialist calls in favour of 'humanitarian' intervention. Nor should we offer 'critical support' to this or that regional dictator or Islamist group ('moderate' or otherwise): we should rather stand alongside those sections of the working-class movement that have not been tainted by either social-imperialism or false anti-imperialism.

Only by adhering to basic principles can we stand any chance of regaining support amongst the working class in the region. It is foolish to seek short cuts. There are no easy solutions.

II: From the Sykes-Picot agreement to the twenty-first century

The new caliphate

In 2014, the jihadist group Islamic State, or Isis, announced its name-change in a promotional video, 'The End of Sykes-Picot'.[12] This was a reference to the 1916 agreement between Sir Mark Sykes and François Georges Picot, which marked the end of the Ottoman Empire after decades of decline. It saw the establishment of two zones of influence in the Middle East: one British, one French. 'The line in the sand' drawn on the map by the two diplomats went from the A in Acre to the second K in Kirkuk. The region to the north, including modern-day Syria and Lebanon, went to France; everything to the south – including the provinces of Basra, Baghdad, Transjordan and Palestine – became British zones of influence.

The agreement had its critics: T.E. Lawrence, who knew a lot more than Sykes about national and religious differences in the Arab world, warned of conflicts within the region. US president Woodrow Wilson commented that:

> Peoples and provinces are not to be bartered about from

> sovereignty to sovereignty as mere chattels and pawns in a game ... Every territorial settlement involved in this war must be made in the interest and for the benefit of the populations concerned.[13]

But Britain and France paid no attention. Many of the regional wars, civil wars and conflicts in the region can be traced back to the imposition of arbitrary borders and creation of many new 'states' in the region to suit the colonial carve-up that followed Sykes-Picot. The current civil wars in Syria and Iraq, decades of conflict between Kurds in Iran, Iraq, Turkey, Syria and the central government in these countries, the establishment of the state of Israel and the Israeli-Palestinian conflict all have their origins in this era.

The rise and fall of the Ottoman Empire[14]

The Ottoman state was established under Osman Bey in Anatolia in 1299. In 1453 Memet II, who had conquered Constantinople, declared the establishment of the Ottoman Empire. Its territories were expanded in the fifteenth and sixteenth centuries and control over the majority of land trade routes between Asia and Europe brought economic prosperity. When, in 1520, Sultan Selim I defeated the Persian Safavid dynasty's Shah Ismail, he also conquered Egypt. All this consolidated the empire as a regional power, with further expansion coming from the capture of Belgrade and overall control of large parts of Hungary.

The decline of the Ottoman Empire began in the late eighteenth century when Selim III was deposed by Mustafa IV. Rebellions by many ethnic groups ended with the Treaties of Jassy and of Lausanne. But the empire had already been weakened by economic devastation and wars against Russia. Attempts to reform and modernise (*Tanzimât*) failed. Covering a vast area (at times from Vienna to today's Iran, and from Yemen to Algeria) and home to many nationalities and religions, the theocratic Ottoman Empire relied on a military bureaucratic apparatus to keep control. The corrupt and ill-equipped state – the 'sick man of Europe' – only survived because of inter-imperialist conflict.

In its heyday the empire had used the concept of *millet* (nation, people) to rule. The concept is referred to in the Koran but the Ottoman interpretation had its own nuances. In the Ottoman Empire, each religious group was categorised as a *millet*, including Orthodox Christians and Jews considered as whole groups. Each *millet* was allowed to elect its own religious leader and enforce its own religious laws. Sharia or Islamic law had no jurisdiction over non-Muslims. The 32 provinces of the empire were treated as Ottoman *elayats* (provinces) governed by a *vali* (administrator). As the empire weakened towards the end of the eighteenth century, the Western notion of nationalism stimulated differences amongst larger groups and the long-drawn-out decline began.

In July 1908, the Young Turk Revolution changed the political structure of the empire; but the revolutionaries understood that the capitalist powers' enthusiasm for constitutional reforms and moderation was driven by their own desire to expand their colonies.[15] The Turkish revolution was praised only because it was weak and hostile to proletarian struggles. Throughout this period, the British colonial authorities were plotting the demise of the Ottoman Empire with various Arab tribal leaders. In 1908 both the regime of Abdul Hamid, which had lasted more than 35 years, and the autocratic system developed under his control were destroyed.

The groups that fought each other sought unification with the aim of salvaging a common country – Macedonia, Greece, Bulgaria and Armenia. One of Abdul Hamid's main policies was to promote peace between Muslims and Christians – an unachievable aim. Religious and ethnic strife continued, leaving the new government no time to deal with the declining empire's other problems. In July 1908, a month after a Young Turks rebellion in Macedonia – supported by an Albanian uprising there and in Kosovo – escalated into widespread insurrection and mutiny within the imperial army, Sultan Abdül Hamid II agreed to demands made by the Young Turks and restored constitutional rule. Albanians hoped for autonomy within the empire, and the Young Turks lifted the Ottoman ban on Albanian-language schools and on writing the Albanian language. A meeting of Albanian intellectuals in Manastir in 1908 chose the Latin alphabet as a standard script.

Dissatisfaction with the constitutional regime

Once the initial enthusiasm about the constitutional system died down, the lack of progress towards democracy led to evident dissatisfaction as early as 1909. The newly established political system was based on the assumption that the citizens of the empire could unite under a single flag representing Ottomanism, but the process of replacing the imperial institutions with constitutional administration and electoral policies was neither as simple nor as bloodless as had been regime change itself. The imperial periphery continued to witness local revolutions.

Nine months into the new government, fundamentalists united to overthrow the second constitutional government and to reinstate the caliphate with a new monarch, Sultan Abdul Hamid II, who had promised to eliminate secular policies and restore rule of the Sharia. A counter-coup, on 31 March 1909, failed, but on 27 April Abdul Hamid II was deposed and Mehmed V became Sultan, proclaiming the equality of all subjects in the matter of taxes, military service (allowing Christians into the military for the first time) and granting political rights for religious minorities. The new constitution aimed to increase popular sovereignty but, because of their international character, it could not address areas such as the Ottoman public debt or the Ottoman Bank. Moreover, companies established to construct or perform public services – such as Baghdad Railway or the two major French tobacco and cigarette companies, Régie Compagnie interessée des tabacs de l'empire Ottoman and Narquileh Tobacco – were exempt from constitutional change. The Sultan, while retaining powers such as the right to declare war, became largely a figurehead.

The war with Italy over the control of Tripoli in 1911 and the Balkan Wars of 1912–13 brought further territorial loss and weakening of the empire. By World War One, the Ottoman Empire was also bankrupt. British forces in the Persian Gulf declared Kuwait an 'independent sheikdom under British protectorate', ignoring the Anglo-Ottoman Convention completely.

Capitulations and public debt

One could argue that contemporary sectarian divisions go back to the 'Capitulations' during the Ottoman Empire – the privileges that were based on religion and on the right of foreigners to be subject to legal proceedings only on the basis of their native jurisdiction and conducted in their own country's consulate or embassy. Foreign firms and individuals, moreover, were exempt from taxation at a time when most of the financial sector, industry and railway construction in the empire were in the hands of non-Muslim people – Armenians, Greeks, Jews, Italians, French, Germans and English. These 'Capitulations' became a source of discontent and paved the way for more corruption, as law-makers associated with various non-Islamic jurisdictions took bribes and maintained a discriminatory tax system.

In the Middle East, World War One lasted from 29 October 1914 to 30 October 1918. The combatants were, on the one hand, the Ottoman Empire, with some assistance from other Central Powers (including Germany and Austria-Hungary); and on the other, the Allied forces of Britain and Russia. On the Allied side were Jews; Arabs, who participated in the Arab Revolt; and the militia who participated in the Armenian Resistance, and who – with volunteer units – formed the Armenian Corps of the First Republic of Armenia in 1918. The Assyrians also joined with the Allies following the Assyrian genocide, instigating a war of independence. The Turkish Ottomans had the support of Kurds, Turcomans, Circassians, Chechens and a number of Iranian, Arab and Berber groups.

There were five main campaigns – in the Sinai and Palestine; Mesopotamia; the Caucasus; Persia; and at Gallipoli. There were also minor actions in North African, Arab and South Arabia. Russian participation ended with the Armistice of Erzincan (5 December 1917) even before the Bolshevik government withdrew from the war with the Treaty of Brest-Litovsk (3 March 1918). The Ottomans accepted the Armistice of Mudros with the Allies on 30 October 1918, and signed the Treaty of Sèvres on 10 August 1920 and later the Treaty of Lausanne on 24 July 1923.

In summary, during World War One the Ottoman Empire allied itself with the Central Powers, and at the end of the war was partitioned by the Allies, giving rise to the Turkish War of Independence. In 1923, the central part of the six-centuries-old empire was replaced by what we know now as the Republic of Turkey. The Sykes-Picot deal provided the basis for these post-World War One developments, while, in June 1919, the newly created League of Nations issued the mandates granting protectorates over the Ottoman territories of Mesopotamia and Syria to Britain and France – modern Iraq to the British Empire, Palestine and the regions of Syria and Lebanon to the French.

Nearly a century later: what was wrong with the Sykes-Picot Agreement?

The treaty-drawn straight lines divided nations and religions across borders. Lebanon was supposed to be a land for Christian and Druze; Shia were supposed to stay in the Bekaa Valley. Palestine was promised to the Arabs, while remaining home to a sizeable Jewish community. The secrecy surrounding the deal, moreover, meant that the Arab allies of Britain and France knew nothing of its content. Since 1910, Britain had promised many Arab tribes that rebellion against Ottoman rule would bring them independence. Not only did this not happen but arrogant colonial interventions continued right through to the 1940s, fuelling nationalist struggles in North Africa, Syria and Iraq.

The debates about Sharia law versus secularism, traditions and customs versus modernity started during the latter years of Ottoman rule. Following partition they were interrupted and diverted into other issues. France and Britain used religious and national differences to divide and rule. Victims of constant colonial and later imperialist interventions, the numerous nationalities and religious groups, formerly under Ottoman rule, reverted to sectarian, regional politics. The modernisation imposed from above in Turkey, Syria, Iraq and elsewhere faced religious challenges, mainly because it never addressed the division between town and countryside, between wealth and poverty. Fundamentalist groups in rural, provincial areas were able to gain support amongst the dispossessed. In an ever-changing world, as economic competition with the West became impossible, many wanted continuity and security in what they knew best: religion and Sharia law.

The Middle East after World War One

In understanding the contemporary Middle East, then, we need to remember that, with the exception of Egypt, most Arab states were created less than a century ago. (Egypt, a 'khedivate' – autonomous tributary state – until 1882, then effectively a part of the British Empire, became a British protectorate in 1915 and gained formal independence in 1922 under Muhammad Ali.) Although the mass media are keen to blame recent Middle Eastern conflicts on a 'Sunni–Shia divide', the story – of arbitrary borders dividing nationalities, of local rulers deliberately chosen from religious minorities and imposed by colonial powers, and of elites from minority religions being promoted as the economic and financial partners of imperialist countries – is more complicated.

British and French rule between the two wars

The US President Woodrow Wilson had produced his 'Fourteen Points', a plan to create a 'changed political atmosphere'. The idea was that, rather than acting like colonial powers, Britain and France would teach and guide administrators and politicians in these territories; a policy of which the 'flower was independence and democracy'. The legal and moral duty of the mandate powers was to facilitate the path to independence.

However, the French – after 1918 facing major economic problems with their exports at 20 per cent of pre-war levels – were keen to maintain control of their mandated territories: the 'maintaining and strengthening ... [of our] presence in the area' was emphasised by growth of the Army of the Levant to some 70,000 by 1921. The British, for their part, wanted to control oil-rich Mosul – not least so that they could secure fuel for the British navy. This brought them into conflict with the newly established Turkish Republic. Britain also needed control of trade routes to the Indian subcontinent, emphasising the importance of the Suez Canal, through which nine to 14 per cent of all British trade passed. The strategic importance of the Persian Gulf and the Straits of Hormuz necessitated the maintenance of air bases in Basra and Baghdad. Throughout the 1930s, the Anglo-Iraq treaty and later the maintenance of garrisons in Egypt directed British policy in the region.

French and British attitudes towards their protectorates were, however, different. France saw itself as protecting Christians and propagating French culture. In Lebanon they promoted pro-Maronite (Christian) policies, whilst in Syria the policy was to supervise *waqf* (endowed) land, aiming at weakening the power of the Muslim clergy or Ulema. Franco-Muslim secondary schools were expanded. (I myself went to one such school in Tehran with strong links to Lebanon, and by my second year was so angered by the constant comments about the superiority of French culture that, although born into a secular family, I became an Islamist for a short period.) Britain, on the other hand, did not see the need to take on any cultural role and – contrary to some historical claims regarding the reasons for British support for Zionist immigration to Palestine – it seems unlikely this had anything to do with attempts to extend 'Western civilisation'. But what the two powers had in common was the promotion of economic development for their own gain.

The British government owned a 51-per-cent share in the Anglo-Persian oil company and wanted a better deal in its mandated territory, Iraq, for the Mosul oilfields. In Syria, during their mandate, the French established a vast bureaucracy of their own officials, portioning the country into five separate states.[16] The British sought to avoid partitioning but neither colonial power honoured the agreements they signed promising independence. Arab resentment grew.

World War Two and after

In June 1940, the French in Syria recognised the capitulatory Vichy government, ending hostilities with Germany and Italy. By 1941 German aircraft flying to the Persian Gulf were being refuelled in Syria. To combat this, British and Free French army troops invaded, staying until 1946 when Syria gained independence under the auspices of the United Nations, and became a founder of the Arab League. After a humiliating defeat in the Arab-Israeli war of 1948, however, the country looked inwards, trying to maintain a stable division of power within the elite between different national and religious groups. The main division in the country, however, remained between the wealthy, urban owners of capital and the poor in the countryside. The Sunni-Alawi divide was expressed in the differences between the National Party headed by Shukri al-Quwatli – Sunni-dominated, supported by Saudi Arabia – the People's Party, representing the interests of noble businessmen, whose main support came from Aleppo, and the secular Arab nationalist Ba'ath Party, which recruited mainly from students, technocrats and army officers, particularly amongst the Alawite and other minorities.

In Iraq under Nūrī al-Sa'īd, who had been prime minister since 1930, the initial reaction to World War Two was to strengthen the Anglo-Iraqi alliance and declare war on Germany. However some government ministers feared backing a loser: Syria was declared neutral. After the French defeat, public opinion in Iraq changed dramatically and long-term hostility to Britain meant that Germany found allies in pan-Arab forces. Some Arab nationalists advocated alliance with Germany, hoping for genuine independence. In the spring of 1941 British military reinforcements entered Iraq from the H'abbāniyyah air base, inaugurating the British-Iraq war. The Iraqi military was defeated by the end of May and the governments that followed were mainly dominated by Sunnis – in a country where the majority population are Shia. The Iraqi-British agreement of 1948, signed by Iraqi premier Jabr and British Foreign Secretary Ernest Bevin, promised equality between the two countries, stipulating that 'each of the high contracting parties undertake not to adopt in foreign countries an attitude which is inconsistent with the alliance or which might create difficulties for the other party'.

Nationalist and Ba'athist regimes gained prominence during

the Cold War, when they benefited from Soviet financial and political support. Pro-Soviet 'official' communist parties, some with considerable working-class support, were instructed by Moscow to dissolve and join the Ba'athists. After the collapse of the Eastern Bloc in the late 1980s, nationalist bureaucrats slid easily back into the Western fold, becoming semi-dynastic dictators. They emerged as authoritarian supporters of the neo-liberal economic agenda – protagonists for IMF-style restructuring programmes and the privatisation of state-owned assets – often enriching their own supporters. Contrary to what the 'democratic' defenders of the 'free market' economy tell us, authoritarian regimes not only embrace neo-liberal economic policies, they can carry them out with little or no opposition, having suppressed secular, left-wing forces and labour activists. Islamists themselves, moreover, often associated with the bazaar and industry, also benefit from free-market economics, whether they are in power or in opposition. The repressive measures of rulers such as Mubarak in Egypt, Tunisia's Ben Ali, Assad in Syria and Libya's Gaddafi have generally meant the decimation of the revolutionary left, with Islamists untouched.

In the absence of serious secular organisations in Egypt at the time of Mubarak's downfall (most left-wing groups were banned, their members arrested and in some cases executed), the Muslim Brotherhood (MB) was the largest, best-organised political force in the country. Its success in forming the government was not proof of the popularity of political Islam: it was a reflection of the weakness of other political forces. The workers' strikes and popular opposition to Sharia law that brought down the MB government in Cairo in the summer of 2013 testify to this.

Civil war and conflict in Iraq and Syria

On 3 July 2014 the Iraqi Ministry of the Interior (not the most reliable source of information) put out a statement maintaining that Abu Bakr al Baghdadi (otherwise known as Ibrahim al-Samarrai), the Islamic world's new Caliph – or Amir Almuminin ('commander of the believers'), successor to the prophet Muhammad – had been wounded in an air strike and had been transferred to Syria for medical treatment. The same day the militant Sunni group also issued video footage showing the destruction of dozens of places of worship in Nineveh province in northern Iraq. Shia, Sunni and Christian sites were destroyed, with images placed on social media. In line with IS's claim that it was abolishing the arbitrary borders drawn up by Britain and France in 1916, the group symbolically blew up border posts between Syria and Iraq. On 8 July the Al Arabia news agency was reporting the circulation of a new IS passport in the name of 'the State of the Islamic Caliphate' – the first caliphate, or succession to Islam's prophet Muhammad, having been established in the seventh century when, according to Sunnis, Abu Bakr succeeded Muhammad as the commander of the believers. Sunni Muslims claim that Abu Bakr was chosen by Muhammad – the dying prophet having asked him to lead prayers as indication of his choice. Followers of Shia Islam, however, hold that Ali ibn Abi Talib, Muhammad's cousin and son-in-law, was the designated successor and that previous caliphs are irrelevant.

The Ottoman emperors (1451–1924) were originally secular conquerors. Fatih Sultan Mehmed, however, in 1481, claimed caliphal authority and his grandson, Selim I, who conquered further Islamic territories, continued the title as the defender of Islam's holiest shrines. The final collapse of the Ottoman Empire in 1923 marked the end of the caliphate. Iran's Islamic Republic, of course, portrays itself as the true Islamic state for both Sunnis and Shias, while the Moroccan king calls himself 'commander of the faithful'. Fringe groups like IS, moreover, have sometimes declared their territory a caliphate. But the specific problem with IS's declaration is not just that it has left itself open to accusations of overreaching itself, but also that it has put itself on a collision course with al-Qaeda. The conflict between the two groups has become an open one and in Syria they have taken up arms against each other.

In Iraq, the government of Nouri al-Maliki, after the US-led invasion of 2003, was rightly blamed for sectarianism and incompetence: it was certainly largely responsible for creating the political stalemate that paved the way for the current crisis in Iraq. Throughout his two spells as prime minister, the Iraqi leader made no serious effort to reach out to either Sunnis or Kurds. On the contrary, his 'counter-insurgency' policies aimed to reduce the influence of Sunnis in both state and military – a policy unsatisfactory to Sunnis in the northern provinces. The Iraqi army became dominated by incompetent, unpopular officers loyal to the Shia prime minister. Maliki turned a blind eye to reports of corruption and even torture. One general, already sacked in 2009 for failing to protect Baghdad from terror attacks, was put in charge of defending part of the northern territories and is believed to have been amongst the first deserters. As a result, the military was quickly sapped of morale and cohesion, compromising the local population's confidence in the central government.

In the 2010 elections, the more or less non-sectarian, mainly Sunni, Iraqiya coalition gained a plurality of parliamentary seats, but Maliki used the courts to stop it from attempting to form a government. By delaying tactics – false accusations of corruption against Sunni rivals – he manoeuvred himself back into power. Then, between April and August 2014, the Iraqi parliament failed to agree nominations for the country's top posts. By late summer, Maliki, no longer prime minister, had made powerful enemies of the USA, Britain and some factions of Iran's Islamic Republic; and they were looking for an alternative figure.

Tribal leaders and Sunni politicians in northern Iraq have also been blamed for the crisis. Without the active cooperation or acceptance of locals, IS would not have been able to capture so many cities. Those Sunni leaders who think they are preparing the ground for an Islamic state have clearly not thought through the implications of being part of an IS-led 'rogue state', with little or no access to oil – a state where self-appointed 'caliphs' will interfere forcefully in the private and social lives of Iraqi citizens, irrespective of their religious and cultural backgrounds.

For all the hype about IS's military gains, we should remember that the last time jihadists, in the shape of al-Qaeda forces led by Abu Musab Al-Zarqawi, controlled a large chunk of northern Iraq, they did not hold it long. Their brutality alienated the majority of the local population, and also the Sunni tribes who had backed them.

It must also be remembered that – for all the attention focused on IS – that *the working classes in Iraq and Syria have not joined the jihadist forces* and that the urban industrial population constitutes the most committed opposition to the reactionary Islamists.

Kurdistan

In the midst of this political and military chaos, the incompetent, corrupt and deluded leaders of the Iraqi Kurds also hope to benefit, calling for Kurdish independence. Having secured (temporary) control of the Kirkuk oil refinery on 1 July 2014, Massoud Barzani, the president of Iraq's autonomous Kurdistan region, announced an imminent referendum: Iraq, he added, was already 'effectively partitioned'. Israeli prime minister Binyamin Netanyahu immediately promised cooperation with any new Kurdish state. This initiated postings on social media about the historical background to Israeli-Kurdish relations, including photographs from the 1960s showing Massoud Barzani's father, Mustafa, embracing the then Israeli defence minister, Moshe Dayan. In 2004, moreover, there was a meeting between Israeli officials and Kurdish political leaders, where Massoud Barzani, Jalal Talabani and former Israeli prime minister Ariel Sharon publicly affirmed good relations.

Soon after the Netanyahu statement, social-imperialist groups echoed Israel's position on the establishment of an independent Kurdish state. Iran then warned its former allies in Iraqi Kurdistan, the Kurdish Democratic Party and Patriotic Union of Kurdistan, against independence. Iran's foreign ministry spokeswoman, Marzieh Afkham, was quoted as saying: 'Undoubtedly the vigilant Iraqi people will not allow the Zionist regime and enemies of a unified Iraq to carry out their plots and realise their immature fantasies in the region'.[17] Deputy Minister for Arab and African Affairs, Hossein Amir-Abdollahian, said that the USA wanted a Ukrainian scenario in Iraq.

Anyone getting excited about an 'independent Kurdistan' (limited to Kurdish territory in Iraq, of course), moreover, should remember that the biggest obstacles will be economic. Barzani clearly hopes to benefit from oil revenues, but the Kurdish authorities are currently in dispute with the central government, with Baghdad withholding payment of its share of the national budget to the Kurdish regional government. Serious attempts at separation will reduce the chances of the Kurdish authorities' economic survival. The territory is landlocked and the 'independence' plan is based on income from the export of oil resources through Turkey, which will depend on lengthy negotiations with Ankara. A new Iraqi Kurdistan will be in the hands of Ankara (not the Kurds' best friend), and will no doubt include conditions aimed to silence aspirations for independence in Turkish Kurdistan.

Meanwhile, exaggerated stories about the role of KDP peshmergas in fighting IS in northern Iraq conflicted with reports from the region. Barzani's initial order to his peshmergas was to avoid conflict with IS. It is the PKK and Pejhak guerrillas who have been taking the lead against IS advances in Kurdish territory in both Syria and Iraq. Furthermore, Barzani's supporters must be aware that IS's ambitions go far beyond defeating the Shia government in Baghdad and that it is violently opposed to semi-secular Iraqi Kurdistan, where there is no state-imposed sexual segregation, some women dare go out without a headscarf, alcohol is openly sold and so on. Then there are the problems posed for Iraqi Kurdistan by the fiercely nationalistic, anti-independence Sunni Arabs and the Turkmen around Kirkuk who also dislike Barzani's plans and oppose the Kurdish regional government's attempts to fully integrate Kirkuk. No one should take Netanyahu and his cheerleaders in the Iranian and the British left seriously when they talk of the 'birth of a new Kurdish nation' in Iraq. To unilaterally declare the current Kurdish region independent would unleash civil war.

More about the 'Arab Spring'

Over four years after the 'Arab Spring', there was little sign of the kind of political and social change called for by the protestors. In Egypt a military court had sentenced 528 supporters of the Muslim Brotherhood to death. After July 2014, when the army deposed Mohammed Mursi, hundreds died. Egyptian writer Ahdaf Soueif, speaking to the BBC in 2014, summed up the mood:

> Basically, this isn't the third anniversary for the revolution that we were hoping for. The security state is back and also a great many activists are in jail. Ironically the official gatherings to celebrate the 2011 uprising, in Tahrir Square and elsewhere, were organised by the military, who are keen to portray themselves as the saviours of the nation – in reality they are the saviours of the ruling elite.[18]

In Tunisia and in Egypt opposition to the rulers, whether 'moderate' Islamists (Tunisia) or the secular military (Egypt), was not tolerated. The jails were full of political prisoners and the banning of oppositionists had become integral to the new order. There was a catastrophic economic situation with unemployment on the rise and the majority of the population unable to afford many basic goods. Yet there remained at least some kind of political life.

In Syria however – where in the early days of the uprising, opponents of the Assad regime raised demands for political freedom – the 'revolution' had been hijacked, creating the circumstances for the war by proxy between Iran's Islamic Republic and Saudi Arabia discussed above. Having declared that the use of chemical weapons was the 'red line' the Syrian leadership should not cross, the USA accepted Russian proposals for a 'diplomatic solution'. If the original decision to launch a 'limited military strike' was unpopular, the retreat from it proved no less so, with critics in the USA and beyond claiming the climbdown was an expression of indecision and weakness.

The US administration had little choice, however. First, there was cynicism in most Western countries generated by the use of the discredited 'weapons of mass destruction' *casus belli* in Iraq in 2003. Austerity and the continuing effects of the financial crisis also helped generate a mood of opposition to a Syrian war. Parliamentarians in the UK voted down Prime Minister Cameron's attempt to join a rapid US attack and the signs were that Congress was likely to adopt a similar position. In many ways the Russian proposal for a compromise, a few days after the USA had tried to gain the support of allies at the G20 conference, saved the Administration from further humiliation. But against this, and irrespective of the specifics of the Syrian conflict, US backtracking had international repercussions. The *Washington Times* summarised the situation as follows:

> Obama's 'red line' vow turned a lighter shade of pink, with secretary of state John Kerry saying a US military strike 'might' be necessary if talks led by Russia fail to compel Syria

to turn over its chemical weapons.[19]

There is anger in the Middle East itself, principally amongst America's Sunni allies, the Gulf emirates, Saudi Arabia and Jordan, and the jihadists in the Syrian opposition. If, as has been argued above, the threat of war against Syria was directly linked to USA-Iran relations, subsequent negotiations with Iran, since late 2013, have suggested historic changes in USA's Middle-East policy. For the first time in 34 years, a US president has spoken to his Iranian equivalent, and the foreign ministers have negotiated by phone and face-to-face. Contrary to the claims of the reformist movement in Iran, the dramatic changes in Iran-USA relations are not simply a consequence of the election in June 2013 of a 'moderate' Iranian president. We now know that secret meetings between US and Iranian officials took place in Oman in the latter stages of Mahmoud Ahmadinejad's presidency.

The point is that these secret, then open, talks and negotiations mark a radical change in US policy. For most of the last three-and-a-half decades, since the coming to power of the Islamic Republic in Iran in 1979, US foreign policy in the Middle East has been to keep its two main allies, Saudi Arabia and Israel, at loggerheads with the Islamic Republic. This policy has had one strategic focus: preventing a repetition of Iran's Islamic revolution in another Muslim country. Ironically it was the 'Arab Spring' – the rise and subsequent failure of political Islam in the Arab world – that alleviated this fear, allowing the US to move towards rapprochement with Iran.

In Libya, the situation could not be more chaotic. Genuine opposition to the regime of Muammar Gaddafi had no chance of surviving once the USA, France, the UK and Italy got involved – cheered on by sections of the European 'left'. The new 'democracy' the USA brought to Libya is in reality chaos-at-gunpoint masquerading as government, while armed militias –

some political, others just criminal – including appendages of al-Qaeda, rule the country. The militias are powerful enough to kidnap the country's prime minister and half of the Egyptian embassy staff. In fact the new 'democratic government' in Libya is itself a coalition made up of political representatives of the various militias.

My argument is not, of course, that the uprisings in Libya or Syria resulted from a conspiracy by the Western powers or the Gulf States – the view put forward by some supporters of Gaddafi and Assad. On the contrary, the 'Arab Spring' was a real inspiration to those opposing the dictators. Sections of the media, including some left-leaning reporters, suggest that social media – Twitter, Facebook and other new forms of communication – are responsible for the spreading of the uprising from one Arab capital to another. The truth is more complicated.

Grasping it, as we have seen, involves an understanding of, amongst other things, the colonial legacy of artificial borders and dictatorial rule. Minority Alawis found themselves in power in Syria, and minority Sunnis in predominantly Shia Iraq, while Kurds were separated in different states, and Christians and Jews were uprooted from their country of origin. Also significant were the 1980–88 war between Iran and Iraq, fuelled by US interests and leaving at least half a million dead; the civil war in Lebanon; and Israeli attacks against Palestinians. On top of all this history came the transfer, after 2008, of the burden of the economic crisis from the West to the periphery. Mass unemployment sparked events in Tunisia, Egypt and elsewhere. The intensification of socio-economic crisis, and the increase in the cost of living, particularly food, helps to explain the timing of the Arab awakening. Since 2008, Western capitalists have been far more cautious about investing in the Arab world, affecting both the Gulf economies and those of Egypt, Tunisia and Syria. Migrant workers from these countries who used to send money home have had to return, adding to massive unemployment.

Syria, moreover, suffers the consequences of sanctions on Iran, which hamper its ability economically to prop up the Assad regime and its regional ally Hezbollah with, for example, the subsidised oil provided since 1982, when Damascus agreed to close its pipeline through Syria. For some years the Syrian currency has been losing its value and its 'managed decline' further reduces the regime's ability to hold down food prices. All these are important factors, though they do not, of course, negate the fact that the rebellion was fuelled by mounting political opposition.

For France and Italy in 2011, and for Obama, Cameron and the French government of François Hollande, the desire for military intervention has also been about diverting attention from internal problems. There is no appetite whatsoever for full-scale war, only an ever-present eagerness for air strikes. The USA is open as to why it would get involved: its action, says the White House, 'will be guided by what is in the best interests of the United States'.[20] Under normal circumstances both the Americans and Israelis would have preferred to keep Assad in power; but two years into the civil war, according to some reports, Iranian Revolutionary Guards were running the Syrian military, with Iranian heavy artillery deployed in Damascus. If that is so, the USA and Israel are likely again to favour regime change in Syria: imperialist intervention is never separate from considerations about the current international political and economic situation, which – not 'saving lives' – is always the determining factor.

While all this makes it difficult, in mid-2015, to talk of the 'Arab Spring' in the present tense, the mass protests, strikes and other events of the last three years, including the coming to power of 'moderate' and not-so-moderate Islamists, will have long-term effects in the region, and I now turn in greater detail to the political and economic reasons for the upsurge and the consequences of the defeat of its aspirations.

Background

On 17 December 2010 Mohamed Bouazizi, a 26-year-old fruit seller, set himself on fire in front of a government building, sparking riots across Tunisia and beyond. Tunisians, followed by Egyptians, demonstrated against the constant degradation of their living conditions. They had tolerated political dictatorship, corruption and cronyism during the Ben Ali and Mubarak eras, but now felt humiliated and angry at the impotence of their rulers, their subservience to US imperialist interventions, and their acceptance of continued Palestinian oppression. These rulers had also, since the early 1980s, pushed through a neo-liberal economic agenda unchallenged. Economic misery, frustration with ever-increasing unemployment and a growing gap between rich and poor fuelled the revolt.

In countries ruled by semi-secular governments – Syria as well as Egypt and Tunisia – the super-rich were identified as pro-Western, decadent and anti-Islamic. But the ruthless suppression of the left by these governments had created a situation where Islamists, often supported by Saudi funds, could benefit from the political vacuum created when pent-up frustrations brought protestors onto the streets. Many outside the region were surprised that demonstrations starting in Tunisia spread to Egypt and beyond: the reason lies in the common colonial history of the region. We have seen how, with the exception of Egypt, the Arab states are relatively recent creations; and how attempts by the media to blame contemporary conflicts on a 'Sunni-Shia divide' miss the more complicated story of colonial map-drawing and imposed, divide-and-rule regimes. During the Cold War, moreover, nationalist and Ba'athist governments benefitted from Soviet aid and Moscow instructed communist parties – some with considerable working-class support – to dissolve and join the Ba'athists. Then the collapse of the Soviet bloc saw nationalist bureaucrats returning to the Western fold as semi-dynastic dictators and authoritarian promoters of inflicting the international neo-liberal agenda on the masses.

The impact of the 2008 world crisis on Egypt, for example, is revealed in International Monetary Fund figures showing the rate of growth falling from 8.7 per cent in 2006 to 4.6 per cent in 2009 and 1 per cent in 2010–11, and such overall figures conceal the growing gap between rich and poor. Egypt's foreign currency income relies on exports to Europe, but in 2008–09 goods exported dropped from 33 to 15 per cent. Major European and US transnationals such as Orange, IBM and Xerox – beneficiaries from cheap labour in Cairo and Alexandria – closed, or cut back production. Tourism, accounting for 11 per cent of the country's GDP, saw visitor numbers in the first half of 2010 drop from 1,029,000 the year before to 732,000. The negative impact on remittances from the Gulf countries – 5 per cent of Egyptian GDP prior to the crash – was also significant. Egyptians faced additional hardship, as the cost of food, including rice, wheat and corn, increased sharply in international markets from 2006 to 2008.[21]

American aid was also affected. Its disbursement depends not only on US self-interest but also on the succour the dictatorships offer Israel. Regimes prepared to deal with Israel, notably Mubarak's Egypt, were rewarded – for example with duty-free exports to the USA. Qualified Industrial Zones (QIZ), intended as an extension of the USA-Israel Free Trade Agreement, and supposedly to 'broaden support' for the Middle East peace process, produce 'tangible economic benefits' for Jordan, the West Bank and the Gaza Strip as well as Egypt – stimulating their economies and employment; but they have to import at least 12 per cent of their goods from Israel.[25] But political obedience could not fully offset the financial impact of the world crisis. For Egypt, between 2005 and 2008, QIZ exports had grown 57 per cent, accounting for up to 40 per cent of exports to the USA by 2010, particularly benefitting 700 companies in the textile sector.

The crisis has seen major reductions, with a serious impact on foreign currency incomes. The fact that the oil-producing countries – Saudi Arabia and the Persian Gulf states, all with small indigenous populations – have played a significant role in the economy of the Arab countries has also been a factor in making Washington rethink. These powerful countries remain the main sources of funding for the Muslim Brotherhood and the more jihadist Islamic forces. Nor has their support for the Islamic movement been purely reactionary, given popular resentment at Anwar Sadat's and then Mubarak's subservience to the USA and their peace deals with Israel on which the QIZ agreement depended.[22]

Despair resulting from the economic situation, anger at the role of the army and the police, and at the impotence of Arab rulers in dealing with the Palestinian issue, the psychological effects of the defeat of Ba'athism in Iraq, seen by many Arabs as an insult to their national and regional Arab pride – all have been crucial factors behind the uprisings.

The Muslim Brotherhood

In the absence of serious secular organisations when Mubarak fell, the Muslim Brotherhood (MB), was, as we have seen, the largest, best-organised political force, successful *faute de mieux* rather than widely popular. Inevitably, when it tried to impose Sharia law on every aspect of society and it became clear that it had no real alternative to the continuation of neoliberal economics, it lost much of its support. Talk of economic justice was forgotten; and the religious rhetoric became ever more hard-line.

When the MB's political arm, the Freedom and Justice Party (FJP), won 47 per cent of the seats in the Egyptian parliament in January 2012, reporting focused on policies such as imposing Sharia law, banning alcohol and gender segregation. But

Egyptian business, optimistic for economic recovery, largely welcomed the victory. The MB's idea of Islamic capitalist economy, as in Iran's Islamic republic, was based on compromise between interventionism and laissez-faire. For all the talk of 'moving towards an Islamic economy' (complete with interest-free banking), Egyptian banks and the stock market saw no economic threat. The Brotherhood's economists were well aware that Islamic banking encompassed less than 4 per cent of the sector and the FJP was not likely to change that soon. On the contrary, the party encouraged depositors and borrowers. A powerful group of Islamist industrial and commercial leaders, headed by Khairat el-Shater – a multimillionaire businessman and former political prisoner of the Mubarak era who had been a victim of assets confiscation in the past but was, by 2010, an FJP strategist and senior MB leader – favoured a liberal, market economy and a 'business-friendly' climate. People like him were in charge of the 'Renaissance Project', the MB's ambitious scheme to oversee economic planning, public administration, health and education. At the same time the MB's interventionist faction pursued a policy of export substitution in cooperation with the private sector. This called for control of the budget deficit and public debt, restrictions on public spending, and measures to strengthen competition, anti-trust legislation and the raising of the ceiling for tax exemptions.

Most damaging for the MB was its attitude towards poverty, involving a top-down approach, relying on charity rather than enhanced wages and worker rights (although the minimum wage was increased). In opposition, the MB had developed far-reaching, organised charity work, financing social support often with Saudi and Gulf-states funding. Some FJP supporters also advocated making *zakat* – a form of charitable donation, equivalent to 2.5 per cent of Muslims' income, to help the poor – compulsory, but the MB was not in power long enough to implement this. Throughout, the FJP separated the issue of poverty from economic development and planning, classifying the former as 'social justice'; and, while distributing food parcels could be effective during an election campaign, in a country of 70 million (almost a third officially in poverty), it was unsustainable in the longer term.

The FJP promised support for workers in tourism, but its drives to ban alcohol and swimwear and impose gender segregation did little for either cheap resort holidays or the upper end of the travel market. When, in June 2013, Mursi appointed as governor of Luxor province a hard-line Islamist from the Al-Gama'a al-Islamiya group, which claimed responsibility for the murder of dozens of tourists in 1997, infuriated tourism workers blocked the entrance to the local government offices in protest. The MB also eagerly attacked the democratic gains of the 2011 uprising, often relying on its ally, the army – ironically the force that was to depose it. When Mursi adopted, as part of a new Islamic constitution, a 'Constitutional Decree' allowing him to modify legislation in line with Sharia law, over 70 per cent of the population boycotted the referendum to approve it.

There was discrimination against the 10-per-cent Christian minority, facing new forms of sectarian intimidation, including the criminalisation of so-called blasphemy – enshrined in Mursi's Islamist constitution. Islamic gangs enforced the Sharia law imposing financial levies known as *jizya* (originally a ninth-century form of taxation on non-Muslims) on Copts.

Mursi himself became more of a hate figure when he denounced all opponents as foreign agents. In his last speech in office, he lamented: 'How can the best of leaders make major achievements in such a poisonous atmosphere?' By the time of the summer 2013 coup, therefore, the MB had lost much of its support, only to have it partially restored when it in turn was banned, its members repressed and arrested. Islamist hard-liners can play victim when in opposition, even though, as has been seen, they can be willing and ruthless dictators when they have a cosy relationship with the army.

The 2013 military coup – like the one in 2011, when the armed forces intervened to depose Mubarak – had one aim: to end the revolutionary process. The longer the protests continued, the stronger the fear of genuine revolution. Saudi Arabia, Kuwait and the United Arab Emirates continued to pour billions of dollars into the Egyptian economy; but – as in Tunisia, Syria and Libya – the endemic economic and political problems are too serious to be resolved in the short term even by huge sums.

Tunisia: an exception?

The situation in Tunisia, in mid-2015, was slightly better, but only because the Islamists backed down from many of their Sharia-based proposals. On 27 January the Tunisian parliament voted by 216 votes to 200 for a new constitution, the first since Ben Ali's overthrow and the result of a compromise between the Islamists and the secular opposition. However, conflict continues, with opposition leaders assassinated, soldiers and policemen killed and, reportedly, suicide attacks at beach resorts. As in Egypt, tourism is badly affected by new Islamic legislation, lack of security and political uncertainty.

There are reports of torture and deaths in custody. Harassment, assaults and even death threats were still facing anyone expressing views Islamists dislike or any woman wearing 'inappropriate' clothes or leaving home after dark. The mass media presents Tunisia as a rare exception to the disappointments of the 'Arab Spring': many of those living there think otherwise.

What lessons can be drawn

Overall, it is too soon to judge the significance of the 'Arab Spring' for the revolutionary process in the region as a whole, for

Arab unification or in the light of the threat of war. But some preliminary conclusions about aspects that affect both imperialism and the peoples of the region can be attempted.

First, three-and-a-half decades after the first Islamic revolution – in Iran in 1979 – it can be predicted that, if Islamists come to power in another Middle Eastern country (as in Egypt), they are not likely to ally with Iran's Shia regime: antagonism towards non-Arab Iran is more likely. Shia supreme religious leaders in Iran, Ayatollah Khomeini and Ayatollah Khamenei, promised their people and the world that future revolutions in the region would emulate the Iranian events, and, at first glance, events in Egypt and Tunisia in 2012–13 seemed to confirm this. But, even as the MB moved towards power, it became apparent that the Shia-Sunni divide meant they were unlikely to ally with the Islamic Republic. Tehran's hostility to the pro-Saudi MB Cairo government was no less than to Mubarak. US strategists had to accept that any subsequent regimes controlled by political Islam are likely to have their purse strings controlled by their own Saudi and Gulf-states allies rather than the Iranian foe. The Iranian model would not be repeated.

Second, political Islam is unlikely to retain power, as Egypt exemplifies. The Islamists, lacking any perspective outside neoliberal capitalism, cannot keep their promises about 'social justice'. The failure of the MB and the workers' strikes and mass demonstrations of the summer of 2013 show that, in the first quarter of the twenty-first century – unlike Iran in 1979 – the life of Islamic governments will be short. The Islamists misunderstand the political and economic reasons behind the upheavals of 2011 to 2013, underestimate the anger of the youth movement and fail to realise that empty promises of 'equality and social justice' – even when buoyed up with Saudi-financed propaganda and apparently effective in elections – become the source of disillusionment when promises are not delivered. The army's marriage of convenience with the MB ended in bitter divorce when it saw that the Mursi government was fuelling the flames of another uprising. Its American funders can see that political Islam no longer has the staying power of Iran's Islamic Republic.

Nor, thirdly, will Saudi Arabia – for all its lavish expenditure – be able to control the plethora of Islamic movements it finances, a matter of real concern in the USA. As we have seen, the post 9/11 US 'war on terror' produced a Shia government in Iraq which, ironically, made Iran more powerful in the region. Since then Iran and the USA have, despite themselves, been forced together to prop up the occupation-friendly Shia government in Baghdad, giving Iran even more – indeed unprecedented – political influence. For all the hysteria in the USA about Iran's clerical regime, the overthrow of Saddam Hussein has aided the creation of a 'Shia belt' from the eastern borders of Iran to the Mediterranean – via Iraq, Syria and Lebanon.

Initially the 'Arab Spring' found genuine supporters in Syria (Iran's second main ally in the Arab world) and the protests by students, youth and Kurds against Assad's dictatorship gained momentum – a genuine expression of the hopes of the Syrian people. But Saudi Arabia and its allies also saw their opportunity, aiming for the overthrow of Assad's Alavi regime and the consequent weakening of Iran's regional role, only to be surprised when Iran came to Assad's aid. Then, in 2013, the inability of the Saudis to control the Islamic jihadists they finance in both Syria and Iraq when they engaged in systematic car-bombing in Shia civilian areas (and the growing influence of these 'holy warriors' in Libya and elsewhere) became a source of major concern for US strategists. It was a turning point in the USA's Syria policy, perhaps even more significant than the administration's failure to get support for limited military intervention. As far as the survival of the Iraqi regime was concerned, Iran and the USA turned out to have more in common than they had thought.

Last, but not least, the USA knows that sanctions have destroyed Iran's economy. The punitive measures imposed by the West might have failed to stop the nuclear programme, or greatly affect the private wealth of senior clerics, but they have been effective enough to ensure that Iran is no longer in a position to become a real threat to US strategy in the region.

All these issues have had dramatic political consequences: the change in US foreign policy towards Iran and Syria; negotiations with Iran on the nuclear issue and the Geneva talks on Syria; a new desire in Washington to urgently 'resolve' the Palestinian issue. This was the background to a revival of US Secretary of State John Kerry's 2014–15 shuttle diplomacy, rushing between nuclear deals, Syrian talks and the Palestine-Israel negotiations. For the peoples of the region there will be further consequences. The political and economic issues that caused the Arab uprising are as pertinent today as they were in 2011, but political Islam is no longer held in such widespread esteem as the agent for fundamental change. There could even be a small window of opportunity for the revolutionary left.

For socialists, every war, every local conflict, has a history: it is, as Clausewitz taught, 'the continuation of politics by other means'. Faced with complicated scenarios playing out in the Middle East and the north of Africa, the left must beware the consequences of support for 'humanitarian' foreign intervention or aid to whichever dictatorship seems least objectionable for the moment. Media reports, including random eye-witness statements and the evidence of short visits, must be treated sceptically. Both sides in a civil war – in Syria the reactionary regime and the religious-fundamentalist opposition – exaggerate atrocities to win allies. Every statistic, every report of brutality or mass murder must be carefully scrutinised.

It is untrue, for example, that Washington has refused to deliver weapons to the Syrian opposition. By March 2013, according to the *New York Times*, the CIA had smuggled in, via

Turkey, '3,500 tons of military equipment'.[23] According to Robert Fisk, 'Saudi Arabia and Qatar make no secret of the funds and weapons they are running into Turkey and Lebanon for the opposition',[24] and it is no accident that some of these weapons have found their way to jihadists. The progressive forces who initiated a popular uprising in Syria are under attack by Shia/Alawi forces associated with the Assad regime, as well as Sunni Jihadists and al-Qaeda, and the left is in no position to exercise influence. Brutal and reactionary Islamist forces have the upper hand and no amount of wishful thinking will change this.

For Marxists in the UK, France or the USA, the main struggle is against global capitalism. Imperialism is the main enemy that must be defeated. Western governments cannot 'impose peace' in Libya, nor will they 'arm the revolution' – the genuinely progressive forces – in Syria. What kind of 'revolutionary' force will seek Western arms to fight a dictator whose very survival until now has depended on the global interests of imperialism? Even if this could successfully be done, would it not simply create the conditions for regime change from above? What kind of conditions would be imposed on the Syrian opposition in exchange for this support? Already one Syrian opposition leader, the National Coalition's first president, Moaz al-Khatib, has resigned, complaining of the conditions attached by foreign powers to their aid.

To make my argument absolutely clear: there can be no support for reactionary anti-Western forces (such as Iran's Islamic Republic or its proxies in the region, including Assad and Hezbollah). There is, of course, a global hierarchy of states and the politics of the Middle East are enormously complex. But there is no reason to choose between support for Western intervention and becoming apologists for reactionary states or Islamist forces, Shia or Sunni. Advocating any form of intervention – military, economic (sanctions), judicial (participation in imperialist 'tribunals' to condemn dictators or whatever) is ultimately not simply to compromise with imperialism but, in practice, to support it. It is to argue for regime change on imperialist terms.

III: Iran's Tudeh party, the story of the Fedayeen and the legacy of Stalinism

In February 1971, when young militants took over a gendarmerie in a forest in the north of Iran, they were rebelling not just against the Shah's regime, but also against the Tudeh Party, the 'official communist' pro-Soviet party of Iran, whose name had become synonymous with compromise and betrayal following its passivity in the 1953 Western-organised coup against the elected government. The Soviet Union did not support the revolutionary movement against the Shah and naturally the Stalinist Tudeh Party adopted the USSR's line, advocating class collaboration and a peaceful road to socialism. This was what prompted the revolutionary youth to rebel against it.

Taking up arms was a suicidal act and many of the rebels were killed; 13 out of the 19 who were considered to have constituted the original cell of the Fedayeen died fighting and other members and supporters were later executed. Although crushed, however, the rebellion marked a historic challenge to both the Shah's dictatorship and the shameful record of the Tudeh Party. It proved to be the beginning of a struggle that inspired a culture of revolutionary resistance, poetry and art for the new generation, which included poets like Ahmad Shamlou and Shafiee Kadkani. The demise of the Tudeh contributed to the momentum that led to the overthrow of the Shah in 1979.

The background

The birth of the communist movement in Iran can be traced to the development of the capitalist mode of production in the late nineteenth and early twentieth centuries. Although underground cells were set up in many major urban areas, including Tabriz, Tehran, Isfahan and Shiraz, the most important political group active in the anti-dictatorial protests was based in the northern provinces close to the Russian border.

The seasonal workers in the Caucasus and those in Baku's oil industry were amongst the first Iranians to become familiar with social democracy. They established a number of left-wing Iranian groups in Baku, Tabriz, Mashad and elsewhere. These groups played a vital role in the constitutional revolution and grew in numbers between 1905 and 1917. The downfall of Tsarist rule in Russia allowed the formation of the Iranian Social Democrat Party Edalat (Justice) in Baku. The uprising in Gilan and the congress of Iranian social democrats in Bandar-e Anzali in 1920 led to the founding of the Communist Party of Iran. The Party played a crucial role in setting up workers' and women's organisations, amongst them the Union of Iranian Oil Workers, Peyk-e Saadat-e Nesvan (Voice of Women's Prosperity) and Bidarye Ma (Our Awakening). By 1922, some 15,000 Iranian workers were members of trade unions and the Communist Party had around 1,000 members. In the late 1920s and early 1930s, the Party bore the brunt of Reza Shah's repression. Its publications and organisations were banned, its activists imprisoned, its leader murdered in prison and its remaining cadre forced to flee to the Soviet Union.

The Tudeh Party in the 1930s

There is little information about the plight of party members in the Soviet Union during the purges. The historian Cosroe Chaqueri, however, quotes a letter from the Cadres Section of the Comintern to Iranian leftist author Noushin:

> Most Iranian Communists had perished in the purges; a few, such as the Communist poet Lahouti, had been living in exceptional comfort in Moscow or in the Asiatic republics, no doubt due to their collaboration with the Soviet secret police against their compatriots persecuted by the NKVD.[25]

The rise of fascism in Iran and plans for a united front

In 1936 the government of the Third Reich, advocating the common Aryan ancestry of the two nations, issued a special decree exempting Iranians from the restrictions of the Nuremberg Racial Laws. This was done on the grounds that they were 'pure-blooded Aryans'. In various pro-Nazi publications, lectures, speeches and ceremonies, parallels were drawn between the Shah of Iran and Hitler, and the charisma and virtue of the *Führerprinzip* were highly praised.[26] By 1941, Reza Shah was entering into an alliance with Nazi Germany and, consequently, on 25 August 1941, the Allied Forces entered Iranian territory. The north of Iran was occupied by the Soviet Union and the south by British and American forces. Reza Shah was forced into exile and the British brought his son, Mohammad Reza Shah, to power.

In the first years of his reign, while his grip on power remained weak, a large number of political prisoners were released. These included communists in Dr Arani's group (also known as the Group of 53), who adhered to socialist ideology but appeared to be unaware of the plight of their comrades in Russia. The basis for the establishment of the Tudeh Party of Iran (TPI) was laid down with Soviet encouragement. On 29 September 1941, the founding conference of the TPI was held in Tehran under the chairmanship of Soleiman Mohsen Eskandari. There are conflicting opinions about the role of the Soviet Union in forming the party, summarised by Cosroe Chaqueri in his article 'Did the Soviets play a role in the founding of Tudeh?',[27] where he quotes a report by Brigade Commissar Il'ichev, Colonel

Seliukov of the Red Army Intelligence division, about his meeting with Eskandari. On the day of the founding conference they discussed setting up a 'national-democratic party' to 'obtain democratic liberties and an easier life for the Iranian people'.[28] Further reports sent by Seliukov to the Soviet Union show that details of the new party's programme, Eskandari's previous political activities and the offer of financial help from the Soviet Union were discussed subsequently. According to Chaqueri, the Red Army intelligence officer told Eskandari on 10 October 1941 that the new party's programme was in accordance with 'our' opinion, but hesitated at the request for legalisation – presumably because of Anglo-Soviet relations at the time.

Eskandari and Seliukov had monthly meetings during which every aspect of the activists' preparations for the new party was discussed. Opponents of the 'united-front', bourgeois-democratic, anti-fascist party were also contacting Moscow, seeking support. The author Noushin wrote to Moscow about rebuilding the Iranian Communist Party, whilst Avanessain and Rousta, recently released from prison, favoured further Communist initiatives. There is evidence that Dimitrov informed Stalin and his associates (Beria, Molotov and Malenkov), who approved Tudeh's united-front initiative in Iran and were against any Avanessian-Rousta communist initiatives. Iranian communists were instructed 'to work in the Popular Party of Soleyman Mirza ... At the present stage [they] must not display socialist and Soviet slogans; [and they] must not abandon the framework of democratic platform.'[29]

At the same time, the Comintern embarked on a plan of setting up 'united, anti-fascist fronts' not only through the Tudeh in Iran, but also in neighbouring countries. For the execution of the plan in Iran, groups of cadres were designated by the Executive Committee of the Communist International (ECCI) to go to Iran. They were to organise lines of contact one way or another – through Basra or Iraqi territory; the Iranian ports of the

Persian Gulf; Afghanistan or British Baluchistan (now Pakistan) – with the Communist parties of Arab countries (Syria, Palestine, Egypt and Iraq), and of India. They were also to organise direct relations with Iran and establish their own radio transmitter, while assisting Iranian Communists in creating mass organisations and eventually re-establishing the Iranian Communist Party.

In 1942 the Tudeh gained official recognition and launched its paper *Siasat* (*Politics*). The worsening economic situation helped the party recruit activists quickly; and party cells and trade unions were formed in many provincial industrial centres. County organisations were set up in Azerbaijan, Esfahan, Gilan, Mazandaran and Khorasan. Chakeri's conclusion, accordingly, is that Tudeh was a creation of the Soviet Union and that it was primarily set up to suit Moscow's interests. It should be added, however, that Iranian communists who had survived prison in Iran and those left alive after Stalin's purges supported the establishment of this particular 'united front'.

The Democratic Republics of Azerbaijan and Kurdistan

On 26 November 1945, the Soviet troops occupying the north-western provinces of Iran prevented the Iranian army from reaching Kurdistan and Azerbaijan, where Soviet-backed groups had taken control and declared the independence of two separate republics, headed by the left nationalists, Ghazi and Pishevari. This took Tudeh members by surprise, although presumably the leaders closest to Red Army intelligence had some prior warning. In response to a complaint submitted by Iran, Andrei Vyshinsky, the Soviet representative to the United Nations, asked the Security Council not to interfere with ongoing bilateral talks (a reference to the 1907 Anglo-Russian Entente, which had already divided Iran between two spheres of influence, installing puppet regimes in the oil-rich areas). The Soviet proposal offered the recognition of the independent state of Azerbaijan by Iran, the acquisition of north oil concessions and Soviet military presence in a buffer zone consisting of five major provinces north of Iran.

By early 1945, the Tudeh had gathered considerable support, with an estimated 2,200 members and tens of thousands of sympathisers in its students' and women's organisations. The party claimed to have 100,000 sympathisers in affiliated trade unions. Its main newspaper, *Rahbar (Leader)*, boasted a circulation of more than 100,000, triple that of the 'semi-official newspaper', *Ettela'at*. The British ambassador, Reader Bullard, called it the only coherent political force in the country and the *New York Times* reckoned its allies would win up to 40 per cent of the vote in a fair election. From the beginning, the Tudeh had portrayed itself as the champion of patriotism and constitutional liberties against foreign imperialism and the threat of royal dictatorship; but it was forced to change tack and support the partition of northern Iran and oil concessions to the Soviet Union. Predictably, many members resigned.

In Azerbaijan and Kurdistan, the Tudeh Party branches were dissolved and party members were instructed – presumably by the Soviet Union – to join either Firqua Democrat Azerbaijan or Firqua Democrat Kurdistan (left nationalist organisations). Although Pishevari had joined the Tudeh in the early 1940s, he had independent links with Moscow and did not obey.

In April 1946 the Iranian government of Prime Minister Ghavam signed an oil agreement with the Soviet Union and agreed to appoint Tudeh ministers to the government in exchange for a promise of Soviet troop withdrawals from Iran's northern provinces – a policy reversal that saw Moscow favouring the Tudeh again. Partly as a result of pressure from the USA and Britain, Soviet troops withdrew from Iranian territory. Ghavam took three Tudeh members into his cabinet. Later the same year, however, he was able to reclaim his concessions to the Soviet Union, using the excuse of a tribal revolt in the south to dismiss Tudeh cabinet members. When Ghavam and the Shah's troops arrived in Azerbaijan in December 1946, the Firqua Democrat government, deprived of Soviet support, collapsed and Pishevari fled to the Soviet Union. Stalin's letter to Pishevari sheds light on aspects of their disagreements:

> *May 8th, 1946*
> To comrade Pishevari,
> It seems to me that you misjudge the existing situation, inside Iran as well as in the international dimension.
>
> First, you wanted to meet all revolutionary demands of Azerbaijan right now. But the existing situation precludes realisation of this program. Lenin used to put forth revolutionary demands ... as practical demands only when the country experienced a grave revolutionary crisis aggravated by the unsuccessful war with external enemy ... You here want to emulate Lenin. This is very good and laudable. However the situation in Iran today is totally different. There is no profound revolutionary crisis in Iran. There are few workers in Iran and they are poorly organised. The Iranian peasantry still does not show any serious activism. Iran is not waging a war with external enemy ... Consequently, there is no such situation in Iran that could support the tactics of Lenin in 1905 and 1917.
>
> Second, certainly, you could have counted on a success ... for the revolutionary demands of the Azerbaijani people had the Soviet troops continued to remain in Iran. But we could no longer keep them in Iran, mainly because the presence of Soviet troops in Iran undercut the foundation of our liberationist policies in Europe and Asia. The British and Americans said to us that if Soviet troops could stay in Iran, then why could not British troops stay in Egypt, Syria, Indonesia, Greece, and also the American troops – in China, Iceland, Denmark. Therefore we decided to withdraw troops from Iran

> and China, in order to seize this tool from the hands of the British and Americans, to unleash the liberation movement in the colonies and thereby to render our liberationist policy more justified and efficient. You as a revolutionary will certainly understand that we could not have done otherwise.
>
> Third … there is no profound revolutionary crisis in Iran. There is no state of war in Iran with external enemies, and, consequently, no military failures which could weaken the reaction and aggravate the crisis. So long as Soviet troops stayed in Iran, you had a chance to unfold the struggle in Azerbaijan and organise a broad democratic movement with far-reaching demands. But our troops had to leave and left Iran. What do have now in Iran? We have a conflict of the government of Qavam with the Anglophile circles in Iran who represent the most reactionary elements of Iran. As reactionary as Qavam used to be in the past, now he must, in the interests of self-defence and the defence of his government, carry out some democratic reforms and seek support among democratic elements in Iran. What must be our tactics under these conditions? I believe we should use this conflict to wrench concession from Qavam … to spit on everything, to break with Qavam and thereby ensure there a victory of the Anglophile reactionaries … would not have been a tactic, but stupidity. This would have been in effect a betrayal of the cause of the Azerbaijani people and Iranian democracy.[30]

The dismantling of the Communist Party in Iran in favour of the Tudeh followed by the adventures of the Stalinist regime in Azerbaijan and Kurdistan and then the support for nationalist separation resulted in confusion, anger and frustration in Tudeh ranks, the two Firquas and among communists and socialists in Iran. In Azerbaijan, Firqua Democrat made some progress towards land reform and fighting corruption amongst civil servants, but its rule was short-lived and the Shah's army ensured a speedy reversal of these policies. There are contradictory reports about the level of local support for Pishevari and his government; however there can be no doubt that military occupation encouraged the growth of right-wing royalist and later fundamentalist tendencies in the region, particularly around Orumiyeh. In 1948 the Tudeh Party faced a large split under the leadership of Khalil Maleki, who blamed the Central Committee for the Azerbaijan crisis.

Tudeh and the 1953 CIA coup

Worse was yet to come for the Tudeh. The party's indecision vis-à-vis a range of issues during Mosaddegh's premiership and the CIA coup of 1953 had disastrous consequences for Iran and the left. When Mosaddegh came to power in 1951, his first proposal was the enforcement of the Oil Nationalisation Bill to terminate British ownership of Iran's oil industry. The British reacted by issuing a lawsuit against Iran in the United Nations Security Council and at The Hague International Court – which voted in Iran's favour. The Anglo-Iranian Oil Company (AIOC) was dissolved and the 1933 oil agreement between Reza Shah's government of Iran and the British was declared void. The National Iranian Oil Company (NIOC), the first national oil company in the Middle East, was established on 19 March 1951.

Throughout this period, Tudeh's policy towards Mosaddegh fluctuated from one extreme to another: first they attacked him as 'an agent of American imperialism', and then supported him during and after the July 1952 uprising. Tudeh supported nationalisation of the British AIOC oil fields, or 'southern oil fields only', but opposed nationalisation of the northern oil fields owned and operated by the Soviet Union. On 15 August 1953, an attempted coup against Mosaddegh was thwarted thanks in part to information uncovered by the network of the Tudeh Party

Military Organisation. Some believe demonstrations called by the Tudeh two days later to pressure Mosaddegh to declare Iran a democratic republic inadvertently helped destabilise the nationalist government, since Mosaddegh reacted by calling on troops against the protestors. Ironically, the party demobilised late the next day, just as the CIA coup was unfolding.

On 19 August, the democratically elected government of Iranian Prime Minister Mohammad Mosaddegh was overthrown in a coup orchestrated by UK and US intelligence agencies, code-named Operation Ajax. CIA agents worked with pro-Shah military officers led by Fazlollah Zahedi, bribing thugs, clerics and politicians to participate in an anti-Mosaddegh propaganda campaign. A pro-Shah mob marched to the prime minister's office. According to declassified CIA documents, some of Tehran's most feared mobsters were paid by Zahedi and the CIA to stage riots, while Shah supporters were also transported into Tehran to take over the streets.[31]

Mosaddegh was arrested, tried and convicted of treason by the Shah's military court. On 21 December, he was sentenced to three years in jail, and then placed under house arrest for the remainder of his life.[32] Zahedi became prime minister in a military government following a royal decree.[33] Mosaddegh supporters were imprisoned, tortured or executed. After the coup, Pahlavi ruled as an authoritarian Shah for 26 years, until he was overthrown in 1979.

If the coup marked the end of the nationalist government, it also destroyed the Tudeh, which was by then the largest 'socialist' party in the Middle East. Its networks were smashed and its cadres mostly arrested or forced to flee to the Soviet Union. Of course the perceived threat of the Tudeh and the possibility of Iran's rapprochement with the Soviet Union was part of the rationale behind the coup. In his *Iran Between Two Revolutions,* Ervand Abrahamian questions the size of the party and whether the Tudeh military officer corps was in a position to influence events.[34] CIA reports suggest that, on the eve of the coup, the Tudeh had a core membership of around 20,000 and a network of officers within the Iranian armed forces organised by Sazman Nezami Hezb. It acted as a semi-legal political force, publishing three daily papers and organising supporters under the banner of the Iranian Society for Peace (Jamiyat Irani Havadar-e Solh).

Regarding the history of Tudeh's military organisation, Maziyar Behrooz points out that its officers did act independently of Party leadership:

> Between 1944 and 1946, the Military Organisation was involved in two episodes which led to an attempt to disband it and to sever ties with the Tudeh. In the first, in August 1944, around 20 army personnel in the Khorasan division of the army rebelled and attempted to reach the Turkman areas of West Khorasan and East Mazandaran in order to wage war against the central Government... Many ... were killed before they reached their destination and others ... fled to the Soviet Union. In the second, the Military Organisation sent aid and officers to Azerbaijan at a time when the province was rebelling against the Teheran Government. The defeat of the Azerbaijan movement ... caused the party's leadership to attempt to disband the organisation or at any rate cut all contacts with it ... The party asked the organisation back into its ranks in 1948, as a result of active Soviet pressure, and the reunion was finalised the following year.[35]

Iranian Marxists have blamed the Tudeh and its military organisation for inaction during the 1953 coup. Many believe that, even if – as party loyalists argue – defeat was inevitable, it would have been preferable for Tudeh officers and the party to have actively resisted. Some in the officer corps have disputed the claim that Tudeh's military organisation was too weak to make any difference. Fireidun Azarnur, a high-ranking officer, believes that

Tudeh allies occupied important military posts and estimates that 491 Tudeh military personnel had the ability to work with the Party to defeat the coup.[36] Abrahamian, however, notes that none of the Tudeh officers were in the 'crucial tank divisions around Tehran' that could have been used for a left-wing counter-coup, and that the Shah had them carefully screened. He also suggests that one great irony was that, even for a time after the coup, a Tudeh colonel was in charge of the Shah's personal security – as well as that of Vice President Richard Nixon when he made a triumphal visit to confirm American approval of the new regime – which means that the Tudeh had the opportunity to assassinate the Shah and the US Vice President but not to launch a bid for power.[37] And, as for the officer corps' other main task – to protect the Party – that was made impossible by its decimation after the coup.

Irrespective of debates about the strength of the Party, it is clear that the Tudeh (and by extension the Soviet Union) did not come out of this period well. Throughout the early 1950s, party leaders appeared confused about their attitude towards the nationalist government, leading to charges that it was 'khaen' (treacherous). The party was commonly referred to as 'Hezb Khaen Tudeh'. After the coup, it faced a serious crackdown with mass arrests and the execution of some 40–50 leaders: 'Between 1953 and 1957, Iranian security forces tracked down the whole Tudeh underground and more than half the party membership'.[38] Following the Sino-Soviet split, a Maoist group broke away from the Tudeh in the early 1960s and another smaller faction left in 1965.

In 1966, several party members, including Ali Khavari and Parviz Hekmatjoo of the Central Committee, as well as Asef Razmdideh and Saber Mohammadzadeh, were arrested and sentenced to death. This sparked international outcry from sister parties and forced the government to reduce the sentences to life imprisonment. Throughout the 1960s, the Tudeh remained a constitutionalist, reformist party that parroted Soviet dogma about 'peaceful coexistence' and even went so far as 'detecting' progressive aspects in line with the 'non-capitalist road to development' in some of the Shah's policies.

Frustration with Tudeh and the birth of Fedayeen

The Fedayeen organisation was formed through the merger of two groups on the Iranian left, both opposed to the Tudeh. One was led by Massoud Ahmadzadeh. His politics were a combination of Maoism and the espousal of guerrilla warfare. One of his closest allies was Amir-Parviz Pouyan, a man influenced both by *les évènements* in Europe in 1968 and by ideas of armed struggle. Ahmadzadeh's book, *Armed Struggle: Both Strategy and Tactics*, was for many years the bible of the Fedayeen.[39] Amir-Parviz Pouyan also wrote a book on *The Necessity of Armed Struggle and Refutation of the Theory of Survival*, the 'theory of survival' being a reference to the Tudeh's passive line, since 1953, of trying to survive by refraining from offensive action and avoiding arrest. Pouyan argued that this was tantamount to accepting defeat:

> We must demonstrate that the theory of 'let us not take the offensive in order to survive' is in fact no more than saying 'we shall allow the police to destroy us in embryo without the slightest resistance'. If defeatism is the same as liquidationism, then there is no room for asking, 'why should we survive?' All the same, posing the question helps us recognize the opportunistic nature of the theory ... [which] wishes to limit the struggle to meagre possibilities not controllable by the enemy; that is, a simple gathering of elements not significant in numbers, in fact not exceeding one's fingers; and then occupying oneself with the study of Marxism and history in total secrecy.[40]

Ahmadzadeh also attacked the illusion that the national bourgeoisie could have a revolutionary or progressive role. On the role of proletariat he wrote: 'The proletariat [in Iran] is numerically weak, but its special qualities and capabilities to organise are stronger than any other class.'[41] Another leading figure, Bijan Jazani, came from a different tendency – the youth organisation of the Tudeh Party – but he rebelled against Tudeh and agreed to bring his small forces into the new organisation.

To sum up the politics influencing the Fedayeen in this period, one can say that a unique version of guerrilla-ism dominated, along with a simplistic critique of the Soviet Union going little beyond rejection of 'peaceful coexistence'. The Fedayeen's founders were against the changes brought about by the 22nd Congress of the Communist Party of the Soviet Union and adopted a line claiming to be independent of both Russia and China. In reality, however, they remained greatly influenced by Stalinism. In debates with Communist Unity, a middle-of-the-road student organisation, the Fedayeen's position was that, until 1962, the USSR was 65-per-cent good and 35-per-cent bad – a Maoist view.

However, as China adopted the theory of social-imperialism and later the 'three worlds' theory, the Fedayeen and other Iranian left-wing groups distanced themselves from Maoism but only in a way that softened their critique of the Soviet Union.

Those Fedayeen who lost their lives in the 1971 operation had a considerable impact on the youth and student movement in Iran, and this new, emerging left was also very influential among young workers. The years 1971 to 1979 are important because they shaped the political thought of the generation that came to the Iranian revolution as leaders of the Fedayeen. The organisation was mainly underground, preparing for armed warfare and organising occasional bank robberies. Its activities were sporadic. It suffered losses, particularly because, as an armed organisation, members of the Fedayeen could simply be killed in the streets. This endangered known supporters (regarded as part of the armed movement by association), denying the movement a mass base, for example amongst university students. Around 370 left-wingers were executed in this period, 60 per cent of whom were Fedayeen.

In prison, Fedayeen members debated issues such as united fronts, intervention in working-class struggles and the merits of armed struggle. Jazani shifted ground. In his *United Front Against Dictatorship,* he clearly rejects earlier positions taken by Ahmadzadeh and Pouyan, arguably moving back to the Tudeh's stance. But in his *Capitalism and Revolution in Iran,* he presents a valuable analysis of the Shah's regime.[42]

In 1975, Jazani was killed in Evin prison, making it difficult to assess whether some of the writings and ideas attributed to him were truly his opinions. Others around him – released from prison – became leaders of the Fedayeen. By 1979, there was a mass revolutionary movement in Iran. Fedayeen members were released, many during the February uprising when jail doors were broken down. The Fedayeen had become a real force amongst students and young people, gaining popularity through its reputation for actions, some of which were more popular in myth than reality. But the organisation was now very divided, with Jazani's supporters following one political line and Ahmadzadeh's another.

Jazani supporters contended that the armed struggle line, as both strategy and tactic, was mistaken. In that they were right, as it had separated the Fedayeen from its potential mass base. On the other hand, some supporters of Jazani were now excusing Soviet foreign policy and even saw a positive role for the national bourgeoisie. Because little new theoretical work had been done, everyone read the book that, as one Fedayeen elder said, told them 'everything' – Lenin's *What is to be Done?* This gave the Fedayeen their stance against sectarianism, economism, syndicalism and anarchism. Their entire analysis was based on it, but that did not mean it was properly understood – especially given the problematic Farsi translation by the USSR Academy of Sciences, which emphasises centralism over democracy.

The Fedayeen, moreover, had failed to make headway in the working class or in wider Iranian society. Only in the universities did they have substantial support, as became clear during the revolution. Amongst the intellectuals and especially the poets (some of them famous), it attracted remarkable admiration. But it is clear now that it had no strategy about what to do when the revolutionary situation arrived. That was the problem of February 1979.

While the clergy had used the period of economic crisis from 1974 to 1979 to build its base, make propaganda and mobilise, the imprisoned Fedayeen debated in very abstract terms issues like the united front against the dictatorship. The Shah's regime, moreover, was more lenient towards the religious groups than the left, for whom building a mass organisation was accordingly the more difficult. Attempts to go to the factories never went beyond the distribution of propaganda and rapid departure. It is not so much that the February 1979 revolution was hijacked as that the left was simply unprepared. Had it come to power, it would have had no effective political plans, strategy or, above all, theory about what to do.

The oil workers were crucial. Their strikes broke the back of the Shah's regime. The Fedayeen had some influence amongst them, but were hampered by a lack of experience of working with the class. There was no plan about how to take the strike movement forward. Even so, the Fedayeen's first Teheran rally after the overthrow of the Shah attracted 500,000 people. Despite reservations, they stood in the elections to what was a sort of constituent assembly, receiving a couple of million votes.

Splits

The splits in the Fedayeen started in 1979 and are ongoing. Both before and after the Revolution, they made many mistakes with regard to issues such as militarism and centralism, and developed a culture celebrating the heroic guerrilla fighter and the professional revolutionary. They were confused in their criticism of the Soviet Union. There were myths surrounding the part of Fedayeen guerrilla struggle in the 1979 uprising; but many were becoming aware of their organisation's weaknesses, not least its divorce from the mass movement. The supporters of the armed struggle as tactic and strategy were, and are, in a small minority, now with the slogan: 'The Shah was the running dog of imperialism and so is the Islamic republic'. This minority still exists but lacks both analytical coherence and practical theory and is not the main source of division.

That came with the so-called Minority-Majority split, revolving around a wide range of issues, including the nature of the era we live in. But analysis of the Iranian Republic was central. Was it progressive or counter-revolutionary? In 1979–80, the Majority of the Central Committee held the view that the principal contradiction of the period was one of imperialism, principally the United States against socialism, represented by the USSR! Iran's regime, although Islamic, was held to be objectively moving Iran towards the 'socialist camp'. It was anti-imperialist, so it was given at first conditional, but later full, support. Members of this Majority claimed to have been close to Bijan Jazani in prison, but although they did constitute a majority on the Fedayeen central committee, it was soon clear that they did not have majority support in the country.

Tension grew after the spring of 1979, with the government strengthening itself to a position from which it could impose repression on opposition forces. This allowed for notable events such as the takeover of the US embassy by students – hailed by the Fedayeen Majority and Tudeh (as well as most of the left outside Iran) as an anti-imperialist act, but seen by Iran's radical left as a deliberate diversion aimed at stopping political strikes against – indeed all opposition to – the Islamic regime. It was the embassy occupation that really brought the arguments within the Iranian left to a head. The Minority had walked out of the Central Committee, and it had support from thousands of left-wing students and youth who did not want to follow the Islamic Republic into the abyss. The Majority, however, retained some support in the working class.

The embassy incident was also significant in that the government declared that anyone who did not support it must be a counter-revolutionary or a CIA agent. Counter-revolutionaries could be arrested and even executed: a situation that intensified once the Iran-Iraq war, portrayed as a war against imperialism, started. Some on the left, including the Fedayeen Minority, adopted the line, originally put forward by 'line three' Maoists, that the Iran-Iraq war was reactionary, which meant that any member of the Minority could be arrested, accused of supporting US aggression against Iran and possibly killed as a traitor.[43] The Fedayeen Majority, in contrast, could be invited to Ayatollah Rafsanjani's office for consultations.

Both the Majority and the Tudeh Party supported the government in repressing the rest of the left. The Majority, close now to Tudeh, began following the Moscow line: they said: 'Produce more – this is an anti-imperialist war and a war economy, and Iran is moving towards the socialist camp'. The Minority by contrast told workers that, while fighting imperialism, they also had to fight the regime. (The Iranian Trotskyist groups divided along very similar lines.) From this point on we are talking about two very different organisations. The Majority was able to operate openly until at least 1984, with offices in Tehran until 1982–83. The Minority was considered a proscribed organisation: their homes were raided and many died in those first years.

The first congress of the Fedayeen Minority showed the diversity of forces that had taken a united position against the Majority. There was even a split at this congress, with those in favour of joining the Mujahedin in the National Council of Resistance leaving. There was also a Trotskyist tendency with considerable support amongst young members.

Aside from the political problems there were other concerns. The Fedayeen's secret printing press was raided by the government with many killed. Political debate became confused with security issues, encouraging militarism and centralism – some of the blame for which was unjustly attached to the Trotskyist Tendency. This marked the beginning of a disregard for democracy by those who were preserving the organisation for the sake of it. Fedayeen ideology had always been dominated by talk of professional revolutionaries and heroes, who were considered the elite: dedicated people who had no other life, no other concerns and no interaction outside of the organisation – lest this led to their becoming 'confused' and acting against its interests. For all its faults, however, the Fedayeen Minority was for many years the main left organisation opposing the Islamic Republic.

A further blow to the Majority came when a CIA plant in the Soviet embassy in Tehran gave the names of Tudeh Party members to the Islamic government, leading to some leaders being arrested. This was the beginning of the end for both organisations inside Iran: their remnants survive in exile. Workers who had harboured illusions in the Majority had by then abandoned them. By 1982, leading oil workers, who had gone with them or with Tudeh over the revolutionary nature of the regime, had left.

Kurdistan base

The Fedayeen Minority, meanwhile, was forced to move most of their leading members to Kurdistan, although some key figures who had not been involved in the various security scares moved to other countries. The Central Committee kept one person in Tehran. Ironically, as a woman, she could go undetected because, although the government posted her photograph on every lamppost, it showed her without a headscarf when in reality she was totally covered! She managed to produce a left-wing paper in the middle of Tehran until 1985. It gave prominence to work in the class but the image of the heroic guerrilla persisted.

The period in Kurdistan was both a good and a bad time for the Fedayeen. It was safer than the Iranian cities, but the Marxist organisation was forced to work in the countryside among the peasantry, to whom Fedayeen ideas about building socialism were alien. They were, however, hospitable perhaps more because of their own hostility to a regime founded on Kurdish nationalism than through any understanding of what the Fedayeen stood for. The peasants were not religious in the manner of the Islamic Republic – something also true of the peasants in Iran itself, who have their own ways of expressing their faith.

In Kurdistan, the Fedayeen Minority needed its strength to survive harsh, cold winters and hot, dry summers. When a government clampdown took place, the organisation had to move from village bases to more mountainous, tribal areas without stable settlements. Political debate was limited and what there was usually centred on written questions. As the situation became more difficult, the Central Committee became even more centralised with dissent from the political line viewed as treachery. Dissidents were not expelled, but they were discriminated against. Four months after one congress, for example, members found out about a pamphlet written by the Trotskyist Tendency – but only through the denunciatory insults in a book, *Leninism or Trotskyism*, by a Central Committee member.

This book heralded a U-turn in one of the Fedayeen's longstanding positions when it announced that: 'In a future revolutionary Iran the Soviet Union will help us build heavy industries in order to achieve socialism'. How, members asked the author, was this different from the Tudeh Party's 'non-capitalist road to development' – the line that Fedayeen founders had rebelled against? He responded: 'We are not treacherous like Tudeh!' The majority of members did not share his opinions, but there was no opportunity for debate or the holding of a further congress.

Another corrupting influence was the interference in Kurdistan of the organisation led by Jalal Talebani – now (in 2015) President of Iraq. This group was one of those controlling not only Iranian Kurdistan, but neighbouring areas in Turkish Kurdistan and part of Iraqi Kurdistan. An area between Iran, Iraq and Turkey – known accordingly as the 'valley of the parties' – it was surrounded by high mountains, and therefore safe as a political base, for training schools and radio stations. Talebani's group was dominant there. Even 25 years ago, he had already moved well away from the left, developing as a bourgeois politician with a tribal, feudal background who would meddle in the affairs of political groups, finding a faction in this or that group to support against its leadership.

In Kurdistan, however, there were positives. People who wanted to fight the government arrived in large numbers. But they had no history with the Fedayeen or theoretical background and, unfortunately, no real attempt was made at political education. Most cadres only read the works of Lenin or 'martyred' Fedayeen comrades.

Few things were more symptomatic of the influence of Stalinism than the battle for control of the radio station. Ordinary members wanted a congress but the Central Committee refused, knowing it would lose power. Ignoring complaints about the lack of democracy, it had co-opted compliant members. When an attempt to physically wrest control of the radio station was made by people with a dubious political line – moving increasingly to the right and today in discussions to rejoin the Fedayeen Majority – the Central Committee delayed the congress, preventing proper discussion about strategy and tactics, or about political theory. Where did the Fedayeen stand now that they were no longer guerrilla-ist or Maoist and the Trotskyist Tendency had been expelled? Some in the Central Committee did not see anything wrong with the Soviet Union under Brezhnev. It was this lack of discussion that paved the way for the political decline of the Fedayeen Minority.

Even with these disasters in Kurdistan and their lack of support inside Iran, the Fedayeen remained a powerful force elsewhere, with around 1,000 supporters in the USA and perhaps 100 in each of several European countries. They worked hard, fund-raising, providing publicity and producing their own publications, including a student journal. But Fedayeen membership was quite a different matter. This was an organisation of professional revolutionaries, and because recruitment had slowed to perhaps one a year and many had died, there were only around 40 Fedayeen Minority members left, compared with 60 at the first congress. They had few rights, able only to elect representatives without influence. By the end of the twentieth century this model of organisation – professional revolutionaries aided by supporters – widely discredited elsewhere was still practised by the Fedayeen. Most importantly, they still worked on a 'need to know' basis, so supporters had a distorted view of both the theory and practice of the organisation. It was very hard to do much to change this, because members – I was one – were forbidden to divulge any secrets.

Most members, moreover, were exhausted by activity and could not read or study properly. You could be sent to another continent at a few hours' notice. Even in the Foreign Committee, there was little political discussion. In Kurdistan of course there was at least the excuse that a war was being fought and the Fedayeen did not want the enemy to take prisoners who knew too much. But that hardly applied in Europe.

What, then, are the main lessons of the Fedayeen? It can be too easy to criticise in retrospect. We should not underestimate either the repression of the Shah and the Islamic Republic, nor the real influence of the Fedayeen in the birth of the new left and in the Revolution. A heavy price was paid in fulfilling this historic role. But there were many mistakes too: militarism, the return to Stalinism, centralism, the culture of the heroic guerrilla and the professional revolutionary. For all the heroism of February 1971, the shadow of the Tudeh's Stalinism haunted the organisation that took up the struggle against the Tudeh. Today, at a time of revival of a new revolutionary movement inside Iran, some activists of the left misguidedly lament the absence of 'existing socialism however bad it was'.

Against this, I have tried to explain the disastrous legacy of Stalinism in Iran both in terms of the Soviet-Iranian relationship and the history of Tudeh and the Fedayeen Majority. Its demise can only be positive for the development of a radical working-class movement.

IV: Afterword

The 14 July 2015 deal on nuclear energy – concluded after long negotiations between Iran and the P5 + 1 nations – was the outcome of the changed relationship, dictated by the pragmatism of American policy in the Middle East discussed above, between Washington and the Islamic Republic. It was neither the mistake 'of historic dimensions' claimed by Israeli prime minister Binyamin Netanyahu and his allies in the US Republican Party, nor the 'win-win' announced by Iranian president Hassan Rowhani. As the *Financial Times* summarised it the following day: 'Iran has accepted unprecedented international control and surveillance over its nuclear programme, as well as cuts in its uranium stocks and in the number of centrifuges.' On the other hand the elite running and benefitting from Iran's neo-liberal, dependent capitalist economy, brought to its knees by punitive sanctions, had at least postponed the threat of regime change – the real aim of the sanctions – and the possibility of military attack. And Rowhani could justifiably claim Iran had won the right to pursue its nuclear programme to the extent that low-enriched uranium can now be used to produce fuel for power plants.

Supreme Leader Ayatollah Khamenei, having had to surrender his 'red line' that he would 'not allow inspection of Iran's military installations' resorted to rhetorical denunciation of the USA as 'the arrogant power'. But the reality is that Tehran's pursuance of a neo-liberal economic agenda made its submission to the 'arrogance' of the system's global hegemon inevitable. Iran is now one of the most unequal societies in the region, where what has been called 'a new class of untouchable one-percenters' accumulate wealth while the middle and lower classes suffer the impact of the country's deepening economic crisis. As the corruption of the members of the regime of former president, Mahmoud Ahmadinejad (the 'champion of the poor'), who lined their pockets through privatisation and sanction busting, come daily to light, Khamenei calls for such matters to be played down lest they provoke demoralisation. Our 'third world-ist' Supreme Leader presides over growing inequality, scandalous corruption, massive unemployment and wholesale privatisation, coming out only with occasional slogans about US arrogance and carefully avoiding the term 'imperialism' because of its Marxist connotations.

Forgotten are the promises of the Islamic Revolution to provide economic independence, full employment and a comfortable standard of living for all by the end of the twentieth century. Iran is seen as a regional power because of its influence in Lebanon, Syria, Bahrain and Yemen, but it is economically dependent on international capital. Conditions imposed by the International Monetary Fund and the World Bank in exchange for loans made a mockery of claims of independence. Khamenei ignores the fact that, long before sanctions, Iran was totally dependent on the sale of oil. Rowhani's government is faced with implementing the 'reforms' proposed in the report of the recent IMF inspection team, headed by its assistant director for the Middle East and central Asia, Martin Cerisola, which stresses the need for policies to preserve the advantages of disinflation and support the economy in adjusting to lower oil prices, including restricting the budget deficit in the next fiscal year to around 2.5% of GDP and making reforms in the financial sector.

As the nuclear negotiations progressed, and with the IMF 'reforms' in the background, foreign firms started queuing up to invest in Iran, with its cheap labour, stringent restrictions on workers' rights and a workforce disciplined by years of unemployment.

No wonder France, Germany and the United Kingdom were so keen to find a solution to the remaining points of contention. And the *Wall Street Journal* reported renewed interest amongst major American corporations such as Boeing and General Electric. As the Supreme Leader well knows, Iran's corrupt Islamic Republic will become yet more closely integrated into the capitalist order and its 'world arrogance', of which it is a part.

For all the Israeli hysteria and less-exaggerated Saudi opposition to the deal, both Barack Obama's and Khamenei's statements make it clear that the political situation in the region will not change dramatically. The US will support Turkish and Saudi efforts for regime change in Syria. For once, Robert Fisk is wrong when he writes that 'the overwhelming influence of the Sunni Muslim nations, which ... provided the world with Osama bin Laden, ... [and] supported the Taliban and ... the Sunni Islamists of Iraq and Syria' is over; and that the USA has tired of the 'emirs ... who support Isis ... [the] decrepit princes of the Gulf [with] their puritanical lectures ... tiresome wealth (unless it's paying for US weaponry) and ... grotty civil war in Yemen'.

He is wrong to suppose that 'Shia Iran is now the good guy on the block'. On the contrary, the twin-track policy of containing Islamic State, while promoting failed states in Iraq and Syria, is now supplemented by a policy of controlling Iran. There will not be sanctions against IS's main backers – Saudi Arabia, Qatar and the other Gulf states. Arms sales will continue (with, by some accounts, the Saudi kingdom seeking to develop its own nuclear programme; this aspect of policy at least, it is to be hoped, *not* to be shared with IS).

In Iran itself the people have reasons to celebrate. The deal should mean better access to medication and essential supplies, and, for those able to benefit, the ability to enter into personal and commercial international banking transactions, and this has already seen an improvement in the rate of exchange. Iranian students will be able to continue studying internationally. The employment situation should improve with the removal of the 'targeted sanctions' that impoverished the majority of the population, while bringing massive dollar windfalls to the select few, including the governmental elite, which will no longer be able to blame sanctions for its economic mismanagement. But do not expect improvements in democratic rights. Having reversed the nuclear programme to hold on to power, the regime – all its factions, 'reformist' and conservative – will continue to oppose basic political freedoms, and anything that might help fighters for the rights of workers, women and national/religious minorities. The danger is that progressive movements will now find fewer international allies, as funds for regime change dry up. It is all the more essential that the movement for principled international solidarity from below, which Hands Off the People of Iran represents, continues to be developed and brought on to the agenda of European workers.[44]

PART IV

A Critique of Some Past Guidelines

by Cliff Slaughter

I return here to the question raised at the end of this book's introductory remarks. What is meant by the *theoretical* rearming which is so necessary? Why must we make a critical re-evaluation of earlier writings and formulae – in particular, those of Lenin and Trotsky – which have been studied and used without regard for their historical context? And why, too, is it important to recognise that, in some significant respects, these great revolutionaries made mistakes?

Lenin and his What Is To Be Done?

In their search for an effective guide to action, many of those coming into struggle will turn to the writings of Lenin as the most successful revolutionary and Marxist. *What Is To Be Done?* (1902) is perhaps his best-known work, and has been taken as a guide by those who have wanted to be communists. It is important to look very carefully at what this book says, and to understand the historical and political context in which it was written, and for what purpose – as it has been much misunderstood and misused.[1]

In particular, three simple things should always be borne in mind by anyone wanting to learn from Lenin's text. Firstly, Lenin in his introduction says that it deals with two questions, which are not the same though they are intimately interrelated. One is the matter of the nature of 'social-democratic' (that is, communist) politics. The other concerns how to organise in the prevailing conditions of illegality. On this latter subject, much nonsense could have been avoided had some would-be Bolsheviks noted that Lenin quite explicitly wrote that the organisational methods he described were *not* applicable in circumstances where parties did not have to operate illegally and clandestinely.

Secondly, in the year immediately following publication (1903), a long discussion on *What Is To Be Done?* took place at the congress of the Russian Social-Democratic Labour Party.[2] Lenin was sharply criticised for so-called elitism because of his insistence on 'consciousness brought to the working class from the outside' and on the need for a party of 'professional revolutionaries'. As part of his response, Lenin said that the Economists whom he criticised had 'bent the stick' too far in one direction: it was therefore necessary for someone to bend it the other way in order to get it straight.[3] Much misunderstanding and misuse might have been avoided if these remarks had been printed at the top of every page in subsequent editions of Lenin's book and duly noted.

Thirdly – and most important of all – it is surely necessary to start from the actual experience of Lenin and the Bolsheviks in the conditions of Tsarist Russia and then in the revolutionary months of 1917. The relationship of the Bolsheviks to the working class changed radically in those months, as did the relationship between Lenin and the leaders and rank and file of his own party. Marcel Liebman has described how there was talk of 'de-Bolshevisation' of the party after Lenin's return to Petrograd from exile in April 1917.[4] And for good reason, as we shall see below – under the heading 'class-consciousness'.

Tsarist Russia was a backward country ruled by a repressive autocratic state. Capitalist industry was coming into existence only in the last decades of the nineteenth century. By the 1890s, the newly-born industrial working class, a small minority of the population, was beginning to show its potential strength in strikes and protests (Lenin writes of 'trade union consciousness', though trade unions hardly yet existed; he is referring to the sphere of relations between workers and employers). At the same time, Marxist socialists like Lenin were working to found a revolutionary party. They looked to the Social Democratic Party of Germany as the inspiration for their theory and political programme (social democracy at that time was the party name taken by Marxists, and bears no resemblance to the reformist parties of that name today).

By 1902 different tendencies had formed within the young Russian socialist movement. One of these was known as 'Economism', which advocated a reliance on the spontaneous movement and consciousness of the working class. It was against this tendency that Lenin's *What Is To Be Done?* was directed, attacking the notion that revolutionary class-consciousness could emerge spontaneously from the working class in its day-to-day struggles, and outlining the organisational necessities for a revolutionary party (secrecy, clandestine threads of contact, etc.) in a country with a repressive regime allowing no political freedoms. Some reading *What Is To Be Done?* – or this part of *Against Capital* – today will be working in conditions of illegality and police/military repression, and will do well to heed Lenin's words on organisation. On the other hand, Lenin is at pains to emphasise that in conditions of political freedom and legal existence, a very different pattern is appropriate.

It is important to recall Marx's insistence on the necessity of 'communist consciousness on a mass scale', which surely means that there will have to be anything but clandestine forms of organisation. On the other hand, it is now a commonplace that state agencies are using electronic 'surveillance' on a massive scale in all countries, so that movements of resistance and revolt are having to learn how to protect their methods of communication, and this they are doing. Furthermore, as the structural crisis of capital deepens, democratic freedoms come under attack, and state repression intensifies, such that in the 'advanced' countries the contrast with the authoritarian conditions faced by Lenin does not look so sharp.

Lenin was convinced that the 'Economists' were diverging widely from Marxism and must arrive at the same 'revisionist' standpoint as that of the German Social Democrat Bernstein. Bernstein and his followers saw the achievement of socialism as merely the culmination of a gradual process of reforms within capitalism. The Economists, argued Lenin, thought that the socialist revolution would develop from the immediate, 'spontaneous' movement of resistance by workers to their conditions of work and life.

For Lenin, political work based on this 'worship of spontaneity' falls far below the level required in the practice of revolutionaries. Far from restricting themselves to economic (typically 'trade union') struggles, revolutionaries must act to expose and mobilise against *every* manifestation of oppression and exploitation – that is, all issues at the level of politics, of the state and its institutions and measures, as well as struggles over wages and working conditions.

In his insistence on this position, Lenin presents approvingly a passage from the work of Karl Kautsky, at that time recognised as the authoritative voice of Marxist socialism and leader of the German Social Democratic Party. Kautsky had written:

> The vehicle of science is not the proletariat, but the *bourgeois intelligentsia*: it was in the minds of individual members of this stratum that modern Socialism originated, and it was they who communicated it to the more intellectually developed proletarians who, in their turn, introduced it into the proletarian class struggle where conditions allow that to be done. Thus, socialist consciousness is something introduced into the proletarian class struggle from without and not something that arose within it spontaneously. [5]

When Lenin endorsed this statement, he did *not* say, as has often been alleged, that at all times there can be no socialist consciousness in the working class unless it is 'brought from the outside, by bourgeois intellectuals'. He says no more than that it was the 'bourgeois intellectuals' Marx and Engels who founded modern socialism, and that a revolutionary party must fight to take the struggles of the working class beyond the economic, trade-union sphere to a practical consciousness of the need to overthrow and surpass the rule of capital. Thus:

> 1. [After characterising the wave of strikes in the 1890s]
>
> We have said that *there could not yet be* Social-Democratic consciousness among the workers. It could only be brought to them from without. The history of all countries shows that the working class, exclusively by its own effort, is able to develop only trade union consciousness, i.e., the conviction that it is necessary to combine in unions, fight the employers and strive to compel the government to pass necessary legislation, etc. The theory of Socialism, however, grew out of the philosophical, historical and economic theories that were elaborated by educated representatives of the propertied classes, the intellectuals. According to their social status, the founders of modern scientific Socialism, Marx and Engels, themselves belonged to the bourgeois intelligentsia.
>
> 2. ... the organisation of revolutionaries must consist first, foremost and mainly of people who make revolutionary activity their profession (that is why I speak of organisations of *revolutionaries*, meaning revolutionary Social Democrats). In view of this common feature of the members of such an organisation, *all distinctions as between workers and intellectuals*, and certainly distinctions of trade and profession, must be *utterly obliterated*. [The emphasis is Lenin's.]
>
> 3. ... by 'wise men', in connection with organisation, I mean *professional revolutionaries*, irrespective of whether they

> are trained from among students or workingmen.[6]

From these sentences it is clear that what Lenin envisaged as the driving force of a 'Social-Democratic' working-class consciousness was a party of 'professional revolutionaries', with no distinction between intellectual (students, etc.) and worker members. Furthermore, Lenin insisted at the Congress of April 1905 that the proportion of workers in the committees be raised to 80 per cent. Six months later he declared, 'now we must wish for the new Party organisations to have one Social-Democratic intellectual to several hundred workers', and weeks later he called for the building of 'a mass party'.[7] Against the members of his own party who were suspicious of the emergence of the Petrograd Soviet, he wrote of the December 1905 insurrection: 'The proletariat sensed sooner than its leaders the change in the objective conditions of the struggle and the need for a transition from the strike to an uprising'.[8] It is also worth noting that in 1923, just before his death, Lenin insists on the urgent need for working-class leaders coming from the working class itself.[9]

'From the outside...'?

The phrase, 'from the outside, by bourgeois intellectuals', has been the main source of the misunderstanding of *What Is To Be Done?* and of Lenin's politics to which we have already referred. Is it true that revolutionary consciousness must be brought to the working class 'from the outside, by bourgeois intellectuals', because the working class can by itself arrive only at 'trade union consciousness'? Certainly it was the bourgeois intellectuals Marx and Engels who from the 1840s, through a thoroughgoing critique of the most advanced thinkers in philosophy, history and political economy, were able to carry out their work of discovering the 'laws of motion' of the capital system and the revolutionary role of the working class. It was a fundamental breakthrough to show that the capitalist order is not at all the natural outcome of humans' need to produce and exchange, and this insight could not arise simply from the experience of the exploited working class. Engels, in his *Condition of the English Working Class in 1844*, had described and analysed the life and work of the proletarians of his day, but only he and Marx were able to show that the proletariat was not just an oppressed and exploited class but the revolutionary class that must overcome the rule of capital and take humanity towards socialism. In this sense, and only in this sense, was socialist revolutionary consciousness brought to the working class 'from the outside, by bourgeois intellectuals'.

It would be perverse to think that from the time of the young Marx and Engels onwards, the working-class movement would have to depend on 'bourgeois intellectuals' *coming from the outside* to develop the necessary socialist revolutionary consciousness. And such a notion is completely contrary to the political and organisational life work of Lenin. His revolutionary party was to be, and became, a party not *for* the working class but *of* the working class, consisting of workers who grasped revolutionary theory (Marxism) as they became leaders of their fellow workers ('professional revolutionaries'). At the same time, as Engels had insisted, the workers' class struggle, besides the 'economic front' (against employers, for wages and better working conditions) and the 'political front', must also be continuously fought on the 'theoretical front'. This means building and renewing Marxist theory as an understanding of the way in which the contradictions of the capital system develop in new ways, with all the implications of these changes for the strategy and tactics of the working-class movement. Here the words of the *Communist Manifesto* are directly relevant:

> In times when the class struggle nears the decisive hour, the process of dissolution going on within the ruling class, in fact

> within the whole range of old society, assumes such a violent, glaring character, that a small section of the ruling class cuts itself adrift, and *joins the revolutionary class, the class that holds the future in its hands* ... a portion of the bourgeoisie goes over to the proletariat, *and in particular, a portion of the bourgeois ideologists, who have raised themselves to the level of comprehending theoretically the historical movement as a whole.* [Emphasis added.][10]

Rather than their 'bringing revolutionary consciousness from the outside' these intellectuals do indeed go over to – that is join – the working class, and the work they do there, in practice and in theoretical work, is from the *inside,* not transmitting their ideas to this or that worker, but, with the workers, together forging what Marx referred to as the necessary *practical consciousness* of the revolutionary class. Marx's critique of bourgeois ideology, moreover, led him to insist on this practical consciousness, so that, as he later stressed, his ideas are *'not a theory, but a guide to action'*!

It was firmly on this basis that Lenin and his comrades, despite his commendation of Kautsky's 'from the outside, by bourgeois intellectuals', did their political work. Once this is understood, the essential content of *What Is To Be Done?* falls into place with Lenin's political life's work as a whole. This essential content of the work was to politically arm the young working class to lead the Russian people in overturning Tsarist oppression and founding a democratic republic. Until the revolutions of 1917 Lenin wrote of such a democratic republic as providing the best conditions for the working class to conduct its struggle for socialism. Only with the upsurge of workers' soviets (workers' councils) in the months before the October revolution did he abandon his idea of a 'revolutionary democratic dictatorship of the proletariat and the peasantry', recognising that the actual alternatives were either a military dictatorship or a proletarian, socialist revolution. (In this he came to the position long held by Trotsky, who at that point joined Lenin and the Bolsheviks.)

Returning to his difference with the 'Economists' on the general question of the content of working-class politics, there can surely be no argument with his insistence that:

(a) a proper understanding of society and of political tasks can only come from studying the totality of the relationships between the classes, and not simply from worker-employer relations and experiences; and so,

(b) socialist revolutionaries must work in all spheres of those relationships, all classes and social groups in order to 'bring political knowledge to the workers'.

Class-consciousness

As we have seen, it was the 'bourgeois intellectuals' Marx and Engels who discovered the revolutionary role of the working class, through a critique of the most advanced thinking of their day. But the *knowledge* thus gained by *individuals* is *not* class political consciousness; it is a theory, a set of ideas in the heads of individuals, and it can be transmitted, yes, to other individuals. *Class* political consciousness is something else: it is the *practical consciousness* of the working class in movement; and it develops in the course of the actual struggle of the class, its practice and experience.

And so Lenin's injunction to 'go among the workers and all strata of society, etc.' must surely mean not merely the inculcation of communist ideas in the heads of individuals but an immersion in the class struggle, learning from it as well as fertilising the workers' struggles and consciousness with Marxist theory. In summary: class political consciousness is therefore a practical consciousness, and the task of socialists/communists/Marxists is to *engage* in this conscious practice, learning all the time that class consciousness is a process of the unification of theory and practice. Thus class consciousness develops *inside* the working class in movement, and absolutely does *not* arrive to the working class ready-made in the brains and mouths and writings of Marxist intellectuals, bourgeois or otherwise. Once again Marx: not a theory, but a guide to action.

I believe that this conclusion fits better with Lenin's actual politics than does his approval of Kautsky's 'from the outside, by bourgeois intellectuals'. Of great importance for the way the communist movement later developed, is the way in which the latter formulation has been taken out of context and has thus distorted (with disastrous consequences in the case of Stalinism, and with the consequence of fundamental mistakes in the case of Trotskyism) the relationship between party and class. It has contributed very significantly to the subordination of the interests and struggles of the working class to the conceived interests of the party ('building the party', etc.). Once the young Soviet republic was isolated by the betrayals and defeats of the revolutions in Europe, and the Communist Party found itself compelled to substitute itself for the working class as the holder of state power, the stage was set for 'Leninism' to be interpreted as the theory and practice of an elite attempting to determine the interests of the working class. 'From the outside' became 'from above'.

How could Lenin succeed in 1917?

Before tracing some of those consequences, we should ask how it was possible for Lenin and his party to be able to lead a successful revolution in October 1917, and to suggest a comparison with the very much changed situation in which Trotsky attempted in the 1920s and 1930s to stop the Stalinist degeneration and put the international working-class movement on the revolutionary path. This should make clearer the absolute need in our present struggles to work on the basis of the very different situation faced by today's movements towards socialism, and not start from past formulae appropriate only in their given context.

Why then were Lenin and the Bolsheviks able to go forward with the Russian working-class movement in 1917 to lead the October overthrow of the Tsarist autocracy and the classes it represented, the capitalists and large landowners?

First, the power of the Tsarist state was critically weakened by its involvement in World War One; and the Prince Lvov and then the Kerensky governments installed after the February 1917 uprising proved utterly ineffective. Second, the Bolsheviks had by 1917 established a nationwide organisation able to work in every decisive section of the working class. Third, Lenin proved able to recognise and firmly grasp the significance of the rapid changes taking place in 1917, in particular the formation and power of the workers' soviets. And when Leon Trotsky returned to Petrograd from exile in April 1917, Lenin had already begun to abandon his old perspective of a 'revolutionary democratic dictatorship of the proletariat and the peasantry' and move rapidly towards Trotsky's own programme of a socialist revolution led by the working class, its fate to be determined by the hoped-for successes of proletarian revolution in Europe. They both moved forward with this perspective, and Trotsky very soon joined the Bolsheviks. Fourth, and finally: once this change had been made, Lenin and his comrades were sufficiently alert to the rapidly deteriorating conditions and the mood and militancy of the masses to be able to put forward slogans and calls to action which made possible the decisive struggle: 'Peace, Bread and Land! All power to the Soviets!'

Only at this point, and only in a way not expected, was Lenin's aspiration of 1904 fulfilled: 'We are the party of a class inasmuch as we *in fact* direct almost the entire, or even the entire, proletarian class in a Social-Democratic way.'[11] Lenin's Bolsheviks did not exactly 'direct' the working class in its revolutionary action to take power in October 1917. On the contrary, as Lenin himself pointed out, the Bolshevik Party found itself in April 1917 *behind* the workers' soviets.

Was the Bolsheviks' success in October 1917 the product of the building, since 1902 and *What is to be Done?*, of a 'monolithic' party constructed in conspiratorial conditions? The answer is a categorical 'No!' The internal life of the Bolshevik Party in the months between the February and October Revolutions of 1917 bears not the slightest resemblance to the attempted 'monolithic' parties aimed at by those who in later years sought to follow the path of Lenin and Bolshevism. In summary: in the course of those months, the 'old Bolshevism' had to be fought against, above all by Lenin, and defeated. This could come about only by the most intense and bitter inner-party struggle, in the context of a rapidly changing relationship between the Bolshevik Party and the working masses. I summarise Marcel Liebman's account of this historic and dramatic transformation in his meticulously researched *Leninism Under Lenin*.[12]

Both Bolsheviks and Mensheviks (the 'majority' and 'minority' tendencies of the Russian Social-Democracy) had always shared the view that the necessary revolution to overthrow the Tsarist autocracy was a 'bourgeois-democratic' one, bringing into being a democratic capitalism in which the working class would have the political conditions in which to organise and fight for socialism. Trotsky had led a far smaller group (in 1917, some 4000), the Mezhrayontsi, with the perspective of 'going over' from the bourgeois-democratic to the proletarian revolution – in what he called 'permanent revolution'. (Compare this, as suggested above, with the South African Communist Party's insistence on the overthrow of the apartheid regime as the beginning of a 'national-democratic revolution' which must be supported and completed before there could be a working-class struggle for socialism.)

Lenin's letters from exile in March and April 1917, then his speeches on his return, came like a bombshell to the Bolshevik Party. He rejected totally the perspective and programme on which the party had always worked, denouncing the Provisional Government emerging from the February Revolution as a government ruling in the interests of capitalists and big landowners. It was the workers who had overthrown Tsarism, and their victory had been usurped by the bourgeoisie. The aim must now be a new revolution to establish the rule of the working class and its allies (above all the poor peasantry). It was to take a bitter struggle against the existing Bolshevik leadership to break the party from the old line of bourgeois-democratic revolution. Lenin was opposed as a hothead and adventurist making premature and dangerous demands. His opponents insisted on a policy of pressure on the Provisional Government to fulfil the programme of democratic reform. Lenin characterised such demands as like asking a brothel-keeper to abstain from sin.

Lenin's battle took place against a background of revolutionary ferment in the working class. Thousands of workers joined the Bolshevik Party between February and October, increasing its membership some tenfold. The story of the internal party battle against the Bolshevik old guard bears no resemblance whatsoever to the myth of a united 'monolithic' party. Until Lenin's return from exile, only a tiny left grouping in the Bolshevik Petrograd Conference of March 29, 1917 could see beyond the old 'bourgeois-democratic' perspective: 'The Russian Revolution can secure for the people of Russia a maximum of democratic liberties and social reforms only if it becomes the point of departure for the revolutionary movement of the Western European proletariat against their bourgeois governments.' They insisted on the need to prepare for a struggle against the Provisional Government and the formation of a Workers' Red Guard to conduct this struggle, with the Soviets as 'the embryo of revolutionary power'. The conference defeated this resolution overwhelmingly, against Stalin's affirmation that the Provisional Government 'has in fact assumed the role of consolidator of the conquests of the revolutionary people'. Contrast Lenin: 'Our tactics, no trust in and no support of the new government.' Two days earlier he had declared categorically that the Provisional Government 'has wrested power from the proletariat' and 'represents the class of capitalist landlords and bourgeoisie'.

Lenin began to draft his 'April Theses' on 17 March. He wrote of the necessity of establishing in Russia 'a workers' government that relies, first, on the overwhelming majority of the peasant population ... and, second, on an alliance with the revolutionary workers of all countries in the war ... The revolutionary proletariat can only regard the revolution of 1 March as its initial, and by no means complete, victory.' The working class must 'fight for a democratic republic and socialism'.

Perhaps most significant for the purposes of our present inquiry is Sukhanov's reference to Lenin at this time considering 'systematic work on a party of a *new* type'. It was indeed that systematic work that he set about doing on his return. It meant a head-on collision with the old guard, the 'old Bolshevism', as he called it. Sukhanov writes of Lenin's 'complete intellectual isolation, not only among Social-Democrats in general but also among his own disciples'. Lenin won his battle only after a whole series of meetings and conferences, and it was a matter of only a few days before the October uprising that he won over the majority to his position. In the course of the struggle, Kamenev and the old leadership repeatedly reaffirmed, explicitly and publicly, against Lenin: 'As for Lenin's general schema it seems to us unacceptable, insofar as it proceeds from the assumption that the bourgeois-democratic revolution is finished and counts on the immediate conversion of the revolution into a socialist revolution.'[13]

The Petrograd Committee of the Bolsheviks rejected Lenin's Theses by 13 votes to 2 on 8 April. One week later, Lenin won the day at the April Conference, notwithstanding Kamenev's amendment attacking the 'disorganising consequences' of the slogan 'Down with the Provisional Government!'[16] Lenin was proceeding in the firm conviction that 'old Bolshevism' must be discarded, attacking those 'old Bolsheviks who more than once have played so regrettable a role in the history of our Party by reiterating formulas senselessly *learned by rote*'.

The Bolshevik Party which led the October Revolution was not the same party as had existed from 1902 to early 1917. That party, as we have seen, had needed to be turned inside out. At one point, Trotsky referred to the 'de-Bolshevising' of the Bolshevik Party in 1917. Marcel Liebman's comment on this perhaps serves as a fitting conclusion here:

> Later on, when anxious to present himself, in his struggle with Stalin, as an unconditional Leninist, and to take upon himself the whole heritage of the dead leader, Trotsky, yielding through tactical calculation or political weakness to the growing orthodoxy and the cult of Lenin, was to refrain from ever taking up again this thesis of the 'de-Bolshevised party'. And yet, although schematic, perhaps apologetical in purpose and certainly undialectical, this thesis of the 'de-Bolshevisation' of the Bolshevik Party as a result of the February revolution of 1917 and all through its most turbulent and most triumphant phase has much to be said for it. The contribution made by the past, by the dozen years that Lenin and his followers had devoted to building the Party, did not of course evaporate in 1917 – far from that. But if Bolshevism in its original form meant, above all, on the organisational plane, centralism, discipline and the 'Party spirit', then the formula of 'de-Bolshevisation', whatever its shortcomings, does indeed illuminate the process of genuine transformation that

> Lenin's Party underwent in the great revolutionary period opening with the fall of Tsardom in February 1917.[14]

Is there not an obvious parallel between Lenin's understanding and action over the need to go beyond the democratic revolution of February to proletarian revolution – against those forces which had usurped the victory won by the workers in February – and the problems faced by those workers who removed the rulers of Egypt, Tunisia, Southern Africa, only to find themselves still oppressed and exploited?

Yes, *but* ...

Lenin was able to act in the context of the world war and the expectation of imminent revolutionary struggles in Western Europe, and thus able to hope that the Russian workers would not be isolated. But what is the context of the development of international workers' struggles when the question arises of overthrowing those who have usurped the power in, for example, the 'Arab Spring' or Southern Africa? What are the prospects for NUMSA's declarations for working-class political independence, a break from the ANC, socialism – in Africa and internationally? How do we estimate the depth of the damage done to working-class internationalism by the decades of betrayal by Stalinism and social democracy, not to mention the mistakes of those of us who tried to make an alternative? How do we begin to overcome these obstacles? What is the objective basis for overcoming the problem? These are the questions before us – questions that include the not inconsiderable matters of overcoming the decimation of the working-class movement in Western Europe and North America and of the debris of Stalinist rule in the Soviet Union and China.

Trotsky and Trotskyism on 'party and class'

Leon Trotsky took up the principled fight against Stalinism and the reactionary idea of 'socialism in a single country', and was to pay with his life for doing so. His critique of Stalinist politics, in particular the subordination of the interests of the international working-class movement to those of the Stalinist bureaucracy, was an unequalled and historically vital struggle. It is essential for our struggles today, however, to question thoroughly his views and his practice on the question we are dealing with here, that is, the relation between the working class and the revolutionary party. Why?

The issues were clarified in the article – first published in Paris in the journal *Carré Rouge* – which follows. In it the socialist activist Janos Borovi, in commenting on work by the Russian historian and militant, Alexei Gusev, shows how the opening of Soviet archives after 1991 made possible politically highly relevant historical research.[15]

On the *Partiinost* of Yesterday and of Today

by Janos Borovi (translated and edited by Cliff Slaughter)

In an article [published in French in *Cahiers Leon Trotsky*] on the Left Opposition led by Trotsky [the Russian historian, Alexei Gusev concludes]:

> [In 1928] the Opposition's dogmatic clinging to *partiinost* (party spirit), its political *attentisme* (waiting to see what happened), its hope of reforms within the [Soviet Communist] Party, as well as its belief in the possibility of compromise with a section of the bureaucracy, these four factors prejudiced the development of a real struggle by the Opposition against the party-state. It had every chance of going that way if it had allied itself with the spontaneous working-class struggle. The Opposition suffered defeat, notwithstanding the fact that its

activity would go down in history as the ultimate attempt at organised political resistance to the advent of totalitarianism.

Gusev shares the view of one section of the Opposition in 1928 (the 'Sapronovists') who, having merged with the Opposition led by Trotsky, split from it at the end of the 1920s, because they did not share Trotsky's analysis of the nature of the Soviet regime, of the state, or of what remained of the Bolshevik Party. They considered that this state had already developed into a bureaucratic one, that it retained nothing of a working-class character, and that therefore a new party must be formed to prepare a social revolution. Against this, Trotsky and his supporters, the 'Bolshevik-Leninists', considered (a) that the forming of a new party would attract anti-Soviet elements, and (b) that it was possible to reform the Stalinist parties and the Third International (the Comintern). They held this position until the coming to power of Hitler and the Nazis in 1933. And for decades afterwards most Trotskyists, at least until the fall of Stalinism in 1989, were for the political (not social) revolution in the USSR and/or the Eastern European countries. They attributed a 'dual nature' to these states, states which were instruments of oppression of the working class, but at the same time instruments for the defence of the (of course imperfect and degenerating) 'conquests of October'...

The fact that only one tendency in Bolshevism survived and has been embodied in Trotskyism(s), does not by any means dictate that this tendency is (or was) right.

It is not a question of blaming anyone – that is not the problem – but of acknowledging that, in the face of Stalinism, the Trotskyists felt the need to close ranks, which led to a certain 'monolithism' concerning not only the disagreements that had existed in the communist movement before the victory of Stalinism, but also another profound problem, namely that of the nature of Stalinism (did Stalinism have only a single nature, i.e.

counter-revolutionary through and through, or did it have a 'dual nature', counter-revolutionary but also 'working-class', that is to say 'positive', because of its supposed links with the 'conquests of October in the East and with the working class in the West?'). This debate was there already while Trotsky was still alive, and is far from over. We shall see its political implications in the context of today's tasks.

Here it is useful to reflect on some new historical elements introduced by Gusev in his study. With documentary evidence, he shows that in 1927–28 the Left Opposition had relatively wide support in the working class, where many workers saw it as an alternative to the Stalinists; however, the Opposition, because of its analysis of the extent of the degeneration of the Bolshevik Party at the time, did not want to go beyond certain limits.

The decision to do no propaganda work among non-Party members, who were nonetheless the majority in the working class, inevitably gave the propaganda of the Bolshevik-Leninists a highly abstract character. They regarded the non-Party workers as having the role of merely providing pressure to improve the situation within the Party.

When working-class discontent mounted, the Bolshevik-Leninists rejected 'political strikes' because, they said, they harmed the 'workers' government'. Gusev cites the case of one of the big factories in Krementchoug, Ukraine, where, during a dispute arising from a cut in wages in the spring of 1928, an Oppositionist informed Sosnovsky (one of the leaders of the Opposition):

> As a result, numerous unhealthy things happened. For example, in campaigns against the Opposition, the rumour was circulated that it was working to organise a parallel political second party, and the workers replied: 'If they do organise one, and it becomes clear that it defends the working class, then it will not be us who are sorry.'

And Gusev concludes:

> The deliberate and conscious self-isolation of the Bolshevik-Leninists, which cut them off from large sections of the population, was to become one of the principal reasons for the relative facility with which the Stalinist organs of repression succeeded in wiping it out.

Gusev's analysis may appear shocking to Trotskyists. However, what it does is complete the 'classical' Trotskyist explanations, i.e. the defeat and crushing of the Opposition were due to the falling back of the world revolution; the isolation of Soviet Russia, backward and exhausted by the Civil War; the demoralisation and demobilisation of the working class; loss of the best fighters; and so on. Certainly these objective and subjective reasons did exist, and Gusev's analysis does not contradict them, only relativises them. On the basis of hitherto-unknown historical elements, he emphasises the point at which the Opposition became self-limited in its relations with the working class, the point at which it did not sufficiently base itself on the struggles of the workers in its battle against the rising Stalinist bureaucracy.

In underlining one of the aspects, relatively unknown, of the Opposition's struggle, it is out of the question to underestimate that struggle. If men of the stature of Trotsky and Rakovsky – such as whom we cruelly lack today for the renewal of revolutionary Marxism – could underestimate, in 1928 when Stalinism was emerging, what this historically unique monstrosity was to become, who can blame them? We need to be duly modest before those millions of men and women who paid with their lives for their heroic fight against Stalinism. But for them we would not be here today.

But is there any better way to pay homage to them than to draw lessons from their history in order to understand our own epoch and to better define what it means today to be a revolutionary communist? Are the difficulties for Trotskyists today, in trying to aid the attempts at self-determination by workers and youth, not due to a restricted view of our traditions, to a reduction, a one-sided vision of Bolshevism, an approach that prioritises 'building the party', opposed to or at best alongside the interests of developing the autonomous movements of the class?

After the fall of Stalinism in 1989 some people entertained the illusion that the path was now clear, that workers and Trotskyists would come together spontaneously in a joyous and historic reunion. Had not the Fourth International's Programme foreseen that 'the conquests of October lived in the consciousness of the masses'? And that the crisis of humanity is reduced to the crisis of revolutionary leadership? Consequently, it was enough to construct/reconstruct the Fourth International and so the road to socialism was laid out. And so 'we' (at that time the present writer was one) 'represented' the historical continuity of the Bolshevism of Lenin and Trotsky against Stalinism; we, the vanguard, would be recognised by millions of workers as their 'leading party' in a spontaneous, automatic and inevitable process ...

It is true enough, as people say, that 'it was not socialism that failed (in the Soviet Union) but a caricature of it', but all the same it is difficult to be comfortable with this form of words. It convinces nobody, and it allows one to avoid embarrassing questions like what does it mean to be political today? What kind of socialism do we want? What relation does it have to the workers' own, spontaneous movement? How does it relate to the 'socialist' past, littered as it is with millions of people dead, and billions of tonnes of steel produced (supposedly having proved the 'superiority of really existing socialism to capitalism')? We know where that came from – from a 'socialism' based on statisation of the means of production and on a savage anti-working-class dictatorship. This police regime was the negation of the road to true socialism, which can be opened only by socialisation of the means of production, by a regime where the producers direct and decide everything. The fact is that along with Trotsky we believed that in the Soviet Union and Eastern Europe, despite the Stalinist police dictatorship, we had a solid base for a socialist renewal.

Whether Trotsky was right or wrong on this question is certainly important. But what really must be discussed is why, in the year 2000, Marxist revolutionaries have not managed to go beyond the perspective of 'Bolshevism versus Stalinism', which was justified, with whatever reservations, in the past, but once Stalinism disappeared, became meaningless.

Where are the resources for the socialist alternative?

Let us try to break from that Manichean view of history which has so poisoned our past: 'All are traitors ... except for my own sect, the only ones who understand and know, etc.' It seems to me that, very simply (ah, if only it were so simple!), the problem is the difficulty of getting away from the alternative 'Bolshevism or Stalinism' in general or, to be more precise, from one variety of Bolshevism as it was defined in a particular situation by Trotsky and which forms part of Trotskyists' heritage. In reality the question is not what is Bolshevism; are all Bolshevisms good or bad; which is the 'good' Lenin, the Lenin of *What is to be Done?* or the Lenin of *State and Revolution*; or whatever: but to define what is the relation between the building of one's group or party and the self-emancipation movement of the masses. What is the meaning today, after the collapse of Stalinism, of Marx's sentence in the Communist Manifesto: 'The emancipation of the working classes is the task of the workers themselves'? And if we start from this base, how do we, militants who call ourselves revolutionaries, make ourselves useful to the self-emancipation of the masses?

For the moment, the balance-sheet is not very encouraging. Certainly there have been a few electoral successes for Trotskyists, showing, no doubt, sympathy for their ideas, but in a situation where the electoral system, parliamentarism, is not only of little interest to but is actually rejected by the most oppressed and exploited workers, such successes must not be overestimated.

In the face of the capitalist offensive there has been a series of movements, resistance struggles of varying breadth, form and social composition, but all characterised by a profound desire for democracy, for control, for independence from governments left or right. In France, these have included the struggles of the '*sans-papiers*', of the teachers of Seine St. Denis, of high-school students and the unemployed.

In these important struggles of the post-Stalinist period, Trotskyist organisations have done very little to fill what should be their role, i.e. to spread these struggles as independent movements, bringing every assistance possible from their own resources and experience. Rather, they have kept their distance from these movements, or they have participated in them but tried to channel them towards the political and trade-union bureaucratic machines. Let us take two of the most typical examples. Firstly, Lutte Ouvrière, for whom all of these struggles are never 'good' because they do not fit in with the schema of a supposed 'general demoralisation of the working class'. Consequently they are never 'working-class' enough, always too 'petty bourgeois', and so, waiting for the great day, the Lutte Ouvrière leadership preaches abstention. Secondly, the Ligue Communiste Revolutionnaire: typically, it played the student union leadership's card when the students tried to self-organise and enlarge their movement. One could write at length on Lutte Ouvrière's role in the struggles of high-school students and *sans-papiers*.

This situation is worth discussion, because it is not merely a matter of a few mistakes but rather of an attitude, a general approach of mistrust of anything not mapped out beforehand, anything not resulting in 'building the party', a narrow, mechanical, penny-pinching approach. An attitude which puts the building of the party far away from the real life of the oppressed and exploited, which gives the impression that a regroupment of revolutionary Marxists would be a collection of zombies or people suffering from delusions of divine guidance.

Do these 'post-Stalinist' struggles fit in with the schemas established by our predecessors? Certainly not, and that is not the fault of those engaged in the struggles. The world has changed, the bourgeoisie has reorganised, in order to attack the working class in the 'globalised' reality, and Stalinism, which presented itself in the name of the October Revolution, is no more. Today no revolutionary ideology or programme can presume to have the confidence of significant sectors of the proletariat, in France or anywhere else. In the face of the internationally organised bourgeoisie, there exists no meaningful international revolutionary resistance.

However, there have been autonomous struggles in France and to a lesser extent elsewhere. There was the 'divine surprise' of Seattle! It is in these struggles that revolutionary Marxists must find their place, from them that they must draw strength; it is there that they will find new allies for their ideas, but only if they break with a certain conception of '*partiinost*', of 'party spirit' badly understood, cold if not hostile to everything that calls into question those 'certainties' that their group represents, and at the same time (or because of that) complacent about the bureaucratic apparatuses. One can discuss Makhno, or Kronstadt. One can talk about our history. Was it necessary, as early as 1928, as maintained by Timofel Sapronov's Decemists (part of the Left Opposition), to base oneself entirely on the workers, against the party which ruled in their name, when opposition communists were already in the camps? But all that discussion is worthless unless we can draw political conclusions for our own day. Are we agreed that today in no case whatsoever must workers be fired on, even if their struggles appear to us opposed to what we, the organisation, the party, consider to be in the interests of the working class? Do we agree that the renewal of democratic socialism, its credibility as the alternative to capitalism, is impossible without participating, without assisting every attempt of workers to organise themselves? This would have to be true for movements starting from the base, but also, and this is not in contradiction, for those sparked by calls from above, from the political and trade-union bureaucracies.

Such support and assistance to self-organisation inevitably means a confrontation with those bureaucracies. Such a choice might sometimes perhaps be painful, because it means breaking from tactics trying to make bureaucrats 'turn to the left', to be 'the left of the left'. But the ideas of democratic socialism will not advance along any other path.

Let a hundred flowers bloom!

In October 1999, one hundred militants in France, men and women, launched an appeal entitled 'For a resolute alternative, for the development of our struggles, and for the independence of the social movement'. The appeal declares that there is 'a loss of legitimacy of political institutions, a crisis of democracy, a crisis of delegation of power, a crisis of the form and function of "party", all based on a crisis of society'. Who can argue with this? The signatories opened an interesting discussion, which they concluded by affirming the following:

> We, members of associations and trade unions, are convinced that from this social movement can emerge the elements of a new society, if it succeeds in bringing together into association

all its demands. It is by putting forward together all the alternative projects arising from the struggles that we really can drive back neoliberalism, the logic of capitalism, the world of 'profit before everything'.

If it is true that these movements have brought enormous riches, in the sense of the content and practice of democracy and of programmatic advances, it seems to me that the organisations, networks, parties – never mind the form, the name – have an indispensable role to play in the development and renewal of Marxism, of a programme for the exploited. For everyone there is a place; all means, all programmes, all experiences which help to take forward the struggle are good.

Unfortunately this appeal, with few exceptions, produced only skin-deep reactions from Lutte Ouvrière and the Ligue Communiste Revolutionnaire. Instead of seeing allies, with whom they could 'march separately, strike together', or better still march together while discussing fraternally, they cried: beware, the signatories represent no one but themselves, they are against political organisations!

We have posed, above, the loss of credibility of Trotskyist organisations among what are today called social movements. If it is true that the appeal bends the stick a little in one way, if it charges with too many tasks the emerging social movements, politicals like us should be happy that such an appeal was issued, must respond modestly, bringing our own contribution to the elaboration of a new project for a socialist society, and understanding that anyone who raises such questions is not an 'enemy', or one of those dreaded 'anarchists'.

The problem is to have an understanding of '*partiinost*', of 'party spirit', which is not (is no longer) sect spirit, but an opening towards the world as it now is. Not to abandon one's programme (rather, develop it), one's organisation, but to abandon the messianic spirit of 'the party which alone expresses the objective interests of the proletariat', to confront the problems and the unforeseen features of struggles. A comrade of *Voix des Travailleurs* has said that it is necessary to construct an organisation in the image of the society we desire. That is a profound thought. We shall have to show that the programme and the methods of democratic socialism, our objective, serve the everyday struggles of the present. We must be not offering 'a free shave tomorrow', but make ourselves useful.

A Critique of Some Past Guidelines (cont.)

by Cliff Slaughter

Trotsky and Trotskyism: the 'Transitional Programme'

Borovi's article – quoted extensively above in my translation – leads me to the following thoughts.

It was 1933 before Trotsky came round to the view of Sapronov and the Group of Democratic Centralism ('Decemists') that Stalin's Communist Party was in every sense an enemy of the working class, that to dream of working to reform it was a fatal error, and that a new proletarian party was necessary. Trotsky now set out to go beyond 'left opposition' and prepared to found a new, Fourth, International.

The stages through which Trotsky's change of orientation developed can best be seen in Jean van Heijenoort's invaluable memoir, *Sept Ans Auprès de Leon Trotsky* (translated as *With Trotsky in Exile*). Until the coming-to-power of Hitler, his orientation did not change:

> [E]ven after he was expelled from Russia by Stalin in 1929, his goal was still to put the Communist International back on the revolutionary track, not to create a rival organization. Though formally expelled from the ranks of the official organization,

> the [Trotskyists] considered themselves as forming an opposition ... which for a time was outside but would some day find its place again within the ranks of the Communist International. 'Our ideas will become your ideas and will express themselves in the programme of the Communist International', Trotsky ... once [wrote].[16]

Only when Hitler came to power in 1933 did Trotsky's orientation begin to change. On 2 March, in an interview reported by Van Heijenoort, he said: 'I am convinced that, if Hitler remains in office in Germany and if the Communist Party fails, it will be necessary to build a new party. But the most important elements constituting this new party will come from the old one.' Van Heijenoort wrote:

> Yet this view still related to a hypothetical situation. After the catastrophe of March 5, Trotsky in the March 14 article rejected as out-of-date [finished, *perimé*] the policy of reforming the German Communist Party, but he clung to the policy of reform for the other parties of the Communist International, in particular for the Russian party. However, the problem of the International as a whole could not fail to be raised. In April, the Executive Committee of the Communist International unanimously adopted a resolution proclaiming that the policy of non-cooperation with the Socialists followed by the German Communist party 'had been entirely correct up to and including Hitler's coup d'état.' ... There were isolated reactions, here and there, in the ranks of the Communist parties, but as an organization, the Communist International was in Stalin's grip. The policy of reform [had lost its *raison d'être*].[17]

On 15 July 1933 Trotsky, under the pseudonym G. Gurov, addressed to the Trotskyist groups an article entitled 'It Is

Necessary to Build Anew Communist Parties and a Communist International'. In it, wrote van Heijenoort, 'the policy of reform was abandoned with respect to all communist organizations dominated by Stalin. This policy, explained the article, had now become "utopian and reactionary".'[18]

The new perspective was discussed on 27 July by a meeting of all those in the Trotsky entourage at Saint-Palais, south-west France, where he found refuge before leaving for Mexico. Van Heijenoort's account, again, is interesting:

> Some remarks made by Trotsky ... reveal the political climate of those days: 'There is the secondary and subordinate question of a name. Fourth International? It is not very pleasant. When we broke with the Second International, we changed our theoretical foundations. Now, no; we remain based on the first four congresses [of the Communist International]. We could also proclaim: the Communist International is us! And call ourselves the Communist International (Bolshevik-Leninists). There are pros and cons. The title of Fourth International is neater. There may be an advantage as far as the [great] masses are concerned. For the slower selection of cadres, there is probably some advantage ... in being called the Communist International (Bolshevik-Leninists) ...' [Note the] hesitation ... in these words through which Trotsky went in passing from the policy of reform to that of a new International. But his doubts did not last long. Although the new organisation had to remain far from the '[great] masses', and to concern itself with the 'slower selection of cadres', he soon adopted the name of Fourth International.[19]

At this point, it is necessary to pose the question: did the 1933 abandonment of the policy of reform of the communist parties and the Communist International bring a correction of the ill-fated *partiinost* of the late 1920s? The answer is 'No'. As he moved to the founding conference of the Fourth International, Trotsky elaborated his 'Transitional Programme'. This was entitled *The Death Agony of Capitalism and the Tasks of the Fourth International* (1938). Starting from the premise that capitalism was in decay and the productive forces stagnating, he asserted that the objective conditions were ripe for socialism.[20]

From this foundation, he concluded, and wrote in the 'Transitional Programme' that 'the crisis of humanity is reduced to the crisis of working-class revolutionary leadership'. This was henceforth to be the basic principle of the Trotskyist movement, and it remains so for the existing Trotskyist groups and parties. Essentially, their activity has been and is concentrated on 'building the party', in many cases seeing this recruitment as the main aim of any political work they do. This attitude, and the party regime it creates, has never built parties of any size or lasting significance, and nearly a century of 'reconstructing the Fourth International' has produced nothing, and will not. There are very good reasons for this.

In the first place, the basic ideas behind Trotsky's 'Transitional Programme' can be seen, especially with the benefit of hindsight, to have been mistaken. (I leave aside for the moment the second reason – that there have been social changes which bring into question any notion of political leadership from above, by some kind of centralised leadership.)

Clearly the historical, structural crisis (economic, political, ecological) of the capital system in the twenty-first century is giving rise and will continue to give rise to massive struggles. In those struggles there will emerge leaderships with the far-sightedness to clarify the line of march, the next steps and the necessity of combining with other struggles for the necessary offensive against the capital system as such. But such is the depth and universality of the system's structural crisis that it cannot be 'reduced' to the need to resolve the 'crisis of leadership'.

It might be argued that in 1938, when Trotsky wrote the Transitional Programme, the 'crisis of the revolutionary leadership' thesis was correct. That argument does not stand up when we consider the way Trotsky understood the objective situation then. Thus: 'The economy, the state, the politics of the bourgeoisie and its international relations are completely blighted by a social crisis ...' So far, so good. But the sentence continues '[a social crisis] characteristic of a pre-revolutionary state of society'. The next section of the *Programme* repeats this evaluation: 'The strategic task of the next period – a pre-revolutionary period of agitation, propaganda and organisation – consists in overcoming the contradiction between the maturity of the objective revolutionary conditions and the immaturity of the proletariat and its vanguard ...'

'Pre-revolutionary situation'? 'Maturity of the objective revolutionary conditions'? Within a year of the 'Transitional Programme' being adopted by the Fourth International, Europe was engulfed in World War Two. This war was certainly a manifestation of the crisis of the system, but the 'objective conditions' resulted in war, not in a revolutionary or even pre-revolutionary situation. Trotsky had concentrated absolutely correctly on the responsibility of Stalinism for the defeats of the working class in Germany, Britain, China and Spain in the 1920s and 1930s. But he surely underestimated completely the strength derived by capitalism from those defeats as well as the demoralisation, disorganisation and in some cases decimation of the working class as a result of the betrayals and defeats.

It was on the basis of this wrong perspective that Trotsky, in the 'Transitional Programme', persisted in that outlook which in 1928, as we have seen, gave predominance to the state of 'the party' rather than the condition and movement of the working class. Hence, again the Programme: 'As time goes on their [the Stalinists' and Social-Democrats'] efforts to hold back the wheel of history will demonstrate more clearly to the masses that *the crisis of the proletarian leadership, having become the crisis in mankind's culture, can be resolved only by the Fourth International.'* [Emphasis added.]

For three-quarters of a century Trotskyist groups have persisted in putting in front of every other consideration their supposed mission of 'constructing the alternative leadership', 'constructing/reconstructing the Fourth International', and 'building the party'. On the few occasions when Trotskyists were able to win influence and members, they squandered these gains by treating them solely as gains for their 'party-building'. There were two important examples in the history of the Socialist Labour League (SLL)/ Workers Revolutionary Party (WRP) in Britain. Work in the Labour Party (the famous 'entry tactic') made it possible to win the leadership of its youth section, the Young Socialists. When the inevitable crackdown came from the Labour Party bureaucracy in 1964, the Young Socialists and their newspaper *Keep Left* became independent, with SLL leadership. Soon it was possible to hold a Young Socialists (YS) rally in London with some 4,000 youth attending, and there were branches all over the country. Very soon all momentum was lost, because of the concentration on 'building party branches' and taking on young people as full-time party workers, 'professional revolutionaries'. The YS disappeared.

In the 1984–85 miners' strike, the WRP found itself with only a tiny handful of its members in the National Union of Mineworkers. I spoke about the history behind this in 2012 at a conference of former WRP members and others to discuss revolutionary working-class 'agency'.[21]

> The strike of Spanish miners brings to mind a lesson from the practice of the SLL and WRP. We could have had a very different and more positive part in the British miners' strike in the 1980s but for what was a very mistaken perspective some

years earlier. Jim Allen led a group of miners at Middleton colliery in Lancashire, with support from Ron Thompson in Wigan and others, to found a paper, *The Miner*. This paper, carrying news about mining communities and about the NUM, and confronting head-on the National Coal Board management and the NUM bureaucracy, became very popular in Lancashire and Yorkshire as well as other coalfields. It was not a 'party' paper but a paper which reflected and engaged with the real-life struggles and the consciousness of miners, and it changed the consciousness of many.

Comrades in Yorkshire, for example, led by Albert Field, sold the paper at pitheads, often selling over 100 at a single pit. It was possible through this work to establish miners' branches of the SLL and to bring together some of the best militants in the coalfield. From being individual militants in their own collieries, they were able to come together as a force to oppose the right wing and the Stalinists in the area.

What happened to this work? Why was it not built up into a force which by 1985 could have been of great value in the miners' strike? The explanation is that Gerry Healy (WRP Secretary) decided, against all advice, that *The Miner* was a rival to the party's daily paper, and that party members must sell that daily paper and not *The Miner*. Given 'democratic centralism', those of us who disagreed accepted the 'majority decision'.

I give this as one example of a notion of 'building the party' which was wrong and at the heart of the Trotskyist movement (indeed, the work with *The Miner* did build the party, and the decision to abandon it severely weakened the party). There was too much of 'building a party *for* the working class', rather than 'building a party *of* the working class'.

In this light, and at the expense of being denounced as a revisionist, I think we need a harsh critical look at the founding document of the Fourth International, Trotsky's

> 'Transitional Programme'. This was written in the belief that there existed a 'pre-revolutionary situation'. This idea was nowhere near as stupid as Healy's crass declaration that we must change the name of the SLL to Workers Revolutionary Party in the 1970s because we were in a 'revolutionary situation', but all the same it was not valid. The fascist victory in Spain sealed a period of defeats, of counter-revolution (including the suppression of the Left Opposition and all other threats to the regime in the Soviet Union).
>
> The central proposition of the 'Transitional Programme' was that 'the crisis of humanity is reduced to the crisis of revolutionary leadership'. This 'reduction' was the rationale for a practice concentrated entirely on 'building the alternative leadership', the Fourth International, which would be able to bring revolutionary consciousness to a working class driven into action by the conditions of the 'pre-revolutionary situation'. Even if the central place given to 'crisis of revolutionary leadership' had been right in 1938, it would certainly not be right today. What is at issue is the rebuilding (I would today say 'reconstitution') of the working-class movement itself (a self-movement of the working class, in which communists make their own contribution), and not, as some of us used to think, the rebuilding of the Fourth International.

Was 'the crisis of humanity reduced to the crisis of working-class revolutionary leadership'? Was it true that 'the crisis in human culture is the crisis in the proletarian leadership'? What is the heritage of Trotskyism and Trotsky?

It must never be forgotten that Trotskyism's struggle against Stalinism and the understanding of its wholly counter-revolutionary nature was unique, unequalled. But look again at the 'Transitional Programme', beginning with its title, *The Death Agony of Capitalism*, a death agony shown by the fact that 'mankind's productive forces stagnate'. The 1930s was the decade of the Great Depression, but even if then, the formula 'stagnation of the productive forces' could carry some weight, that cannot be said of the 75 years up to our own day. The productive forces have developed at an unprecedented rate, no matter how you define 'productive forces'.

A workers' state?

According to the 'Transitional Programme', the Soviet Union was a 'degenerated workers' state'. This was plain wrong. The state is an instrument of the oppression of one class by another. The working class in the Soviet Union was brutally oppressed by the state machine. It was an oppression carried out by the counter-revolutionary Stalinist bureaucracy. In the interests of what class? The answer: the capitalist class everywhere in the world. According to Trotsky, the Soviet Union was a 'transitional' state, in transition to socialism on the basis of state ownership of the means of production, but in danger of a restoration of capitalism if the working class did not make a 'political revolution' to overthrow the Stalinist bureaucracy.

The Stalinist state was at war with the working class, brutally suppressing any questioning of the state's role and power. It inflicted mass murder to remove any obstruction or opposition to the creation of an industrial infrastructure and a rigidly disciplined working class. These formed the necessary basis for a fully-fledged capitalism when the Soviet Union collapsed in 1989. The existence of a dispossessed and disciplined working class has been the essential prerequisite of every capitalist regime since the end of the Middle Ages. The historical perspective now possible indicates clearly that in the twentieth century it was only on the basis of a revolution/counter-revolution that a backward country like Russia could create those preconditions for a capitalism of the modern age. Yes, the Soviet Union was a 'transitional' state, a state of an original type – transitional to capitalism on the foundations laid by a proletarian revolution in a backward country. If further proof were needed, it was provided by China, Mao and the 'Cultural Revolution'.

The same internally contradictory characterisation of the Soviet state was carried into the post-war years when the Eastern European countries under Stalinist rule were christened 'deformed workers' states'. The *Communist Manifesto* was surely clear enough as a judgment on that definition: 'Political power, properly so called, is merely the organised power of one class for oppressing another'.

A fitting conclusion here, showing the connection between the '*partiinost*' problem and that of the so-called workers' state, was provided by Victor Serge, writing about the position of Oppositionists in 1928:

> As for the idea that the bureaucratic counter-revolution had attained power, and that a new despotic state had emerged from our own hands to crush us, and reduce the country to absolute silence – nobody, nobody in our ranks was willing to admit it. From the depths of his exile in Alma Ata Trotsky affirmed that this system was still ours, still proletarian, still socialist, even though sick: the party that was excommunicating, imprisoning, and beginning to murder us, remained our party, and we still owed everything to it; we must live only for it, since only through it could we serve the revolution. *We were defeated by party patriotism: it both provoked us to rebel and turned us against ourselves.*[22] [Emphasis added.]

In this twenty-first century context, we should find a real and revolutionary relevance in the words of the young Marx:

> ... a class is called forth which has to bear all the burdens of society without enjoying any of its advantages, which is ousted from society and forced into the sharpest contra-

> diction to all other classes; a class which forms the majority of all members of society and from which emanates the consciousness of a fundamental revolution, the communist consciousness which may, of course, arise among the other classes, through the contemplation of the situation of this class.[23]

We should prepare to be seeing the birth-pangs of that elusive thing that Marx called 'mass communist consciousness', the essential condition for success of the social revolution. As we shall see, the consciousness here referred to by Marx is not a set of ideas in this or that person's head, or in many heads, but a *practical consciousness.*

> Both for the production on a world scale of this communist mass consciousness, and for the success of the cause itself, the alteration of men on a mass scale is necessary, an alteration which can only take place in a practical movement, a revolution, not only because the ruling class cannot be overthrown in any other way, but also because the class overthrowing it can only in a revolution succeed in ridding itself of all the muck of ages and become fitted to found society anew.[24]

Once again on the 'Transitional Programme': dangerous illusions

Returning to the 'Transitional Programme': putting party and the crisis of leadership before class brought with it another more than doubtful heritage to the Trotskyist movement. Recalling the months between the 1917 February and October revolutions in Russia, Trotsky wrote:

> The chief accusation which the Fourth International advances

> against the traditional organisations of the proletariat is that they do not wish to tear themselves away from the political semi-corpse of the bourgeoisie. Under these conditions the demand systematically addressed to the old leadership: 'Break with the bourgeoisie, take the power!' is an extremely important weapon for exposing the treacherous character of the parties of the Second, Third and Amsterdam Internationals.

No one today could give credibility to posing the existing social-democratic and 'left' parties with the demand 'break with the bourgeoisie', but was it realistic in 1938? And could it do more than create illusions? In 1917 the Russian working class was organised and acting in a revolutionary way, with the Petrograd Soviet and, very soon, Trotsky at its head. The situation in 1938 (as we have already seen, above) was very, very different, and corresponded in no way to Trotsky's notion of it as a 'pre-revolutionary situation'.

Two paragraphs later in the Transitional Programme, we have this poisoned chalice in a slightly different form: 'However, we cannot categorically deny in advance the theoretical possibility that, under the influence of completely exceptional circumstances (war, defeat, financial crash, mass revolutionary pressure, etc), the petty-bourgeois parties including the Stalinists may go further than they wish along the road to a break with the bourgeoisie'. Certainly Trotsky immediately remarked that such a turn is 'highly improbable', but the plain fact is that it was impossible, and that in every case in the following years those parties came to the rescue of the capitalist class. And when, under the terms of Stalin's, Churchill's and Roosevelt's carve-up of post-war Europe, the Eastern European states came under Russian domination, with Stalinist parties in office, the Trotskyist movement characterised them as 'deformed workers' states'. In reality they were, like the Soviet 'degenerated workers' state', in no sense workers' states but police states for the oppression of the working class. Even the brutal crushing of the Hungarian workers' revolution in 1956 by the Red Army was not enough to open the eyes of those who attributed to the Stalinist state a 'dual nature'.

The central meaning of all the examples we have cited, and of the critique we have attempted of some traditional theories and programmes dealing with the relation between the working class and a revolutionary party, is that there is an urgent need to reassert the fundamental truth that '*the emancipation of the working class is the task of the working class itself*'.

PART V

The Theoretical Foundations

by Cliff Slaughter

The reality of social relations ... and sociology's myths

The aim of *Against Capital* is to contribute to the process of clearing the path towards a better understanding of the tasks facing the many movements of resistance and protest arising from the structural crisis of the capital system. In preceding chapters we have concentrated on the need for a thoroughgoing critique of some revolutionary programmes and methods of the past. I turn now to the way in which millions of young people in every country are taught in universities and colleges something called 'social sciences', sociology, etc. What follows aims to pose the Marxist alternative to the way in which these teachings conceal and distort the reality of the social system that we all seek to change fundamentally.

University sociology courses will offer, for example, 'sociology of the family', 'sociology of knowledge', 'sociology of deviance', 'urban sociology', 'rural sociology', indeed sociology of just about anything. The description and analysis in each of these is essentially no more than a mapping of the existing state of affairs in that sphere. With few exceptions (including the recently formed left and Marxist sociology groups in the United States), the underlying theories behind this kind of work are of two types, with in some cases an attempted combination of the two. Functionalism, inherited from Emile Durkheim and his 'social facts', sees the essential meaning of any social phenomenon, mode of behaviour, etc. as the function it has in maintaining the given social system or culture as a whole. The conservative and unhistorical implications are clear.

More prominent in sociology is the 'social action' theory initiated by Max Weber. For Weber and Weberians, 'social action' is the content of social processes and systems. It is defined by Weber as 'action to which the actor attaches meaning'. But it is clear that there are results of social processes, results of the actions of human beings which are unforeseen and unintended by anyone, and often the opposite of the meaning people attached to what they did. The causes of such unintended results obviously must be sought at a different level entirely from that of the intentions of the actors. Even more importantly, no doubt many, many workers see their working activity as virtually meaningless, yet the character of their work as wage-labour exploited by capital has real meaning: it is actually the basic *cause* to the whole social system.

There is no way that knowledge of this essential character of the system could be arrived at by proceeding from 'the meaning attached to their action by the actors'. In this way, sociology based on Weber's theoretical standpoint cannot but obscure the reality of society. For example, Weber's celebrated theory of bureaucracy as a manifestation of social action proceeding on the basis of 'formal rationality' conceals and is an apologetic for the oppressive class nature of state power: the economic base that structures capitalist society and its state is in essence not 'rational' but irrational. In Weber's theoretical system it must be any opposition to or attempt to overcome capitalism that is irrational (or, as Weber puts it, founded on 'emotionalism'). As for an explanation of why the state is necessary, what its relation is to the classes of societies based on exploitation, or why the organs of the state must resort to violence in maintenance of the social order, we have only Weber's matter-of-fact truism that the state has 'a monopoly of violence' and that it is essentially a matter of formulated law, the product of Western jurists. Indeed, Weber's system seems to be bidding to outdo Durkheim and functionalism in its conservative apologetics.

Such conservatism is equally characteristic of the much-taught Talcott Parsons and his 'universally valid'(!) *General Theory*, which injects his 'structural-functionalism' with a pragmatic smattering of Max Weber's 'social action'. Parsons claims that his theory is a summation of what is valid in the basic methodological and theoretical concepts of the disciplines of sociology and economics, and he is right in the sense that what he systematises is the essential conservatism and anti-historicism of both. Parsons typifies what Marx called 'the outlook of political economy', in that he accepts the capitalist social order as corresponding to an unalterable necessity. Thus, 'there must be a property system which regulates claims to transferable entities, material or immaterial, and thereby secures rights in means of life in the facilities which are necessary for the performance of functions'. It would be impossible to invent a more thorough-going apologetics for the existing social order – what we have 'must be'.

In terms of basic theory, social anthropology has for decades been stagnating in the same straitjacket as sociology: functionalism, deriving from Bronislaw Malinowski, was succeeded, especially in Britain, by the 'structuralism' stemming from Alfred Radcliffe-Brown and later from the idealist version introduced by Claude Levi-Strauss. Just as Parsons' 'structural-functionalism' failed to overcome this duality, so did social anthropology, despite more recent attempts to adapt the methods of Michel Foucault and others. Malinowski and all 'cultural anthropologists' are trapped in an anti-historicism, concentrating, like Parsons, on the stable functioning of a given social system. There is no room for contradictions or processes of system-change. The structuralist anthropologists, on the other hand, concentrate on social relationships ('role and status', etc.: in most cases, kinship and descent rules), paying little or no attention to the processes of production and social and cultural reproduction that go on in the framework of kin relations. For them, the function of every activity is its contribution to the maintenance of the social structure. They proceed as if there can be structure without a history – past, future and *present*. And, as in Parsons' system, if this appears to be circular, that appearance is not deceptive. Thus, the 'structure' is the framework and necessary starting condition of every social activity, and the 'function' of each such activity is to sustain and preserve the structure ... and so presumably we should all 'know our place'. Parsons writes

> [It is] possible to isolate specific and manageable action processes for intensive dynamic study. Such processes, that is, are treated as action in relation to institutionalised roles, in terms of balances of conformity with and deviation from the expectations of the socially sanctioned role definitions, of conflicting role expectations impinging on the individual, and the constellations of motivational forces and mechanisms involved in such balances and conflicts.[1]

And so on, *ad nauseam*.

As István Mészáros has written:

> [This] theoretical obfuscation [is] profoundly *anti*-historical, with its ultimate obliteration of the actually existing structural determinations of capital's social-metabolic order ... The fundamental ideological purpose of this theory is the eternalisation of the capital system in a fetishistically camouflaged way, travestied in the form of complicated typologies and schematisms depicting invented structures and disembodied functions. But the barefaced character of these 'grand theories' is revealed from time to time either directly, as we have seen above in the *explicit denial* of class conflict and capitalist exploitation by Talcott Parsons in actually existing monopoly-capitalist society – or indirectly in his abstract formalist

> discourse on 'transferable entities' and 'facilities' required for the permanence of the strictly accommodatory 'performance of functions'. The established – *historically produced and historically changing* – social and economic order of the capital system completely disappears thereby from view, so that the danger of any *significant change in the future* should also disappear with it in an aprioristic and irretrievable fashion from the reader's horizon.[2]

There are sociologists who have thought to combine Marx's concepts with those of sociologists, and in particular of Max Weber. Such an attempt fails to recognise the diametrical opposition between the Marxist and the sociological world-views. In Marx, the starting-point is not 'structure' and 'function', but *mode of production*. Human society originated and has continued to exist and to develop because human beings *create their own unique mode of being*. No longer living only according to how nature had determined their instincts and ability to react to the environment, they applied their labour to the given natural resources, transforming elements of that environment into instruments and systems for producing the means of life. Every generation begins not simply from the natural world confronting it, but from the socially inherited means of production and the social relations hitherto necessary for their implementation.

The mode of production consists, one can say, of the basic social structure (relations of production, e.g. class relations of ownership and control) and the actual process of production and social reproduction (labour, application of the means of production, constituting the *forces of production*). The forms of social life built on this foundation consist of social processes, not fixed routines. The *forces of production* and the social relations of production are a *unity of opposites*. In every hitherto-existing type of social formation (for example, feudal system, capital system, etc.) contradictions between forces and relations of production have developed, until at a given stage the social relations become a barrier to the potential of the productive forces, and a new form of social system must be achieved, unless the society is to disintegrate under the weight of the contradictions (Marx writes of the necessary victory of a new class *or* 'the mutual ruin of the contending classes'). Only a return to this 'historical materialism', in which the necessity of humans' productive activity is the source of culture and of change, can overcome the inescapable dualism and conservatism of the 'social sciences'. This despite Parsons' ludicrous decision to treat Marx's ideas as part of the 'idealist', 'voluntarist' tradition in social thought.[3]

We have considered only the 'sociologies' which offered a general theory of society as a whole (functionalism, social action, etc.). They amounted to an attempted alternative to Marxism. In the late twentieth and twenty-first centuries such 'general theories' (including, of course, that of Marx) were discounted. 'Postmodernist' social theories explicitly deny the possibility of establishing the truth about social reality and of such pretended truth informing effective social practice: in the words of Jean Baudrillard, '[t]he secret of theory is that truth does not exist. You cannot confront it in any way.'[4] The great discovery of the postmodernist sociologists is that all 'grand narratives' must be abandoned and concentration must be on 'small narratives'. Among the 'grand theories' or 'grand narratives' that must be rejected, Jean-François Lyotard lumps together 'the dialectics of Spirit, the hermeneutics of meaning, the emancipation of the rational or working subject, or the creation of wealth'.[5] The 'basis' of all these, including explicitly 'the Marxist narrative of emancipation from exploitation and alienation through the socialisation of labour', 'has been invalidated over the last fifty years'. In this way, our postmodernists are certainly hardly less hostile to the possibility of any emancipatory enterprise than are the structural-functionalists and other 'grand theorists' in sociology.

Constructivism was a strong current in sociology in the last decades of the twentieth century. Here again, any attempt to establish objective truth is dismissed, on the grounds that knowledge is always a social construct rather than a reflection of objective reality.[6] Thus we can know only the meaning of anything as a construct of the thinking of socially conditioned individuals. 'Post-constructivism' attempts to correct this view by emphasising that any aspect of our understanding of social reality is always a mixture of constructed meanings and elements of an objective reality.

The systematic critique of these and similar social theories (or rather, anti-theories) is not the subject of our treatment here, since they are concerned only with the ways in which people are integrated into and conditioned by existing social formations, and with the possibility/impossibility of knowing the truth about social forms and their development, and thus providing no feasible 'guide to action'.

Fashionable in university courses in sociology and social anthropology is the work of Foucault. Although he is characterised as a type of constructivist, his writings have appealed to many socially concerned people because he considers the most important of all the socially conditioning influences on men and women to be that of 'power'. He has been able to show how social conformity, discipline and oppression are enforced not only by state power but also by power that exists as diffused in various institutions, practices, routines, and discourses. On this basis, Foucault was active and influential on radical and progressive issues. This is the case, despite the fact that 'using Foucault's methods' in sociology has meant no more than analysing how power functions in a given society and how it can be challenged (and even turned against established forms) rather than raising any questions about the contradictions in a society's formation/metabolism, its developmental tendencies, or the necessity and agency of social revolution. A thorough investigation of all these theories and anti-theories that succeeded structural-functionalism would be the subject of another book.

Marx

Marx does not begin from any such abstract notion as 'function' or 'meaning attached to action'. On the contrary, he looks for a new beginning, and finds it, concretely, at the point where humans themselves had to begin, and must constantly begin again every day. That is to say: no society can continue to live unless the means of life are produced; and the mode of this production, the starting point of social life, must be the starting point of the understanding of society. Change and development of the mode of production, its functioning and its structural imperatives, are the keys to the social system as a whole. Only when we begin to understand the contradictions and changes in this economic base can we know what the possibilities are of conscious action for fundamental change. Then we will be at the point where men and women, as Marx wrote in *A Contribution to the Critique of Political Economy*, 'become conscious of the contradictions and fight them out'. This can come about not by some mechanical, simple, direct determining of consciousness by the economic base. On that base is built a whole legal, political and ideological superstructure. The institutions of this superstructure, such as the state and the law, reinforce and maintain the economic structure and the rule of the classes that dominate it. Marx's *Capital*, said Engels, deals with 'the relations between capital and labour, the axis on which our entire present system of society turns'.[7]

The imperatives of the capitalist mode of production bring a relentless search for increased profit (surplus value) and this has brought constant and unprecedented development of mankind's productive forces. The capital system has reached the point at which these forces have outgrown the existing relations of production, the exploitation of wage-labour, of the working class, by capital. This is the fundamental contradiction underlying the crisis in every part of the superstructure, every aspect of social life, political, moral, ideological and economic.

It is from this standpoint that the pernicious role of the 'social sciences' like sociology, with their acceptance of the surface forms of social life, can be understood. Some may think that by starting from a 'sociology of work' or 'sociology of industrial relations' they are saying something similar to the ideas of Marx. However, if we look further into the nature of work, labour, we find that that is far from the truth.

Why does a person go to work? Not because he or she likes coalmining, or assembling small engine parts according to a computerised programme, or repeating the same message every three minutes from a call centre, or loading supermarket shelves, or cleaning tables, or keeping an eye on a robot, or ... Marx long ago provided the antidote to Weberian sociology's 'meaning attached by the actor' when he explained the character of the wage-labourer's work (work on which, it must be remembered, the whole social structure is based). Here a lengthy quotation is in order:

> But the putting of labour-power into action, i.e. work, is the active expression of the labourer's own life. And this life-activity he sells to another person in order to secure the necessary means of life. His life-activity, therefore, is but a means of securing his own existence. He works that he may keep alive. He does not count the labour itself as a part of his life, it is rather a sacrifice of his life. It is a commodity which he has auctioned off to another. The product of his activity, therefore, is not the aim of his activity. What he produces for himself is not the silk that he weaves, not the gold that he draws up the mining shaft, not the palace that he builds. What he produces for himself is *wages*, and silk, gold, and

> palace are resolved for him into a certain quantity of necessaries of life, perhaps into a cotton jacket, into copper coins, and into a basement dwelling. And the labourer who for twelve hours long weaves, spins, bores, turns, builds, shovels, breaks stones, carries hods and so on – is the twelve hours' weaving, spinning, boring, turning, building, shovelling, stone-breaking regarded by him as a manifestation of life, as life? Quite the contrary. Life begins for him when this activity ceases, at the table, at the tavern seat, in bed. The twelve hours' work, on the other hand, has no meaning for him as weaving, spinning, boring, and so on, but only as earnings, which enable him to sit down at the table, to take his seat in the tavern, and to lie down in a bed. If the silkworm's object in spinning were to produce its existence as a caterpillar, it would be a perfect example of a wage-worker.[8]

'Everyone knows' that we go to work because we have no other access to the means of life except the money paid to us in wages. Why do we have no access? For the obvious (unquestioned) reason that all means of production of the necessities of life are concentrated in the hands of the class of employers. For sociology ('sociology of work' included) the worker's non-possession of the means of production is taken to be one of 'the facts of life'. In reality it is the historical product of the violent expropriation of those means (especially the land) at the initial stage of the capitalist mode of production. It is the result of theft.

Whatever the many and varied types of work, those who work have this in common: they have no material means of production; their labour-power is a commodity, which has to be sold if they are to live. They thus constitute a *class*. In this relationship between the structural antagonists capital and labour there is a fundamental inhumanity. In what way? Here we return to Marx – in chapter 7 of the first volume of *Capital*:

> We presuppose labour in a form that stamps it as exclusively human. A spider conducts operations that resemble those of a weaver, and a bee puts to shame many an architect in the construction of her cells. But what distinguishes the worst architect from the best of bees is this, that the architect raises his structure in imagination before he erects it in reality. At the end of every labour-process, we get a result that already existed in the imagination of the labourer at its commencement.[9]

At this point we need to confront the most original and at the same time most difficult part of Marx's analysis in his *Capital*: the distinction between 'concrete' and 'abstract' labour.

The labour that Marx writes about when he compares human labour to that of the spider is the basic distinguishing character of humans: what Engels, in *Anti-Dűhring*, refers to as our 'productive labour, this natural condition of human existence'. In capitalist society, the labourer has of course no such creative, direct relation to his work and his product, whereas production in earlier societies is a direct and transparent expression of the social organism. In a patriarchal peasant economy, production is the direct expression of the family organisation with its natural division of labour. In early societies, where kinship and descent form the social structure, 'individual labour appears as a direct function of a member of the social organism', and 'the communal system on which this mode of production is based ... causes individual labour to appear as the direct function of a member of the social organisation'. In society ruled by capital the social relations are entirely different: money is 'the effective bond of society'.[10]

We therefore cannot understand the labour of individuals and the nature of social relations in today's society ruled by capital in the same way as in earlier social formations. The productive labour of individuals is not an expression of their social relationship with other individuals and their place in the division of labour. The social relations are mediated through the market, a market in which their own labour power is itself a commodity (see below). And is it true now that 'at the end of every labour-process there is a result that already existed in the imagination of the labourer at its commencement'? For one thing, it is obvious that today's individual worker is only an operative in a work-process conceived, planned, set in motion, coordinated and completed at a level beyond individual knowledge, control or 'imagination', and that the product escapes the worker. But that is so because of advances in science and technique (advances which of course have been appropriated by capital and imposed on every individual worker). However, there is now another and fundamental difference from the simple labour-process.

In our society, the labourer's work in producing useful things ('productive labour, this natural condition of human existence') is not the basis of his or her social relations, his or her relation to fellow-humans. On the contrary – and this is fundamental – his/her labour-power is not a power directed at free, truly human activity. Labour-power is reduced to being a commodity, to be bought and sold like any other commodity. It has a use-value, and that use-value is labour, productive labour. The employer buys the commodity labour-power (its price is a wage) and from then on possesses its use-value, to be used to produce useful things, to be sure; but besides the 'concrete' (particular) use-value of the product, the employer appropriates the value added to it by the worker's labour. This value is greater than the value of the commodity (labour-power) that he bought. Marx calls this difference surplus-value.

There are many and varied types of concrete labour, but they all have one thing in common: they are labours that produce not only useful things, use-values, but (actually above all, from the standpoint of capital) exchange-value. Marx showed that, 'abstracting' from the differences in types of useful, 'concrete' labour, we arrive at the common substance of them all and of their products. The world of commodities is a world where all human products, the results of all labours, are equal to each other in the sense that they are values, values that can be exchanged and accumulated as products of human labour as such, what Marx called abstract labour (i.e., abstracting from the different 'concrete' types of labour). The exchanges have come to be effected by a universal equivalent, money.

The capital system's whole life-process or metabolism – its process of daily reproduction as a system – is driven by the imperative to accumulate more and more surplus-value, which becomes capital. This capital, invested in plant, raw materials, machinery (constant capital) and in labour-power (variable capital – variable in that it brings about an increase in value) returns to the worker as an alien power to which he or she must sell themselves if they are to live. In this way their own product has created a social relation external and alien to them, returning to exploit them once again. It returns in the form of means of production bought by another class's capital, money: 'The simple transformation of money into the material factors of the process of production, transforms the latter into a title and a right to the labour and surplus-labour of others ... [and] this complete inversion of the relation between dead and living labour, between value and the force that creates value, mirrors itself in the consciousness of capitalists'.[11] Thus, wrote Marx, we have a system in which 'the process of production has the mastery over man, instead of being controlled by him ... As in religion, man is governed by the products of his own brain, so in capitalistic production he is governed by the products of his own hand.'[12]

And, as the opposite of sociology's concepts of the nature of social relations: 'the "social character", etc., of the worker's labour confronts him ... as not only alien, but hostile and antagonistic, and as objectified and personified in capital.'[13] Why? Because 'the power (i.e., capital) dominating labour is the circularly transformed power of social labour itself'.[14]

In future years, people will think it monstrous that humans were dominated by an alienated product (capital) of their own labour and that the whole power of science and technique, the 'social brain', on which society's daily reproduction was based, was daily activated, in a fashion appearing perfectly normal, as a natural property of capital and its personification, the capitalist class. And yet it is this monstrosity that sociology takes to be, without qualification, 'society', in the interests of whose continued 'functioning' the actions of men and women, their social relationships and their institutional life take on meaning and can be explained. Such is the 'objectivity' of our 'social sciences'.

On the basis of Marx's basic discoveries we can see clearly the contrast between the basic and essential labour-process characterising humanity, on the one hand, and production as it has now become, on the other, i.e. production of surplus-value as dictated by the demands of capital.

Marx devotes many pages of his *Capital* to the importance of machinery in capitalist production. For capital, machinery is a means for shortening that part of the working day in which the value of the worker's labour-power is replaced, so that for a greater part of the day he is producing surplus-value. With machine production, the worker more and more becomes 'a mere appendage' of the means of production. The machine as an instrument of production, fixed capital, is of course itself the product of past labour, now in the shape of 'dead labour', confronting and 'pumping dry' the living labour of the worker. The special skill of each insignificant factory operative vanishes as an infinitesimal quantity before the science, the gigantic physical forces, and the mass of labour embodied in the factory mechanism and which, together with that mechanism, constitute the power of the 'master'.

This 'science, gigantic physical forces', etc. is characterised by

Marx as 'the social brain'. In machine production,

> the worker ... steps to the side of the production process instead of being its chief actor. In this transformation, it is neither the direct human labour he himself performs, nor the time during which he works, but rather an appropriation of his own general productive power, his understanding of nature and his mastery over it by virtue of his presence as a social body – it is, in a word, the development of the social individual which appears as the great foundation of production and of wealth. The *theft of alien labour time, on which the present wealth is based,* appears a miserable foundation in face of this new one, created by large-scale industry itself.[15]

This reduction of the labourer to an adjunct of the capital (capital is 'dead labour') embodied in machinery can be seen as the physical and immediately felt completion of the alienation of the wage-labourer, whose labour is used, its product appropriated, purely for the purpose of incorporating value in the product as a commodity. The reality that the labour of individuals was expended on the commodities produced is of course not apparent in those commodities. They have a use-value of whatever kind, and a value in exchange, expressed in price. That exchange-value appears to be a material property or characteristic of the commodity; it is in fact the expression of the labour contained in it. Instead of the fundamental social relation, we see a thing.

If this alienation is to be overcome, it is necessary that the producers become conscious of it. The men and women who produce society's wealth do not start with their own implements and the raw materials available in nature (or made available by past labour), nor with their own conception of what is to be produced and how. On the contrary, they can set to work only when they make themselves available to an employer, because the means of production and the raw materials extracted from nature are in the hands of the class of employers. (These resources, it should never be forgotten, do not 'naturally' take the form of capital; they were forcibly expropriated from the individuals and communities who formerly possessed them.)

Again: the owners of capital confront workers not just as that class of people who have the financial wherewithal to pay wages. They confront them also as the 'personifications' of all the social powers of labour, of the productive forces historically developed by social labour. It is impossible to over-emphasise the fact that these are the powers (means and forces of production) of society – yet they can be called into life only according to the needs (economic imperatives) of capital, as conceived and acted upon by the minority that has appropriated that capital.

The whole meaning of socialism/communism is the overcoming of this alienation of individuals' essential powers, so that the preconditions of the daily reproduction of social life and culture exist as men's and women's own (communal) property, for the use of which they will have to devise collectively shared methods and decisions about priorities. It will be the restoration of the genuinely human form of labour, but collectively as well as individually.

It goes without saying that between our present situation and the realisation of such a prospect stand great obstacles that must be overcome. Not only do the 'personifications of capital' constitute the politically ruling class, with all the state's powers of coercion at their disposal. To this must be added the impact upon consciousness of the reality of capital's all-pervading dominance. All manner of ideological forms, control of the media, educational conditioning, etc. as well as direct propaganda, together with the compulsion and necessity of every day's work, flow from and sustain the existing social order. There can be no fundamental social change without the development of a consciousness of the inhuman (the word is used in its literal sense) nature of capital's usurpation of humanity's powers. The inevitable industrial and political struggles and protest movements of all kinds will need continuity, interconnection and new forms of organisation, and the constant and radical critique of the ruling ideology is essential for this to come about. Marx compared the worker's recognition of capital's usurpation of labour's powers to the slave's self-recognition of his individual humanity, a self-recognition which was to make impossible the continued existence of slavery. (I once devised a university lecture course entitled 'Is capitalism eternal?')

Thus, in the social system dominated by capital, the distinctive and fundamental human relation of individuals to nature (through their conscious productive activity) and to each other is distorted, inverted. Certainly, when individuals engage in work and in their everyday relations, they do so with consciousness, intention and will. But they contribute to a result and totality of their actions which then confronts them as something external, something that no one willed, independent of their wills, alienated from them, as if with the force of inescapable, inevitable, 'natural' necessities of life to which there is no alternative but to conform. Here, as Marx writes, 'the process of production masters men but not yet does man master the process of production'.[16]

As Marx puts it: 'Their own collisions with one another produce an alien social power standing above them, produce their mutual interaction as a process and power independent of them.' And:

> The social relation of individuals to one another as a power over the individuals which has become autonomous, whether conceived as a natural force, as chance or in whatever other form, is a necessary result of the fact that the point of departure is not the free social individual.[17]

In a socialist 'community of free individuals' the labour-power of individuals would be 'consciously applied as the combined labour-power of the community'.

Labouring humanity cannot of course return to the 'original' relation to the object, but must appropriate the 'social brain' (i.e. the conquests of science and technique, the productive forces at present at the disposal of capital) as a collectivity of free individuals. The social order that will succeed the rule of capital will be one with a conscious and direct basis in 'the development of the general powers of the human head'.[18]

PART VI

Some Conclusions

by Cliff Slaughter

In what way can the word 'inhuman' be used to describe the most basic characteristic of the social world ruled by capital? Having begun with Marx's definition of human labour (the comparison with the spider) we arrive at the direct opposite. Instead of the labourer employing the existing resources (tools, raw materials, accumulated knowledge and skills), capital employs labour! The said tools, raw materials, knowledge and skills enter the work-process as capital. The worker's place, from the standpoint of capital, is summed up in the give-away term 'human resources'. He/she is now merely part of the material to hand for capital to buy and set in motion the process of production. But the unique nature of this particular commodity, labour-power, is that it adds value to the product.

The product is not appropriated by the labourer and his fellows but by the owners of capital, another class. Workers organise to get a share of the value of the product. The battle over wages is the elementary form of the class struggle. However, whatever concessions and reforms may at times and under certain conditions be won, the structural opposition between the classes remains untouched, the alienation remains. When the working class begins to organise and act to change the very structure because it exploits and oppresses, then begins a higher form of class struggle, the preparation for revolution. Between the two, there is and has been the formation of political organisations to protect and to find political representation for trade unions and to effect reforms. Again, these steps, though they are political, do not yet touch the basic class relations, which

Marx says, as we have shown, negate humanity. The task is to negate that negation.

Against the system, people are organising and sacrificing in response to the inhumanities of the society in which they live. In the course of setbacks, gains, and the usurpation of their struggles and movements by, for example, religious fundamentalist or militarist forces as after the 'Arab Spring', or by bureaucratic leaderships and parties who accommodate to capital (like the 'business-friendly' British Labour Party) they will need to mobilise to confront the real source of their deeply felt needs and grievances, the rule of capital. That confrontation will succeed only if those class-conscious workers and those who, as Marx and Engels put it, have 'gone over to the proletariat' have been able to immerse themselves and establish strong roots and networks among the masses. That is the question discussed above – in Parts II and III – in analysing the experience of those who have tried to follow the teachings and experience of Lenin and Trotsky.

Marx summed up the difference between his approach and that of the unhistorical and conformist 'social sciences' when he wrote:

> In its mystified form, dialectic became the fashion in Germany, because it seemed to ... glorify the existing state of things. In its rational form it is ... an abomination to *bourgeoisdom* and its doctrinaire professors, because it includes in its comprehension and affirmative recognition of the existing state of things, at the same time, also, the recognition of the negation of that state, of its inevitable breaking up; because it regards every historically developed social form as in fluid movement, and therefore takes into account its transient nature no less than its momentary existence; because it lets nothing impose upon it, and is in its essence critical and revolutionary.[1]

'Practical consciousness' – 'revolutionising practice'

When Marx collaborated with Engels in writing the *Communist Manifesto* (1847) he had already laid the theoretical foundations of the analysis of social relations and class struggle that we have just summarised. The *Manifesto* could not have been written without his theoretical work of the 1840s, in which he undertook a critique of existing philosophy and political economy. This work on 'the theoretical front' enabled him to overturn the idealist philosophy of Hegel and his followers and predecessors, and to go beyond Feuerbach's materialist rejection of idealism. Feuerbach knew that humans are conditioned/determined by their circumstances. Marx had this to say on the matter:

> The materialist doctrine that men are products of circumstances and upbringing and that therefore, changed men are products of other circumstances and changed upbringing, forgets that it is men who change circumstances and that the educator must himself be educated. Hence this doctrine is bound to divide society into two parts, one of which is superior to society. The coincidence of the changing of circumstances and of human activity or self-change can be conceived and rationally understood only as revolutionary practice.[2]

For Marx and Engels, the essence of man was not, as it was for Feuerbach, the individual as formed by his circumstances, but 'the ensemble (totality) of the social relations.' In the *Communist Manifesto,* Marx and Engels sought to show that in the material conditions of the capitalist social world the agent of revolutionary practice was the class formed by and necessary to capital, the working class, this class antagonism being the key to the total social structure.

Without these theoretical conquests, any perspective of a

change to a better society could only remain at the level of idealist aspirations. And that is as true today as it was in 1848. The struggle for a better society depends on a 'revolutionary practice' continually informed and shaped by a continually worked-on analysis and understanding of the changing totality of the social relations in our globalised capital system and the conflicts and class struggle endemic to it. This is what Marx meant in saying that, while a legal and political superstructure develops to protect and where possible regulate the rule of the dominant class in the social system (as in capitalism), there are developed at the same time corresponding 'legal, political, religious, artistic or philosophic – in short, ideological forms in which men *become conscious of this conflict and fight it out*' [my emphasis]. Clearly the monotonous, dismissive criticism of Marx as an 'economic determinist' could not be wider of the mark.

'The emancipation of the working class is the task of the working class itself'

It is on this basis that we may return to the question of the revolutionary role of the working class. Marx and Engels were consistent on this matter from the time of the *Communist Manifesto* to their last years. In the *Manifesto* they wrote: 'the emancipation of the working class is the task of the working class itself'. In his often-reprinted 'Preface' to the 1888 English edition, Engels refers to the programme of the International Workingmen's Association (IWMA) – the First International:

> Marx, who drew up this programme to the satisfaction of all parties, entirely trusted to the intellectual development of the working class, which was sure to result from continued action and mutual discussion ... Our notion, from the very beginning, was that the emancipation of the working class must be the act of the working class itself.[3]

And, in the IWMA's 'Provisional Rules':

> Considering,
>
> That the emancipation of the working class must be conquered by the working classes themselves: that the struggle for the emancipation of the working classes means not a struggle for class privileges and monopolies, but for equal rights and duties, and the abolition of all class rule; …
>
> That the economical emancipation of the working class … is the great end to which every political movement ought to be subordinate as a means …[4]

The *Manifesto* says: 'The Communists do not form a separate party opposed to other working-class parties. They have no interests separate and apart from those of the proletariat as a whole.' Or as Marx put it, in instructions for the delegates of the International's Provisional Council, written in late August 1866: 'It is the business of the International Working Men's Association to combine and generalise the *spontaneous movements* of the working class, but not to dictate or impose any doctrinary system whatever.'[5]

Time now to combine and generalise. Here follows the passage in which Marx says what can here be the last word in relation to the discussion above on 'consciousness brought from the outside':

> The Communists, therefore, are on the one hand, *practically* the most advanced and resolute section of the working class of every country, that section which pushes forward all others; on the other hand, theoretically, they have over the great mass of the proletariat the advantage of clearly understanding the line of march, the conditions and the ultimate general results of the proletarian movement. [Emphasis added.][6]

This book has tried to outline the major problems confronting the many movements of resistance to the manifestations of the globalised capital system, and the need to critically rethink the heritage of Lenin and Trotsky as interpreted by their would-be disciples. In this we have endeavoured to start always from the principles contained in Marx's and Engels' theoretical work, and more particularly from the *Communist Manifesto*. Those looking at Lenin's achievements as their guide will learn that there is a real heritage and an abused one. It is decidedly not enough to base one's work on Lenin's *What Is To Be Done?* (and certainly not on his *Materialism and Empirio-criticism* or *Imperialism, the Highest Stage of Capitalism*). Above all it is Lenin's actual work and achievement, especially between February and October 1917, that rewards detailed study. We have dealt with Lenin's heritage and *What Is To Be Done?* so far as the matter of party and class is concerned. But it is necessary always to understand the historical situation in 1917, in terms of the World War and the problems for capitalism in Europe, the backwardness of Russia and the commitment of all socialists at that time to a 'bourgeois-democratic revolution', together with the stage reached at that time by the international working-class movement. In our own day the context is very different and must be understood if a guide to action is sought. Can we say more than: start from the theoretical foundation laid by Marx and Engels, and, crucially, from the understanding of class consciousness as a *practical consciousness,* together with Marx's insistence that his work was 'not a theory, but a guide to action'?

Recognising that Trotsky and the Trotskyist movement had fought against Stalin's anti-Marxist 'socialism in a single country' and the consequent betrayals of the working class and murderous suppression of all opposition, many workers and intellectuals have looked to Trotsky for theoretical and political inspiration. We have argued that while this is understandable it is mistaken. Trotsky's 'Transitional Programme' is based on an evaluation of the nature of the epoch, the stage reached by the class struggle, and the prospect of proletarian revolution which was wrong. It was wrong then, and it is most certainly wrong today. It was right to say that the revolutionary battles of the 1920s and 1930s were betrayed, above all by Stalinism, but Trotsky completely underestimated the renewal of strength given to capitalism by these betrayals, insisting that the period was one of capitalist decay, stagnation of the productive forces, and so on. The whole of the 'Transitional Programme' is posited on the existence of a 'pre-revolutionary situation'.

Into this characterisation of the objective situation, Trotsky injected the conception that has fatally inspired the Trotskyist movement from the 1930s to our own day: 'the crisis of humanity is reduced to the crisis of working-class revolutionary leadership'. We have tried to show that this conception derives from a completely wrong understanding of the relation between party and class. Trotsky's 'pre-revolutionary situation' was only months later a world war, to be followed by decades of capital's being able to displace or postpone its contradictions and achieve unprecedented growth, with revolutionary developments in the productive forces, until the onset of the structural crisis of the system in the 1970s, a crisis in which 'neo-liberalism' has increasingly imposed attacks on all past gains of the working-class movement and will provoke new struggles. What is at stake is not 'the building of the alternative revolutionary leadership', but the reconstitution of the working-class movement. Critical assessment of past supposed 'guides to action' is an indispensable part of that reconstitution.

What has been the outcome of the many revolts and protest movements of the second half of the twentieth century and then of the early years of the twenty-first century? From the uprisings against Stalinism in Poland and Hungary in the 1950s, then the Czechoslovakian 'Prague Spring' in 1968, through the upsurge of the youth in France in 1968, the Polytechnic revolt against the

Greek Junta and Tiananmen Square in China, the British miners' strike of 1984–85, to the 'Arab Spring' and 'Occupy' – and the many other 'social movements' that could be cited – we cannot avoid a sobering conclusion. These struggles did not achieve their ends. They suffered some or all of the following fates. For the most part they remained isolated in space and in time, and they fizzled out. They were brutally suppressed. Their temporary successes were usurped by reactionary authoritarian military or fundamentalist religious regimes. They were ignored, abandoned, betrayed by the 'official' trade unions and political parties claiming to represent the working class.

It is easy to draw pessimistic conclusions from this history (and even to give this disillusioned pessimism a 'philosophical' dressing, as we saw in the ex-socialist post-impressionist Lyotard's 'each of the great narratives of emancipation has, so to speak, been invalidated over the last fifty years').[7] But there are compelling reasons to reject such conclusions.

First and foremost, the reign of capital has entered its structural, historical crisis, and this means that the exploited and oppressed are certain to find themselves driven into new struggles, as capital must pass on to them the burden of its intensifying contradictions. Secondly, the capital system's threat to the future of the planet and of humanity becomes daily more apparent and must in one way or another affect the consciousness of millions. Thirdly, as we have seen, there are positive signs of a socialist awakening – for example in the NUMSA document cited in the Southern Africa section of Part II – from the nightmare of Stalinist and reformist betrayals and illusions of 'national liberation'. And finally, the resources – means of communication beyond the wildest imagination of earlier movements – exist for the achievement of an internationalist consciousness of what is involved in a challenge to globalised capitalism. I stress again that by consciousness I mean, in Marx's sense, a '*practical consciousness*', not just an idea.

In what follows I shall refer to this consciousness as a 'cognitive map' of our globalised struggle.

A comparison and conclusion from anthropology

I.

'You've never had it so good', 'the affluent worker', 'bourgeoisification of the working class', 'we're all middle-class now', the welfare state, 'full employment in a free society' – these were the myths and surface realities of the decades following the end of World War Two in 1945, the so-called 'golden age' of 'modernity'.

It took two world wars and millions of deaths to set Western Europe and the US on this road. It took a generation of short-sighted politicians and 'social scientists' to see it as a new world. But it has taken only a couple of decades for it to fall completely apart. Politicians, economists, journalists and media pundits have suddenly rediscovered the words crisis and even capitalism. The underlying, stark reality of relative prosperity and security in the 'advanced countries' is now open for all to experience the unprecedented scale and intensity of the political and social crises and conflicts, wars, economic collapses, mass poverty and mortality, and unemployment, insecurity and social breakdown of all kinds.

And yet, alongside these ills, we see previously unimaginable forms of production, scientific knowledge and means of communication, but with not the slightest sign of any prospect of being able to overcome what amounts to a universal crisis of global society, with the overriding threat of destruction of the natural environment and exhaustion of the planet's resources.

For reasons that I hope will emerge, I shall leave this gross contradiction aside at this point and proceed first to consider some important aspects of societies and cultures very distant and different from our own. They differ above all in the fact that they give us some insight into the kind of social life that historically preceded the formation of class societies.

Archaeological research tells that in the first 'human revolution', humans overcame the existing condition of being determined by their natural surroundings and physical constitution and instincts. They did this by taking parts of their environment and fashioning them into tools which then enabled them to *produce* their means of livelihood (food, shelter). This was the 'first human revolution', in which humans went beyond the rule of sheer natural necessity and compulsion, finding ways to consciously *produce* their means of life. Obviously we have no direct evidence of the social organisation and cultural norms of the earliest societies, except what might be deduced from their material remains. On the other hand, we do have evidence of surviving societies which when they were studied were still without class divisions. Such evidence was not available to Marx and Engels when they began their *Communist Manifesto* with the words, 'The history of all hitherto existing societies is the history of class struggle'.

There is by now a large body of anthropological research literature on the lives of tribal societies, their adjustment to their environment, their ordering of social relations, their methods for integrating individuals into society and for dealing with conflicts. Here I shall take two examples, the Mardudjara people of Australia and the Ndmebu of Africa.

Robert Tonkinson's work on the Mardudjara is an excellent example of the many studies of Australian Aboriginal societies. For the Mardudjara, as for the Ndembu, knowledge of the natural environment is assured not only by speech but above all through rituals. Rituals like initiation also establish and reaffirm the relationships between generations and between the individual and society, as well as being the means of resolving conflicts and problems. These relations are defined and experienced, as in all the surviving 'early' societies, by means of a society-wide system of rules of kinship and descent. Among these, very important are rules of gift-exchange and reciprocity.

> [In Mardudjara society] the small amount of trade that exists takes place *within the framework of ritual activities* during big meetings, incidentally as gift exchange between friendly kin when small bands meet, or as part of obligations owed to certain close kin and affines ... The significance of exchange lies far less in the nature or value of the items than in the act of reciprocity itself, which is an affirmation of a continuing bond. The alliances so forged promote an interpersonal and intergroup harmony that is essential in an environment as marginal as the desert.[8]

Finally, the famous Australian 'songlines' give familiarity with sites, which become part of their *cognitive map* of the desert world. All these together constitute a communication system assuring the continuity of the structure of Mardudjara society. The kinship terminology which is so central to the writings of social anthropologists has this function of communication: 'A kin term is simultaneously a status term, so it *encodes* a great deal of information that is useful for framing interaction between individuals'. That this pattern characterises all Australian societies is confirmed by R. M. and C. H. Berndt (quoted by Tonkinson) in their *The World of the First Australians*:

> The kinship system of a particular tribe or language unit is in effect a shorthand statement about the network of interpersonal relations within that unit – a *blueprint* to guide its members ... a code of action which those members cannot ignore if they are to live in relative harmony with one another.[9]

(In the above quotations I have italicised words that are of obvious relevance to our general themes of communication, information and control.)

A striking aspect of Mardudjara initiation ritual (as in *'rites de passage'* – like initiation rites in all societies) is the way in which the individual is first isolated from his existing state, leaving that state behind, forbidden to communicate with his fellows, becoming a non-person or 'dead', then reborn, inducted to his new or proper state (in the case of being ritually treated for a problem, restored to normality): 'Talking is forbidden between ritually dead people (e.g. the initiates in seclusion after circumcision).' An identical rule can be found in Ndembu ritual.

The classic study of the rituals of the Ndembu people of what was then Northern Rhodesia, now Zambia, is Victor Turner's *The Ritual Process,* which, with Turner's linked writings, gives a meticulous description and analysis of Ndembu ritual.[10] The same basic features and functions are present – despite the great distance between them, historically and geographically – in Ndembu and Australian tribal societies (though, unlike those in Australia, most in Africa do not practise initiation rites). And he finds another element in ritual that adds a new dimension to the big question of how our own globalised society can achieve an equilibrium, making possible a truly human existence.

First, the same basic processes as in Australian rituals: 'The neophyte in liminality must be a *tabula rasa,* a blank slate, on which is inscribed the knowledge and wisdom of the group, in those respects that pertain to the new status.'[11] As in all *rites de passage* there is created a condition of the subject in which the role, values and responsibilities of the individual to society are implanted, affirmed. The temporarily isolated and culturally stripped condition to which the subject is reduced is called by Turner 'liminas' (after van Gennep). As we have seen, in this condition there are then imprinted on his consciousness the roles and conduct for which the society needs him to take responsibility, i.e. the rules of behaviour that are part of what constitute the society's *structure*. In considering below the relevance of these rituals to our own present concerns, it should be noted that Turner (referring to Levi-Strauss's work) emphasises another side to them:

> The symbols and their relations ... are not only a set of cognitive classifications for ordering the Ndembu universe. They are also, perhaps as importantly, a set of evocative devices for arousing, channelling and domesticating powerful emotions, such as hate, fear, affection, and grief. They are also informed with purposiveness and have a 'conative' aspect. In brief, the whole person, not just the Ndembu mind, is existentially involved in the life or death issues with which Isoma is concerned.[12]

Within this whole process, Turner sees a sort of dialectical opposite to these structural necessities, an opposite which he calls '*communitas*', a commonality of basic human undifferentiated fellowship and equality. This *communitas* is regularly associated with a feature common to many societies, and not only tribal ones, namely the temporary 'pulling down the mighty from their seats', reduction of chiefs and other powerful individuals to their common human condition, stripped for a time of their wealth, status, privilege and prestige. Role reversal is often a feature of such rituals. For our purposes in the present work, Turner's conclusion from all this is certainly highly suggestive:

> However, even in the simplest societies, the distinction between structure and *communitas* exists and obtains symbolic expression in the cultural attributes of liminality, marginality, and inferiority. In different societies and at different periods in each society, one or the other of these 'immortal antagonists' (to borrow terms that Freud used in a

different sense) comes uppermost. But together they constitute the 'human condition', as regards man's relation with his fellow man.[13]

II.

'White man got no dreaming. Him go 'nother way. White man, him go different. Him go road belong himself.' (W.E.H. Stanner, 1966)[14]

In capitalist societies (as in all class societies) there is erected on the economic structure or exploitative base (capital-wage labour, opposed classes) a political and legal superstructure of control and oppression. This superstructure – the state, etc. – stands over and against the individuals who constitute the mass, as does the economic structure. To make any changes the individuals must, as Marx wrote, 'become conscious of the conflicts and fight them out'.

By contrast, in early societies like the ones to which we have referred, there is no 'legal and political superstructure'. They are classless and stateless. Rather, as we have seen, there are codes and customs, rituals and exchanges, in which the structure of relations between groups, between generations, between the sexes, and between the individual and society and its sub-groups, is reaffirmed. There are mechanisms within these institutions and codes which allow for the treatment and resolution of individuals' problems of adjustment and emotional crises. It goes without saying that there is no 'becoming conscious of the conflicts and fighting them out', because, again, the legal and political superstructure of class societies does not exist.[15]

Is it possible, and if so by what means, to revolutionise our own society in such a way as to create a 'cognitive map' of our social world and its dependence on/relation to nature? This 'nature'/environment is the planet, its potential highly developed but now over-exploited and endangered. Can a true and international community (*communitas*) be built?

I am well aware that the comparison I am now about to suggest is open to criticism, even dismissal, in that it ignores the history of societies that have existed since the earliest tribal societies. Such a history would greatly enrich the thesis here suggested, but I would argue that omitting it does not affect the essence of my argument. In effect, it is not strictly speaking a 'comparison' that is at stake. Ritual, along with and integrated with language and labour, was at the core of the first human revolution, the emergence of culture. Today the necessity confronting us is that of a *second human revolution;* again with control of communication/information/production at the source, to be once again at the disposal of the human collective. The 'information revolution' provides one of the essential objective conditions for this (Marx's 'universal intercourse'). It constitutes an extreme development of what Marx saw as the historically unsustainable contradiction between advanced forces of production and a social metabolism based on the theft of alien labour time.

I begin by asking: where does our own, present 'human condition' stand, in relation to the 'simple' societies in which ritual played such a decisive role? Do we, can we, possessing all the advances made since only tribal societies existed, attain anything comparable to their relationship with nature and with their fellow humans? Chris Knight summed up their achievement:

> In Australian ritual, human society was flexible enough and sensitive enough to attune itself firmly to the rhythms of surrounding life, avoiding helplessness by replicating internally nature's own dance. Nature was thereby humanised, while humanity yielded to this nature.[16]

Surely, the more we are compelled to face up to the destruction of nature threatened by the continued existence of capital's imperatives as the ruling order, the more bells ring. Will it be possible to overcome the power that has disrupted, potentially fatally, the unique conquest of the first 'human revolution', and achieve a culture derived from a relationship based not on instinctive adaptation but on a purposive, active making-over of nature, which husbands nature's resources rather than exploiting and exhausting them, and at the same time establishes a continuity of the social relationships necessary for this activity?

That question can be restated in a slightly different form: the class societies of history have imposed a 'second nature' to which men and women have to adapt. In the case of capitalist society, this second nature is living, labouring humanity's subjection to the imperatives of capital, the rule of dead labour over living labour. And so, by 'the second human revolution' we mean the overcoming of that subjection, that second nature, and the return, at an enormously higher level, to the purposive activity and fruitful relation to nature, of those early societies that established culture, escaping from the merely animal, instinctive relation to nature. Today's great problem of *agency*, i.e. of how the working class can overcome and surpass the rule of capital, must be posed in terms of how popular forms of organisation and cooperation can more and more be inspired by a consciousness of the necessity of becoming consistent with and anticipating the future, truly human society. The first human revolution transcended natural necessity though purposive productive activity. Class society and the state later negated the communal content of that activity. The second human revolution is the struggle to transcend the 'second nature' imposed by class society – the negation of the negation.

Our own 'globalised' society under the rule of capital is of course separated from the earliest cultures, some survivals of which anthropology has been able to study, by hundreds of millennia. In those early societies, humans learned to make and use tools, in the making and use of which (labour) their ancestors' work, skill and knowledge was embodied. The use by groups and individuals of this traditional knowledge carried on for many thousands of years, even after the constructions and estates of ruling castes and classes began to control these skills. By then, advances in knowledge and technique laid the basis for a division of labour, in which, eventually, specialised-skill groups, organisers, architects, etc. emerged. As inequalities and private property subverted the old collectivities, there developed a hierarchical division of labour in which the individual labourer's work was controlled and its product appropriated by ruling classes, This development took many and varied forms, the details of which do not concern us for present purposes. What is certain is that the system in which we now find ourselves was founded upon a brutal and complete separation of the mass of labourers from the actual means of production (above all, the land), their power to work, labour-power, becoming a mere commodity which they had to sell (for wages) in order to survive. From that point on, work and its products are outside the control of the actual producers. On the very contrary, their product is accumulated as capital, and capital's imperatives control the producers. This is the secret of our mode of life today.

Thus, again, the dead (dead labour, capital) rules over the living (living labour). It is the requirements of capital – profit, accumulation – that decide how the historically acquired knowledge and technique of society will be applied. The criteria of this application are only very partially to do with human need, depending first and last on what can be 'realised' as profit.

With the development of industry, science, applied science and technology there arrives the massive 'social brain' of 'collective intelligence', a collective intelligence with no 'intelligent' control but only each part of it controlled by this or that portion of capital and its personifications. Every (public or private) investor of capital calls into activity the relevant part of the 'collective intelligence' (science, technology), but only in order to compete with others and to accumulate capital, and not, of course, to apply it intelligently in the interests of society as a whole. *There is no means or mechanism for 'intelligently' or 'collectively' communicating, coordinating, activating, directing and controlling the collective intelligence for the common good.*

Such is the power of the 'social brain' or collective intelligence (and this power is continuously magnified because of capital's own driving force) that it has created, is creating, the elemental foundations (highly advanced productive forces, universal intercourse) of a future, truly human society. Now, with the 'information revolution', the means of production and the means of communication more and more coincide, so that this promise is even more real. *But* there is a change of fundamental importance since Marx showed how capital's productive drive prepared the material conditions for socialism. Capital must daily reproduce itself and at the same time accumulate; but this self-reproduction has now become a *destructive self-reproduction of capital*. This is the secret of our epoch's threat to the future existence of humanity and of the natural environment, and at the same time the secret of how to begin to counter that threat. We may conclude from this: Marx's assertion that the socialist revolution was 'the human revolution' because unlike all earlier revolutions it was not to replace the rule of one class with the rule of another but to end class and exploitation, can now be confirmed and strengthened, because *the socialist revolution, the second human revolution, is needed in order to save all humanity from the threat of destruction*, and to restore the necessary harmonious, non-exploitative relation between humanity and the rest of nature.

To appreciate the problems and possibilities of such a transformation, it is useful to go back to the elemental processes behind the developments just outlined.

The processes of regular reproduction of society's structural requirements were conducted and reaffirmed by means of ritual in the tribal societies we have taken as examples. If we compare with this the reproduction of structural necessities in the society ruled by capital, we begin to see difficult and complex problems but also the promise of an alternative to our society's headlong rush to disaster. Production, when capital rules, is production of *commodities*, containers of value. The owner of these commodities 'realises' that value when the commodities are sold. To produce the commodities in the first place, the employer must himself possess or buy the elements contributing to the value to be contained in the commodity. These are: his existing fixed capital (plant, machinery, etc.); the raw materials necessary (the two together constituting what Marx called 'constant capital'); and the element which *adds* value, namely labour-power. This labour-power is itself a commodity, existing in the person of workers. Wages are paid for this commodity. This expenditure of 'variable capital' (variable because it reappears in the product as an enhanced value, part of which is surplus to the value of the labour-power, thus *surplus value*) is structurally central to the whole system. What concerns us here is the *reproduction* of this vital element, labour-power, the living source of the life-process of the capital system.

As we have already seen, the production of wealth (which happens to be in the form of a mass of commodities) is today dependent not just on the immediate input of individual labourers but on the application of the accumulated scientific/technological knowledge and the resources of society as a whole. Every employer of labour draws upon a part of those resources. In more and more cases, the labourer becomes only an overseer of the machine. But he/she is necessary, and the daily reproduction of his/her presence and ability is absolutely essential. Less and less is that reproduction assured only by the means of subsistence he/she can purchase with his/her wage. It requires all manner of social resources (welfare services, public utilities, etc) *and* the conditioning to the capital system's requirements: discipline, consent, political apathy and often disenfranchisement, prejudices, artificially created needs and manipulated consumption patterns, in order to send the labourer to the market, where his/her wage is spent and the value of the employers' commodities is 'realised'.

In the twentieth and twenty-first centuries, this economic, political and cultural conditioning/process of reproduction of labour-power includes, very importantly, the political systems which have kept the working class relatively quiet: domesticated trade unions, labour/reformist parties and governments, Stalinist distortion of a communist alternative, fascist and other dictatorships (including colonial and post-colonial regimes).

All of these aspects need to be intact and as stable as possible for the 'wired-up' planetary ('globalised') system to work. Of course, it has unevenness and significant remnants of earlier historical stages, as well as rogue elements and parasites. And any breakdown or break-out is a threat to what has to be a single system, a system with media/communication networks, but riddled with competing interests and dominated by the movements of finance-capital over all productive activity. And, as recent experience has proved, the world of finance-capital and its management is fragile, with its own contradictions. The change to this globalised, 'wired-up' system has, of course, highly important implications for the old, traditional methods of opposing capitalist exploitation. The struggle over wages and the trade unions or 'combinations' built in order to conduct it are still necessary but they will have to be developed as consciously and practically *part* of a bringing together of all the social movements that challenge capital's control and its consequences.

Without the achievement of a working network of these movements and struggles, and a way of assuring their continuity, little can be gained. Such a unity of traditional working-class organisations and other social movements will have to be international if it is to confront and challenge the role of capital. In principle this is surely entirely possible: capital's need to have internationally connected operations with rapid decision-making networks makes those operations vulnerable at every point; and the means of electronic, virtually instant communication (mobile phone, internet, social networking) are in the hands of hundreds of millions of people. It is even the case that capital cannot function today without constantly expanding a mass market for these means of communication. Thus the 'conquest of space by time' is an incalculable advance for capital but at the same time a gift to the forces that oppose it. This has hardly gone unnoticed by those who ask how the existing system can be defended. The Chinese rulers' fear of and attempted suppression of internet communication by their opponents is well known. And Nick Dyer-Witheford in his *Cyber-Marx* writes of Mexico:

> Noting that the Zapatistas and other opponents of [Ernesto Zedillo's government] used the Internet, fax, and video, [RAND corporation analyst David Ronfeldt] suggested: 'At a time when the political and economic crisis has created widespread disaffection ... network style organising will enable the opposition to overcome its traditional factionalism. The greatest threats to the government could be hundreds or thousands of independent groups united in their opposition but accepting of each other's autonomy.' Although the 'decentralization' of this oppositional force meant it could not 'take national power', Ronfeldt suggested its activities could make Mexico 'ungovernable': 'The risk for Mexico is not an old-fashioned civil war or another social revolution ... The risk is social netwar. The country that produced the prototype social revolution of the twentieth century may now be giving rise to the prototype social netwar of the 21st century.'[17]

Bearing in mind the contrasts and problems we have described, can the potential contained in electronic means of communication contribute to a 'practical consciousness' of the way forward from the rule of capital? Recalling the role of ritual in tribal, stateless societies, it is obvious that no 'cognitive map' of our world order today can be learned by an individual. By cognition (knowing, knowledge), here is meant, again, a 'practical consciousness', and not just a set of ideas, just as the 'cognitive map' of early native Australians and Africans was a strictly worked out and tested system of relationships and practices and not only beliefs. Can the 'collective intelligence' ('social brain') create and continually recreate such a map and make it possible for individuals to take from it what they need and to contribute to it? As things stand now, this looks impossible. The world as experienced in tribal societies was relatively unchanging, whereas the world as it impinges on individuals today is changing every second, so any 'map' must be capable of changing with it. Society will have to overcome and go beyond an order where humans are dominated by the imperatives of a force (capital) alien to them. We certainly cannot know in advance how the 'collective' of the future will find ways of organising the total 'intelligence' in such a way as to provide for individuals' free and creative access to it. But, however formidably difficult to envisage, this *is* the problem.

How can men and women move towards this mastery of their own product? This raises all the 'old' questions of how the present economic, political and social order can be overcome, and above all the question of agency, of who will be the force for that change. We may however conclude that the scientific/technical means (the 'information revolution') of a future system of social (collective) control already promise to be a decisive weapon in organising movements against capital and its effects. It has always been essential for socialists to fight for those means of struggle that are consistent with and contribute to the end (i.e. against all notions of 'the end justifies the means'). Such are the internet and other electronic means of communication and networking that they will be absolutely central to those means. They are already proven as a weapon in the hands of those who struggle to expose and make inroads into the power of capital and the forms of oppression that sustain it. In this way the problem of assuring spatial and temporal continuity and unified impact of all the partial struggles has suddenly become infinitely more capable of solution. The information revolution has great significance for almost every sphere of human activity and organisation. And the most decisive of these is its implications for the great problem of agency: how will the movement for social revolution – the second human revolution – be built, and who will do it?

At this point we must revert to our starting-point: the nature of the world of globalised capital that we must confront. What does 'globalisation' mean for the politics of class struggle? Is it necessary to put aside past conceptions? Or should we ask: what remains true of those past conceptions, and in what way is it necessary to go beyond them?

The economy, the basis of the rule of capital, is globalised. In this interconnected, 'wired-up' world, finance capital dominates, and transactions take place at speeds completely unimaginable only a few years ago. Globalised it may be, but the rule of capital means division between an exploiting and an exploited class, it means class struggle, gross inequality, eruptions of protest, degradation of living conditions for large sections of the population, as well as uncontrolled fluctuations in the state of every nation's finances, levels of unemployment, and so on. Between nations there are vastly different levels of living standards and economic resources. The fundamental imperative of the capital system is the ruthless search for profit and capital accumulation. In the pursuit of this end there is a constant drive to appropriate the earth's resources and to gain control, by force where necessary, of strategic areas of the globe. Thus the dominant powers, the United States, its allies and its rivals, indulge in mass destruction of people, and their plunder of nature now threatens the very existence of our environment.

So much for the 'economic' results of globalisation, an immeasurable intensification of the capital system's basic features. However, it would be utterly misleading, and highly dangerous, to be satisfied with just an 'economic' knowledge of what capitalism is today. We have to ask: how is this social-economic order, unavoidably antagonistic and crisis-ridden, particularly now that it has entered its structural, historical crisis, controlled? The answer: it is not! Ever since the origins of class-divided societies in the distant past, right through to the capitalism we know and the regimes (Russia, China) that briefly succeeded it in the twentieth century, there has existed the *state machine*, its role being to 'keep the lid on' the antagonisms, conflicts and struggles inevitably engendered by the exploitation at the heart of the system. 'Keeping the lid on' means imposing, by 'the rule of law' when sufficient, or by force when necessary, the conformity of the masses to the demands of the exploiting system. 'Containing' the class struggle in all its forms has always been the role of the nation-state. Globalisation of the economy notwithstanding, the nation-states of course still exist, from the dominant power in the world, the United States, to the poorest countries.

And here is the great contradiction. The economy is globalised; its political system, the political guardian, the state, is not! From the exploitative and oppressive antagonistic structure of 'globalised' capital there flow, inevitably, struggles, protests, rebellions, all over the world. *But* where is the instrument, the 'global state', shall we say, to 'keep the lid on', to condition men and women to the needs of capital? Every nation-state machine, as we see, tends strongly to become more authoritarian in the attempt to regulate and control the contradictions, struggles and movements resulting from the workings of the now globalised economy. These movements and struggles (working-class actions such as strikes and occupations, 'social movements' of many kinds, revolts of the youth) are at an early level of development, until now, as we have seen, encountering isolation, betrayals, frustration, usurpation by military and religious or reactionary political forces – but they will be fuelled by and are learning from these experiences.

This non-congruence between global economy/society and the political superstructure cannot be overcome so long as the rule of capital continues. Already we have experienced – and we see it more and more – the impotence of the would-be rulers of our new world, however bloody and desperate their interventions in the Middle East, Northern Africa and Afghanistan. These have achieved no result other than the destruction of thousands of communities and the deaths of millions of people. At best, from the standpoint of the ruling class, these 'humanitarian interventions', as in Iraq, Libya, Syria and Afghanistan can be seen as a deadly form of control over the exploited masses by dispersing and killing countless millions of them, reducing the survivors to a condition where they must struggle only to survive. This raging impotence is itself a symptom of capital's structural, historical crisis. Like the rulers of ancient Rome and of every previous class society, they reach the point where they are patently unfit to rule.

Enough! No number of arguments, but only the inescapable reality of what is actually happening, is necessary to show that Rosa Luxemburg over a century ago was right: 'socialism or barbarism!' Today's barbarism, and the real threat of environmental destruction consequent on the imperatives of capital, cannot be overcome by any political system or innovation that leaves intact the cause of humanity's grave predicament – the capital system.

Endnotes

Epigraphs

1 William Blake, from 'Milton' (1804-10).

2 Karl Marx in *A Contribution to the Critique of Hegel's Philosophy of Law* (1844).

3 Karl Marx in his eleventh thesis on Feuerbach (1845).

4 István Mészáros, *The Necessity of Social Control* (2015), p. 297.

Part II

1 Isaac Deutscher, *The Prophet OutcastA Trotsky: 1929-1940* (Oxford, Oxford University Press paperback, 1963), p. 426. Deutscher suggests that Trotsky, provoked by Martin's refusal to condemn the Stalinist lawyer D. N. Pritt's defence of the Moscow Trials, may have exaggerated his real belief. Trotsky also thought Martin 'a drunkard' who had 'stole[n] an hour from me'. Leon Trotsky, *Writings ...: supplement 1934-40* (New York, Pathfinder Press, 1979), p. 737.

2 István Mészáros, *Beyond Capital; towards a theory of transition* (London, Merlin Press, 1995), p. 696.

3 On this history, see the classic Dominique Eudes, *The Kapetanios: partisans and civil war in Greece 1943-1949* (New York and London, Monthly Review Press, 1972).

4 Bob Myers, *Revolutionary Times, Revolutionary Lives: personal accounts of the liberation struggles* (London, Index Books, 1997), p. 4.

5 Myers, *Revolutionary Times*, p. 51.

6 Ibid.

7 Ibid., p. 55.

8 Ibid., p. 107.

9 Mészáros, *Beyond Capital*, pp. 699-700.

10 For the neo-liberal thinking that came to dominate the Liberal Democrats under Nick Clegg, making them natural

allies of the Tories in the coalition negotiations of 2010, see David Laws and Paul Marshal, *The Orange Book: reclaiming liberalism* (London, Profile Books, 2004).

11 A phrase used by Friedrich Engels in his *Condition of the Working Class in England in 1844* and theorised by Marx, notably in *Capital*, vol. I, chap. 25.

12 Mark Duggan was shot dead when police tried to arrest him in the Tottenham area on suspicion of planning an attack and possessing a handgun. The Independent Police Complaints Commission report has been constantly delayed. A jury at a public inquest in January 2014 found the killing 'lawful' by 8 to 2; but the official story of what happened has been changed many times.

13 V. I. Lenin, 'Left-Wing Communism, an infantile disorder', in Lenin, *Collected Works* (*CW*) (Moscow, Foreign Languages Publishing House, 1965), vol. 31, p. 17.

14 Justin Welby (born 1956) worked for over a decade, first for the French oil company Elf Aquitaine and then, from 1984, as treasurer of Enterprise Oil plc, concerned mainly with West African and North Sea oil projects. He experienced 'a calling from God' in 1989, was ordained and rose to become head of the Anglican Church. In July 2013, following a report on banking standards, he explained that senior bank executives avoided being given information about difficult issues to allow them to 'plead ignorance', commenting that he would possibly have behaved in the same way and warning against 'lynch mob' demands that errant bankers should be 'named and shamed'.

15 Tomas Fazi, *The Battle for Europe: how an elite hijacked a continent – and how we can take it back* (London, Pluto Press, 2014).

16 Tamasin Cave and Andy Powell, *A Quiet Word: lobbying, crony capitalism and broken politics in Britain* (London, Vintage, 2015).

17 Owen Jones, *Chavs: the demonization of the working class* (London, Verso, 2012).

18 The question was: 'Should Scotland be an independent country?' Since 1707 Scotland, constitutionally, has been part of an incorporating Union with England, long regarded as providing an exemplary model of political stability between two historic nations during the era of capitalist modernisation. It has survived the Irish War for independence from what properly speaking was the UK – the United Kingdom of Great Britain and Ireland, which existed only from 1801 to 1922 – and the demise of the British Empire. The 2014 demand for what was always going to be a somewhat limited form of independence came from the pro-capitalist Scottish National Party (SNP). Since 2007, it had been the governing party in the administration 'devolved' to Scotland in 1999 (following a decade in which the Scottish electorate decisively rejected Thatcher's Tory party but had to suffer her governments), and had won a surprise overall majority in the Holyrood (Edinburgh) parliament in 2011. But, as these extracts illustrate, the campaign for 'yes' took on a life of its own – showing the potential to be the most significant challenge since the defeat of the miners' strike in 1985 to the neo-liberal regime that has governed the UK since the entrenchment of the Thatcher dogma that 'there is no alternative'.

19 Marx to W. Bracke, 5 May 1875 in Karl Marx and Friedrich Engels, *Selected Works* (Moscow, Progress Publishers, 1970), pp. 11-12. In the 1890s, Engels echoed this sentiment when, at the time of the 'new unionism', he chided sectarians for indifference to movements that did not correspond to their purist measure of socialism.

20 The original sources for this section are in an email discussion list set up by former WRP members following the discussion on 'Agency' in October 2012 and in Gabriel Levy's

blog 'People and Nature', accessed at www.people nature.org.

21 John Curtice, Professor of Politics at Strathclyde University, speaking on BBC television on the morning of 19 September 2014.

22 Some of Paul Mason's articles on Scotland can be accessed at http://www.theguardian.com/commentisfree – see especially 31 August, 21 September, and 5 October, 2014.

23 The Radical Independence Campaign (RIC) was established in 2012 by Greens, various small socialist organisations (including the International Socialist Group and the Scottish Socialist Party), some trade-union militants, anti-nuclear campaigners and republicans to campaign for a 'yes' vote under the slogan 'Another Scotland is Possible'. Supporters played a considerable role in encouraging the movement in working-class areas. The RIC held a mass rally and a capacity conference in the Glasgow Conference Centre some weeks after the referendum; but decided not to run parliamentary candidates in the May 2015 UK general election, effectively leaving the way open for the SNP.

24 The 'High Kirk' is the Church of Scotland equivalent of a cathedral.

25 SNP leader Alex Salmond resigned immediate after the referendum and later announced he would stand for the Westminster parliament. He is now (since the May 2015 general election) one of 56 SNP MPs and the party's Foreign Affairs spokesperson. The new leader, Nicola Sturgeon, signalled a re-positioning of her party to the left by abandoning the policy of reducing corporation tax.

26 Queen Elizabeth II was persuaded to compromise her supposed constitutional neutrality with weasel words, following a church service near her 'Highland home' at Balmoral, urging the Scottish people to 'think very carefully' about their vote. President Obama looked a touch embar-

rassed as he called for the UK to remain a united US ally at a VE Day celebration in June 2014; but was more explicit in a much-reported tweet on the eve of the vote. Pope Francis urged 'caution' and, although issuing no instruction to his flock, evoked memories of the violent aftermath of the break-up of Yugoslavia.

27 Dave Temple's books include the *Durham Miners' Millennium Book* (Newcastle-upon-Tyne, TUPS Books and NUM Durham Area, 2011). He also campaigns, and produces the programme, for the annual Durham Miners' Gala.

28 Lenin, 'The Discussion on Self-Determination Summed Up', section 10: 'The Irish Rebellion of 1916', *CW* (1964), vol. 22; or at https://www.marxists.org/archive/lenin/works/1916/jul/x01.htm.

29 Cameron, in a televised pep-talk to his first exclusively Tory cabinet, talked blithely of being the party of 'one nation'. The phrase is associated with Benjamin Disraeli when, in the prosperous mid-19th century, after the shock of Chartism, he convinced the Tories of the need for policies to attract workingmen, calling them 'angels in marble' – potentially loyal and patriotic Conservative voters, enfranchised in the Reform Act of 1867 – who could be conjured out of anonymity, as a sculptor carves a figure from a solid block. But within Cameron's rhetoric – his bland celebrations of underpaid labour as providing 'dignity' – lurk different and much more sinister historic echoes: *Arbeit macht frei* – work makes us free! That this move was not simply rhetoric was confirmed in the new Conservative government's first budget when Chancellor of the Exchequer (finance minister) George Osborne set out, as the neo-liberal magazine *The Economist* (11-17 July, 2015, p. 25) put it, to 'reshape the welfare state' by 'slashing benefits for poor families' and rebranding the legal 'minimum wage' as a (marginally increased) 'National Living Wage', claiming that this made

the Conservatives 'the party of working people'. Parallel with this went the Government's intention to introduce yet more draconian anti-union laws – work, on any terms, not the right to struggle for better conditions, makes you free!

30 G. W. F. Hegel, 'Preface' to *Elements of the Philosophy of Right* (1821), ed. Allen W. Wood (Cambridge, CUP, 1991), p. 23.

31 Miliband's brother David, whom he defeated in the contest for Labour leader in 2010, was quick to join the Blairite chorus against his leadership.

32 Ross McKibbin, 'Labour Dies Again', *London Review of Books*, vol. 37, no. 11 (4 June 2015), p. 12.

33 *Beyond Capital* is the second volume and the keystone in the formidable and essential theoretical building Mészáros began constructing as capital's 'structural crisis' emerged in the 1970s.

34 István Mészáros, *The Necessity of Social Control* (New York, Monthly Review Press, 2015), p. 297.

35 At the time of writing, the trajectory of the Radical Independence Campaign remains unclear. But some supporters were seeking to reconfigure it as the Scottish Left Project, presumably with the hope of emulating Spain's Podemos and Greece's Syriza as elections to the Holyrood (devolved Scottish) parliament – due in May 2016 – neared. The announcement of a conference to be held in Glasgow in late August 2015 – to discuss a new name and electoral preparations – was reported in the independence-supporting Glasgow paper, *Sunday Herald* (21 June 2015), under the headline 'Scottish Syriza to stage first conference ...'

36 Raul Zelik's essay appears here with permission, in a version slightly abbreviated from Eric Canepa's translation in *The Bullet* (Socialist Project E-Bulletin), no. 1113, 7 May 2015: see http://www.socialistproject.ca/bullet/1113.php.

37 This section is based on a talk by the author at the Anarchist Book Fair, London, 18 August 2014, in a session arranged by

the Real World War I Group.

38 Alexei Gusev, a campaigning militant, is a professor of history at Moscow State University and chair of the Praxis Research and Educational Centre.

39 This section, originally an article in *The Bullet*, no. 981, 11 May 2014 – see http://www.socialistproject.ca/bullet/981.php – appears in this version with permission.

Part III

1 Robert Barsocchini, 'A Critical Examination of the DIA Document on the Dynamics of the Syrian Conflict' at http://levantreport.com/2015/05/26/guest-analysis-by-robert-barsocchini-a-critical-examination-of-the-dia-document-on-dynamics-of-syrian-conflict; and see *Empire Slayer*, 24 May 2015 at www.empireslayer.org/2015/05/point-by-point-analysis-of-declassified.html.

2 Barsocchini, ibid.

3 See *Ynetnews.com*, 'Iran General: US has no will to fight Islamic State', at www.ynetnews.com/articles/0,7340,L-4661052,00.html.

4 See *Al-Monitor*, 'Rafsanjani: Saudi-Iranian Co-operation ...' at http://www.al-monitor.com/pulse/originals/2015/02/iran-saudi-arabia-rafsanjani-cooperation.html#.

5 Sam Charles Hamad, 'Peering into the Faultlines: a response ...', at http://internationalsocialistnetwork.org/index.php/ideas-and-arguments/international/war-and-imperialism/483-iraq-response?showall=&limitstart=.

6 Charles Lister, 'Who Finances Isis?' at www.dw.de/who-finances-isis/a-17720149.

7 Michael Stephens, 'Islamic State: where does jihadist group get its support?' at http://www.bbc.co.uk/news/world-middle-east-29004253.

8 Ibid.

9 Michael Watt et al., 'Middle East Borders Are Redrawn in

Religious War, Says Paddy Ashdown', *The Guardian* (London), 15 August 2014.

10 *Ekurd Daily,* 'How the US-favored Kurds Abandoned the Yazadir when Isis Attacked', 18 August 2014, at http://www.ekurd.net/mismas/articles/misc2014/8/state8339.htm.

11 Ibid. YPG is a People's Protection Unit affiliated to the Turkish-Kurdish PKK.

12 Andy Cunningham, 'New Fault Lines in the Middle East: Isis in a Regional Context', 12 August 2014, at http://rs21.org.uk/2014/08/12/new-fault-lines-in-the-middle-east-isis-in-a-regional-context.

13 Woodrow Wilson's 11 February 1918 'Address' to a joint session of Congress can be accessed at: http://wwi.lib.byu.edu/index.php/President_Wilson's_Address_to_Congress,_Analyzing_German_and_Austrian_Peace_Utterances.

14 For this history, see notably Stephen Hemsley Longrigg, *Four Centuries of Modern Iraq* (Reading, Garnett Publishing, new ed., 2001; first pub. 1926).

15 V. I. Lenin, 'Events in the Balkans and in Persia', *Proletary,* 37, 16 (29) October 1908, in Lenin, *Collected Works,* vol. 15 (Moscow, Foreign Languages Publishing House, 1962), pp. 22ff.

16 'Modern Iraq' in Library of Congress, *Iraq: legal traditions and history,* at http://www.loc.gov/law/help/legal-history/iraq.php.

17 For a slightly different translation, see *FARS News Agency,* 'Iran: Iraqi people will never accept disintegration', 5 July 2014 at http://englishfarsnews.com/newstext.aspx?nn=13930414000919.

18 For Soueif's statement, see http://www.bbc.co.uk/news/world-middle-east-25888916.

19 See report in *Washington Times,* 12 September 2013 at http://www.washingtontimes.com/news/2013/sep/12/obama-now-hopeful-russian-deal-avoid-syria-strike/?page=all.

20 See *BBC News*, 30 August 2013 at http://www.bbc.co.uk/news/uk-politics-23894173.

21 The figures are taken from United Nations Department of Economic and Social Affairs, *The Global Social Crisis: report on the world social situation 2011* (New York, United Nations, 2011) at http://www.un.org/esa/socdev/rwss/docs/2011/overview.pdf.

22 See Office of Textiles and Apparel on Qualifying Industrial Zones at http://web.ita.doc.gov/tacgi/fta.nsf/7a9d3143265673ee85257a0700667a6f/196ed79f4f79ac0085257a070066961d.

23 C. J. Chivers and Eric Schmidt, 'Arms Airlift to Syria Rebels Expands …', *New York Times*, 24 March 2013.

24 Robert Fisk, 'Sectarianism Bites into Syria's Rebels', in the *Independent* (London), 22 July, 2012: see http://www.independent.co.uk/voices/commentators/fisk/robert-fisk-sectarianism-bites-into-syrias-rebels-7964251.html.

25 See Cosroe Chaqueri, 'Did the Soviets play a role in founding the Tudeh party in Iran?', *Cahiers du Monde Russe*, 40/3 (1999): see at https://monderusse.revues.org/22. M. Akhundzadeh, Hasan Hasanov (Pourafar), A. H. Hesabi (Dehzad), Kamran (N. Aslani), Ladbon Esfandiari, Mir A.-Q. Asadi, K. Nikbin and H. Rezaev (Sharqi) were held by the NKVD (The People's Commissariat for Internal Affairs).

26 S. Noble, 'Iran's Unholy Alliance with Hitler Enshrined in a New Name': see http://www.independentsentinel.com/irans-unholy-alliance-with-hitler-enshrined-in-a-new-name. On the Third Reich's influence in Iran, see too Miron Rezun, *The Soviet Union and Iran: Soviet policy in Iran from the beginnings of the Pahlavi dynasty until the Soviet invasion of 1941* (Geneva, Sijthoff & Noordhoff, 1981), pp. 318ff.

27 Chaqueri, 'Did the Soviets …'

28 See Central Intelligence Agency, 'The Tudeh Party: vehicle of communism in Iran (Washington DC, 1949), at http://www.

foia.cia.gov/sites/default/files/document_conversions/89801/DOC_0000258385.pdf.

29 Younes Parsa Benab, 'The Gilan Soviet Republic and Azadistan in Iranian Azerbaijan (1917-1921): a study in delinking' at http://www.iran-bulletin.org/ibMEF-2completed/TheGilan%20Republic.html.

30 J. V. Stalin to Ja'far Pishevari, 8 May 1946, History and Public Policy Program Digital Archive, AVP RF, f. 06, op. 7, p. 34, d. 544, ll. 8-9; translation by Vladislav M. Zubok, CWIHP Working Paper, 15; at http://digitalarchive.wilsoncenter.org/document/117827.

31 American History USA: http://americanhistoryusa.com/topic/1953-iranian-coup-detat.

32 David Sylvan and Stephen Majeski, *US Foreign Policy in Perspective: clients, enemies and empire* (London, Routledge, pbk ed., 2009), p. 121.

33 Tareq Y. Ismael and Jacqueline S. Ismael, *Government and Politics of the Contemporary Middle East: continuity and change* (London and New York, Routledge, 2011), pp. 126-8.

34 Ervand Abrahamian, *Iran Between Two Revolutions* (Princeton, Princeton University Press, 1982).

35 Maziyar Behrooz, *Rebels with a Cause: the failure of the left in Iran* (London, I. B. Tauris, paperback ed., 2000), p. 13.

36 Maziyar Behrooz, 'State of Paralysis: Tudeh factionalism and the 1953 coup', *The Iranian*, November 2001; accessible at Iranian.com/History/2001/November/Tudeh, including 'Interview with Fereidun Azarnur' (an active member of the Military Organisation) in *Rah-e Azadi*, no. 24, September-October 1992.

37 Ervand Abrahamian, *Tortured Confession: prisons and public recantations in modern Iran* (Berkeley, University of California Press, c. 1999), p. 92 (available at http://ark.cdlib.org/ark:/13030/ft3s2005jq/).

38 Abrahamian, *Tortured Confession*, p. 89.

39 Massoud Ahmad-Zadeh, *Armed Struggle; both a Strategy and a Tactic* – see at https://www.marxists.org/subject/iran/ahadzadeh/armed-struggle.pdf – was for many years the bible of the Fedayeen.

40 Amir-Parviz Pouyan, *The Necessity of Armed Struggle and Refutation of the Theory of Survival*; the argument is also reflected in P. Pouyan and M. Māni, *Iran: three essays on the necessity of armed struggle and refutation of the theory of survival* (Florence, Edition Mazdak, n.d.).

41 Ahmad-Zadeh, *Armed Struggle.*

42 See Bizhan Jihani, *Capitalism and Revolution in Iran: selected writings* ... (London, Zed Books, 1980).

43 On 'line three Maoists', see Yassamine Mather, 'Marxism and the Iranian Revolution', at rdln.wordpress.com/2012/09/15/marxism-and-the-iranian-revolution/, 15 September 2012.

44 The main sources for this afterword are: Zack Beauchamp, 'Benjamin Netanyahu is freaking out ...', *Vox World,* 13 July, 2015 (www.vox.com); Thomas Erdbrink, 'In Iran, Fatal Porsche Crash Unleashes Middle-Class Anger at Elites', *New York Times,* 30 April 2015; International Monetary Fund, 'Statement at the End of the IMF Mission to the Islamic Republic of Iran' 9 February 2015 (online); Benoît Faucon, 'Deal Rekindles Business Interest in Iran', *Wall Street Journal,* 14 July 2015; and Robert Fisk, 'Did America Just Change Sides in Middle East's Sectarian War?', *The Independent* (London), 15 July 2015.

Part IV

1 For *What Is To Be Done?*, see V. I. Lenin, *Collected Works* (*CW*), vol. 5 (Moscow, Foreign Languages Publishing House, 1961), pp. 347-529.

2 For the minutes of this 1903 Congress, see Brian Pearce (ed. and translator), *The Second Ordinary Congress of the RDSLP* (London, New Park Publications, 1978).

3 I discuss Lenin's conflict with the Economists below; see too Marcel Liebman, *Leninism Under Lenin* (London, Jonathan Cape, 1975), pp. 30-1.
4 Liebman, *Leninism*, p. 160, discusses the significance of the 'de-Bolshevised party' thesis, to which I return below. Liebman, pp. 125-34, shows how Lenin changed the Party in April 1917.
5 Lenin, *CW*, vol. 5, p. 383.
6 Ibid., vol. 5, pp. 375ff.
7 Ibid., vol. 10 (1962), pp. 29-39.
8 Ibid., vol. 11 (1962), pp. 171-8.
9 Ibid., vol. 45 (1964), pp. 378-82.
10 Karl Marx and Friedrich Engels, *The Communist Manifesto* (Oxford World's Classics, Oxford, Oxford University Press, 1992), p. 13.
11 See V. I. Lenin, *One Step Forward, Two Steps Back* in Lenin, *CW*, vol. 7 (1961), p. 262.
12 Liebman, *Leninism*, pp. 123ff, for all the quotations in the following paragraphs.
13 Ibid., p. 131.
14 Ibid., p. 160.
15 Janos Borovi, *'De la* "partiinost" *d'hier et d'aujourd'hui'* appeared in *Carré Rouge* (Paris), 13, Février 2000, pp. 68-76. For the article by Alexei Gusev (for whom, see note 38 in Part II above), see A. V. Goussev, 'L'Opposition de Gauche en URSS á la fin des années 20' in *Cahiers Leon Trotsky*, 59, Août 1997.
16 Jan van Heijenoort, *With Trotsky in Exile: from Prinkipo to Coyoacán* (Cambridge, Mass. and London, Harvard University Press, 1978; also published as *Sept Ans Auprès de Léon Trotsky*, Paris, Les Lettres Nouvelles/Maurice Nadeau, 1978), p. 2.
17 van Heijenoort, *With Trotsky*, pp. 38-9.
18 Ibid., p. 39.

19 Ibid., p. 54.

20 The Transitional Programme – *The Death Agony of Capitalism and the Tasks of the Fourth International* – is available in many editions and can be read at https://www.marxists.org/archive/trotsky/1938/tp/tp-text2.htm.

21 A transcript of the 28 October 2012 meeting is available from Terry Brotherstone, Department of History, University of Aberdeen, Scotland, UK, AB24 1UU: (t.brotherstone@abdn.ac.uk).

22 Victor Serge, *Memoirs of a Revolutionary*, translated by Peter Sedgewick (New York, New York Review Book, 2012; original French edition, 1951), p. 284.

23 Karl Marx, 'The Necessity of the Communist Revolution' in *The German Ideology* (1845): see, *Marx Engels Collected Works 1845-47* (London, Lawrence & Wishart, 1976), vol 5, p. 52; and at https://www.marxists.org/archive/marx/works/1845/german-ideology/ch01d.htm.

24 Ibid.

Part V

1 Talcott Parsons, *The Structure of Social Action* (New York, Free Press Paperback, 1968), pp. xviii-xix.

2 István Mészáros, *Social Structure and Forms of Social Consciousness*, vol. II: *The Dialectic of Structure and History* (New York, Monthly Review Press, 2011), p. 419.

3 Parsons, *Structure*, vol. 2, chap. XIII.

4 Jean Baudrillard, *Forget Foucault* (new ed., Cambridge, Mass., MIT Press, 2007: originally *Oublier Foucault*, 1977), p. 120.

5 Jean-François Lyotard, *The Postmodern Condition: a report on knowledge* (Manchester, Manchester University, 1985), p. xxiii.

6 See, for example, Peter L. Berger and Thomas Luckman, *The Social Construction of Reality* (Harmondsworth, Penguin Books, 1979; first ed., 1966).

7 Karl Marx, *A Contribution to the Critique of Political Economy* (London, Lawrence and Wishart, 1971), p. 21; Friedrich Engels, 'Review of *Capital* volume 1' in the *Demokratisches Wochenblatt,* no. 12, 21 March 1868, available at https://www.marxists.org/archive/marx/works/1867/reviews-capital/dwochenblatt.hrm.
8 Karl Marx, *Wage Labour and Capital* (London, Martin Lawrence, 1932), p. 19.
9 Karl Marx, *Capital: a critique of political economy* (Moscow, Foreign Languages Publishing House, 1954), vol. I, p. 178.
10 Friedrich Engels, *Anti-Dűhring,* in Karl Marx and Friedrich Engels, *Collected Works* (*MECW*) Vol. 25 (Moscow, Foreign Languages Publishing House and London, Lawrence and Wishart, 1987), III, iii ('Socialism'); Marx, *A Contribution ...,* pp. 33-4.
11 Marx, *Capital,* vol. I, p. 310.
12 Ibid., vol. 1, pp. 81 and 321.
13 Karl Marx, 'Economic Writings 1861-1864', *MECW*, Vol. 34 (London, Lawrence and Wishart, 1975), p. 429.
14 István Mészáros, *Social Structure and Forms of Social Consciousness. Volume I: the social determination of method* (New York, Monthly Review Press, 2010), p. 328.
15 Karl Marx, *Grundrisse*: foundations of the critique of political economy (rough draft) (Harmondsworth, Penguin Books, 1973), p. 705: emphasis added.
16 For this English translation from the first German edition of *Capital,* see Albert Dragstedt (trans. and ed.), *Value: studies by Karl Marx* (London, New Park Publications, 1976), pp. 7-40.
17 Marx, *Grundrisse,* p. 197.
18 Ibid., p. 705.

Part VI

1 Karl Marx, *Capital,* vol. I, 'Afterword to the Second German Edition [Abstract]' (1873), accessed at https://www.marx

ists.org/subject/dialectics/marx-engels/capital-afterward .htm.

2 Karl Marx, 'Theses on Feuerbach', third thesis, in *Marx/Engels Collected Works,* vol. 5: '1845-1847' (Moscow, Progress Publishers and London, Lawrence and Wishart, 1975), pp. 3-4.

3 Friedrich Engels, 'Preface to the English Edition of 1888', in Karl Marx and Friedrich Engels, *The Communist Manifesto* (Oxford, Oxford World's Classics, Oxford University Press, 1992), p. 46.

4 'Provisional Rules of the Association', in *Documents of the First International 1864-1866: the London conference 1865* (*DFI 1864-1866*) (Moscow, Foreign Languages Publishing House and London, Lawrence and Wishart, n.d.), p. 288.

5 Marx and Engels, *Communist Manifesto,* p. 17; 'Instructions for the Delegates of the Provisional Council...', *DFI 1864-1866,* p. 346.

6 Marx and Engels, *Communist Manifesto,* p. 17.

7 Jean-François Lyotard, 'Universal History and Cultural Differences' in Andrew Benjamin (ed.), *The Lyotard Reader* (London, Basil Blackwell, 1989), p. 318.

8 Robert Tonkinson, *The Mardudjara Aborigines: living the dream in Australia's desert* (New York, etc., Holt, Rinehart and Winston, 1978), p. 41.

9 Tonkinson, *The Mardudjara,* p. 44; R. M. and C. H. Berndt, *The World of the First Australians* (Sydney, etc., Lansdowne Press, 2nd impression, 1977; first pub. 1964), p. 90.

10 Victor W. Turner, *The Ritual Process: structure and anti-structure* (Chicago, Aldine Publishers reprint, 2008; first ed., London, Routledge).

11 Ibid., p.103. See too on the liminal period in *rites de passage,* Turner's *Forest of Symbols: aspects of Ndembu Ritual* (Ithica, NY, Cornell University Press), 93-110.

12 Ibid., pp. 42-3; *Isoma* refers to 'when a woman has had a

number of stillbirths or abortions': see Turner, *Forest,* p. 13.

13 Ibid., p. 103.

14 W. E. H. Stanner, 'The Dreaming', in W. A. Lessa and E. Z. Vogt (eds.), *Reader in Comparative Religion* (New York, Harper Row, 1958), p. 513.

15 It should also be clear that the relation between base and superstructure, and the forms of consciousness through which men and women find ways to fight out conflicts and contradictions, will not be the same in different types of class society.

16 Chris Knight, *Blood Relations: menstruation and the origins of culture* (New Haven and London, Yale University Press, 1991), p. 465.

17 Nick Dyer-Witheford, *Cyber-Marx: cycles and circuits of struggle in high-technology capitalism* (Urbana and Chicago, University of Illinois Press, 1999), p. 149.

Contemporary culture has eliminated both the concept of the public and the figure of the intellectual. Former public spaces – both physical and cultural – are now either derelict or colonized by advertising. A cretinous anti-intellectualism presides, cheerled by expensively educated hacks in the pay of multinational corporations who reassure their bored readers that there is no need to rouse themselves from their interpassive stupor. The informal censorship internalized and propagated by the cultural workers of late capitalism generates a banal conformity that the propaganda chiefs of Stalinism could only ever have dreamt of imposing. Zer0 Books knows that another kind of discourse – intellectual without being academic, popular without being populist – is not only possible: it is already flourishing, in the regions beyond the striplit malls of so-called mass media and the neurotically bureaucratic halls of the academy. Zer0 is committed to the idea of publishing as a making public of the intellectual. It is convinced that in the unthinking, blandly consensual culture in which we live, critical and engaged theoretical reflection is more important than ever before.

ZERO BOOKS

If this book has helped you to clarify an idea, solve a problem or extend your knowledge, you may like to read more titles from Zero Books. Recent bestsellers are:

Capitalist Realism Is there no alternative?
Mark Fisher
An analysis of the ways in which capitalism has presented itself as the only realistic political-economic system.
Paperback: November 27, 2009 978-1-84694-317-1 $14.95 £7.99.
eBook: July 1, 2012 978-1-78099-734-6 $9.99 £6.99.

The Wandering Who? A study of Jewish identity politics
Gilad Atzmon
An explosive unique crucial book tackling the issues of Jewish Identity Politics and ideology and their global influence.
Paperback: September 30, 2011 978-1-84694-875-6 $14.95 £8.99.
eBook: September 30, 2011 978-1-84694-876-3 $9.99 £6.99.

Clampdown Pop-cultural wars on class and gender
Rhian E. Jones
Class and gender in Britpop and after, and why 'chav' is a feminist issue.
Paperback: March 29, 2013 978-1-78099-708-7 $14.95 £9.99.
eBook: March 29, 2013 978-1-78099-707-0 $7.99 £4.99.

The Quadruple Object
Graham Harman
Uses a pack of playing cards to present Harman's metaphysical system of fourfold objects, including human access, Heidegger's indirect causation, panpsychism and ontography.
Paperback: July 29, 2011 978-1-84694-700-1 $16.95 £9.99.

Weird Realism Lovecraft and Philosophy
Graham Harman
As Hölderlin was to Martin Heidegger and Mallarmé to Jacques Derrida, so is H.P. Lovecraft to the Speculative Realist philosophers.
Paperback: September 28, 2012 978-1-78099-252-5 $24.95 £14.99.
eBook: September 28, 2012 978-1-78099-907-4 $9.99 £6.99.

Sweetening the Pill or How We Got Hooked on Hormonal Birth Control
Holly Grigg-Spall
Is it really true? Has contraception liberated or oppressed women?
Paperback: September 27, 2013 978-1-78099-607-3 $22.95 £12.99.
eBook: September 27, 2013 978-1-78099-608-0 $9.99 £6.99.

Why Are We The Good Guys? Reclaiming Your Mind From The Delusions Of Propaganda
David Cromwell
A provocative challenge to the standard ideology that Western power is a benevolent force in the world.
Paperback: September 28, 2012 978-1-78099-365-2 $26.95 £15.99.
eBook: September 28, 2012 978-1-78099-366-9 $9.99 £6.99.

The Truth about Art Reclaiming quality
Patrick Doorly
The book traces the multiple meanings of art to their various sources, and equips the reader to choose between them.
Paperback: August 30, 2013 978-1-78099-841-1 $32.95 £19.99.

Bells and Whistles More Speculative Realism
Graham Harman
In this diverse collection of sixteen essays, lectures, and interviews Graham Harman lucidly explains the principles of Speculative Realism, including his own object-oriented philosophy.

Paperback: November 29, 2013 978-1-78279-038-9 $26.95 £15.99.
eBook: November 29, 2013 978-1-78279-037-2 $9.99 £6.99.

Towards Speculative Realism: Essays and Lectures Essays and Lectures
Graham Harman
These writings chart Harman's rise from Chicago sportswriter to co founder of one of Europe's most promising philosophical movements: Speculative Realism.
Paperback: November 26, 2010 978-1-84694-394-2 $16.95 £9.99.
eBook: January 1, 1970 978-1-84694-603-5 $9.99 £6.99.

Meat Market Female flesh under capitalism
Laurie Penny
A feminist dissection of women's bodies as the fleshy fulcrum of capitalist cannibalism, whereby women are both consumers and consumed.
Paperback: April 29, 2011 978-1-84694-521-2 $12.95 £6.99.
eBook: May 21, 2012 978-1-84694-782-7 $9.99 £6.99.

Translating Anarchy The Anarchism of Occupy Wall Street
Mark Bray
An insider's account of the anarchists who ignited Occupy Wall Street.
Paperback: September 27, 2013 978-1-78279-126-3 $26.95 £15.99.
eBook: September 27, 2013 978-1-78279-125-6 $6.99 £4.99.

One Dimensional Woman
Nina Power
Exposes the dark heart of contemporary cultural life by examining pornography, consumer capitalism and the ideology of women's work.
Paperback: November 27, 2009 978-1-84694-241-9 $14.95 £7.99.
eBook: July 1, 2012 978-1-78099-737-7 $9.99 £6.99.

Dead Man Working

Carl Cederstrom, Peter Fleming

An analysis of the dead man working and the way in which capital is now colonizing life itself.

Paperback: May 25, 2012 978-1-78099-156-6 $14.95 £9.99.

eBook: June 27, 2012 978-1-78099-157-3 $9.99 £6.99.

Unpatriotic History of the Second World War

James Heartfield

The Second World War was not the Good War of legend. James Heartfield explains that both Allies and Axis powers fought for the same goals - territory, markets and natural resources.

Paperback: September 28, 2012 978-1-78099-378-2 $42.95 £23.99.

eBook: September 28, 2012 978-1-78099-379-9 $9.99 £6.99.

Find more titles at www.zero-books.net